Digital Strategies

Digital Strategies
Data-Driven Public Relations, Marketing, and Advertising

REGINA LUTTRELL
SUSAN F. EMERICK
ADRIENNE WALLACE

New York   Oxford
OXFORD UNIVERSITY PRESS

Oxford University Press is a department of the University of Oxford.
It furthers the University's objective of excellence in research, scholarship,
and education by publishing worldwide. Oxford is a registered trade mark of
Oxford University Press in the UK and certain other countries.

Published in the United States of America by Oxford University Press
198 Madison Avenue, New York, NY 10016, United States of America.

© 2022 by Oxford University Press

Library of Congress Cataloging-in-Publication Data

CIP data is on file at the Library of Congress
978-0-19-092539-0

Printing number: 9 8 7 6 5 4 3 2 1
Printed by LSC Communications, Inc.,
United States of America

CONTENTS

v

PREFACE

With a mission of bridging academics and business to improve the readiness of students entering the fields of public relations and marketing, we bring our collective years of experience, as practitioners, researchers, and educators. We are a unique triad whose learnings reflect learnings from our distinct backgrounds developing, implementing, measuring, and optimizing communications strategies across various disciplines of the profession for some of the largest global brands. Collectively we have led diverse teams pioneering cutting edge social, data, and analytics programs. With the quest to share our expertise and advance student's knowledge and skills, we have successfully taught courses in public relations, campaign planning, data and analytics, marketing, advertising, social listening, social intelligence research, and strategic communications. We actively serve as guest lecturers, public speakers, and experts within the industry and through mainstream media channels. Students will benefit from our firsthand experience in the field practicing, consulting, and honing our expertise and research in public relations, marketing, and advertising, social media, and emerging technologies.

Our book aims to advance the reader's understanding of the social web and how emerging technologies rooted in artificial intelligence bring new capabilities and insights from social intelligence to the profession. These skills play a critical role in building data-driven strategies to support decisions within public relations and marketing. Readers are prompted to consider what success looks like and methods to measure attainment. In this text, we provide essential knowledge necessary for setting and aligning program and campaign strategies with key business goals, establishing measurement frameworks to track effectiveness of strategies, and evaluating tactical execution.

We explore how the Internet, social networking, social media, and digital have dramatically changed the way that the world communicates and conducts business. These advances in technology have made it possible to reach consumers across the globe at a touch of a publish button, no matter the size of a business. The ease of communication through digital means—especially social media—brings about changes for both the creator and the consumer of information.

Emerging digital and social media technologies provide a multitude of content forms and distribution channels allowing instantaneous two-way communications for brands and consumers alike.

We've entered a new era in which nearly every interaction can be tracked and analyzed. To say that the landscape of communications has changed rapidly would be an understatement. Gone are the days of *Mad Men* and the notion that brands control the message. We are in an age in which the consumer is in control and every interaction creates a piece of data that can be tracked, mined, and analyzed to inform strategic decisions. Those who understand how to harness the power of data driven insights, using techniques such as social media listening and analytics, can then apply data-driven insights to strategy development, precision targeting, engagement planning, content optimization, and more, reaping the benefits and capturing market opportunity.

In a traditional sense, public relations and marketing communications disciplines have long been responsible for driving strategies that shift perception and influence buying decisions through effective positioning of a brand, product, service, or cause. But what separates successful strategies? How do we measure and quantify the contribution of such strategies in achieving business objectives? The most effective strategies are informed from the beginning, supported by business intelligence based on data-driven insights that evaluate:

- historical views that establish a baseline of past performance;
- real time analytics to keep a pulse on the present; and
- predictive analytics, which uses advanced analytics and modeling to anticipate and predict future customer behavior—for example, what a customer may buy next.

WHY THIS BOOK NOW

The rate of change in media and technology since the advent of the 21st century continues to astonish. The market demands that today's graduating students have a keen understanding of the emerging forms of media, as well as an understanding of the practice of using data-driven insights to inform decisions. These skills are expected. What's more, they are differentiating factors for students who can successfully demonstrate how to use them.

Traditional textbooks that emphasize discrete media are less effective in meeting the needs of contemporary students. The evolving landscape of public relations and marketing demands a more interdisciplinary, interactive, and fluid approach of study and exploration. To that end, this book offers a model for integrating skills-based analytical approaches, critical and conceptual learning, and practical exercises to prepare students for a future in which they will need to adapt to ever-changing contexts across multiple media platforms. These platforms are a springboard for the world's creators, with billions of pieces of new content posted and exchanged daily. Students in the 21st century need a solid foundation to understand and execute data-driven strategies that can be measured and deliver on goals.

Comprehensive model: This book was written using an evidence-based approach that explains various strategies and techniques that can be utilized to drive market influence. Students learn the importance of data-driven decision making, continuous measurement, and optimization through the LUPE model, which offers a repeatable model for developing data-driven strategies and maximizing value.

Case studies: The book incorporates detailed case studies that put data-driven decision making at the center of strategic planning, execution, and measurement. The cases are proven examples that will provide the reader with a spectrum of practical examples that explore each of these categories and the measurement standards used to accomplish the goals.

Data-driven: The text provides readers with an understanding about why data-driven decision making matters in developing successful initiatives.

Accessible language: The book is written in a pragmatic tone that is easy to understand, yet challenges the reader to contemplate how to develop a data-driven decision-making mindset and consider measurement, evaluation, and optimization as essential aspects of to end-to-end strategic planning.

End of chapter exercises: Included within are exercises and questions at the end of each chapter that challenge students to apply what they've learned to a variety of situations.

ORGANIZATION OF THE BOOK

Readers are provided the foundation of building data-driven strategies that can be applied to programs and campaigns alike. The first three chapters provide students with the foundational building blocks necessary to understand components that go into developing strategies and tactics based on data-driven insights. Each subsequent chapter presents case studies across industries, categories, and brands that demonstrate strategies while also highlighting how organizations utilized research, planned and implemented sound strategies, and measured the effectiveness of campaigns through analytical techniques.

CHAPTER SUMMARIES

Part 1: Foundations of Data-Driven Insights
Chapters 1–3 provide an essential foundation by which data-driven decision making supports the development of effective marketing, communications, and public relations strategies through repeatable planning, execution, and optimization methods.

Chapter 1: An Era of Artificial Intelligence
Chapter 1 covers the implications of artificial intelligence, anticipated changes impacting the marketing communications field, the role social intelligence and analytics play in making data-driven decisions, and the evolving skills required of public relations and marketing professionals across disciplines.

Chapter 2: LUPE Model—Developing Data-Driven Campaigns

The LUPE model (listen and learn, understand, plan, execute and evaluate) provides a roadmap that will aid readers with tactical considerations and proven techniques on how to put insights into action. The model is introduced early in the text to provide guiding principles and a repeatable methodology for using social media intelligence to inform data-driven decision making practices.

Chapter 3: Anything Can Be Measured; Measure What Counts

Nearly everything we share on social media is in the public domain. This creates a massive opportunity to glean intelligence from publicly shared online discourse through social listening and monitoring techniques, down to the level of an individual, based on personality traits, habits, preferences, relationships, and even political views—all from their digital and social footprints. Chapter 3 shows readers how practitioners use data to make informed decisions.

Part 2: Case Studies

Part 2 presents case studies that illustrate a spectrum of practical examples, exploring various topics and using cases to accomplish the featured organization's goals. Readers benefit from a variety of practical applications, enriching their understanding of how data-driven decision making impacts public relations and marketing.

Chapter 4: Convergence of Social Media, Search, and Content Marketing

Chapter 4 explores the fundamentals of search and social convergence. Students learn how to use data-driven insights and apply them to content optimization.

The chapter includes a case study, "Using Analytics to Inform Holiday Facebook Ad Campaigns for Small Business."

Chapter 5: Data-Driven Influencer Strategy

While there are variations on the definition of an influencer, there are common characteristics that the social media influencer possesses. Chapter 5 explores these while providing readers with measurement frameworks to use when considering which influencers to prioritize.

The chapter includes a case study, "Life Alive: Micro-Influencer Campaign Uses Data to Drive Results."

Chapter 6: Creating Compelling Content through Visual Storytelling

Chapter 6 explains the power of visual storytelling and how to use visual techniques to drive engagement, grow a business, and strengthen a brand's recognition by leveraging photos, videos, infographics, presentations, and other rich media.

The chapter includes a case study, "M.O.M. Squad Storytelling Saves the Day."

Chapter 7: Corporate Social Responsibility and Corporate Activism

Chapter 7 examines the foundations of corporate social responsibility and activism through the exploration of cause-based marketing campaigns launched because of the rapid partnership growth between nonprofits and corporations.

The chapter includes a case study, "Patagonia: Can a Self-Imposed 1 Percent Tax Change the World?"

Chapter 8: Engagement through Crowdsourcing and User-Generated Content

Chapter 8 displays several standout brands that exhibit proficiency in crowdsourcing content, helping to achieve measurable benefits like deepening customer engagement while significantly reducing (eliminating) content production expenses.

The chapter includes a case study, "Crunching the Data: Crowdsourcing and the Lay's Potato Chip 'Do Us a Flavor' Contest."

Chapter 9: Social Customer Experience (CX)

Chapter 9 illustrates measurable return on investment by highlighting how customers are the center of an organization and how organizations need to provide effective social customer care to build strong relationships over time. Themes explored include the social customer care, customer journey stages, brand touchpoints, and social and digital interactions.

The chapter includes a case study, "Lush UK: Can a Brand Survive without Social Media?"

Chapter 10: Crisis Communications in a Data-Driven World

Chapter 10 through in-depth examples, students will learn how brands use analytics to establish metrics-based benchmarks that assess the severity of a crisis and subsequent response, visualize and dissect the anatomy of a crisis, and know how to take the right action.

The chapter includes a case study, "Turning Crises into Opportunities: Examining the Effectiveness of Starbucks' Responses to Its Philadelphia Crisis."

Chapter 11: Geofencing and Hypertargeting Strategies

Chapter 11 explores the fundamentals of developing a localized social media strategy and using such techniques as geofencing and hypertargeting for precision audience targeting.

The chapter includes a case study, "How Sprinklr Unified Its Globally Distributed Workforce through Hypertargeting to Inspire Employee Engagement."

Chapter 12: Future Implications of Data-Driven Decisions

This closing chapter highlights industry trends and challenges readers to contemplate the changing roles and skills necessary for practitioners to become essential leaders pioneering transformation in the years to come. Readers are presented with thought-provoking ideas, short opinion pieces, and predictions from experts across industries—categories and brands that are on the front lines of developing proven public relations and marketing strategies while navigating continued change amid the evolving landscape.

ABOUT THE AUTHORS

Regina Luttrell, Ph.D., is currently the associate dean for research and creative activity and the director of the Emerging Insights Lab at the S.I. Newhouse School of Public Communications at Syracuse University where she also teaches social media and public relations. A contributor to *PR Tactics* and *PR News*, as well as peer-reviewed journals, she is a noted speaker who frequently presents at national and international conferences and business events on topics related to the current social media revolution, the impact of artificial intelligence on news and society, the ongoing public relations evolution, and millennials and Generation Z within the classroom and workplace. As a Knight Foundation Tow Journalism Fellow, she examines attitudes and awareness of artificial intelligence and its impact on society. She is the author of several books, including *Public Relations Campaigns: An Integrated Approach, The PR Agency Handbook, Social Media: How to Engage, Share, and Connect,* and *The Millennial Mindset: Unraveling Fact from Fiction.* Prior to entering the education field, she spent the first portion of her career in corporate public relations and marketing. Her extensive background includes strategic development and implementation of public relations as well as social media, advertising, marketing, and corporate communications.

Susan F. Emerick is a globally recognized business and marketing innovator, building online brands for organizations around the world. She is coauthor of *The Most Powerful Brand on Earth: How to Transform Teams, Empower Employees, Integrate Partners, and Mobilize Customers to Beat the Competition in Digital and Social Media*—a must-read for anyone striving to build brand advocacy. She has been recognized as one of the top 25 Internet Marketing Leaders and Innovators by iMedia, listed in TopRank Marketing's top 25 Women That Rocked Social Media, and honored as one of TopRank's top 50 Influential Women in Digital Marketing. Her thought leadership has been featured in Brand Innovators, Bright Talk, CMS Newswire, Forbes, Forrester, iMedia, PR News, Social Media Today, Social Media.org WOMMA.org, and others. Susan is an instructor at West Virginia University, Reed School of Media, and has been a guest lecturer at Columbia University, Carnegie Mellon University, Oakland University, and Eastern Michigan University. Susan has advised various marketing industry association boards. Susan earned a master of science in marketing research from Michigan State University, Broad College of Business, and a bachelor's degree in advertising from Michigan State University, College of Communications Arts and Sciences.

Adrienne A. Wallace, Ph.D., is an assistant professor at Grand Valley State University (Michigan), where she teaches courses in advertising and public relations. Adrienne has more than 20 years of professional experience in both the public and private sectors ranging in scope from nonprofit, health, education, government, hospitality, politics, lobbying, and finance. She's a frequent contributor to industry publications and a conference speaker on all things related to digital/social media strategy, student-run firms, and experiential learning design. Dr. Wallace earned her Ph.D. from Western Michigan University (WMU), where she studied the intersections of public relations, participation, and lobbying on the creation/implementation of public policy in the United States. She received degrees in health communications/advertising and public relations (BS), communications (MS), and government and non-profit administration (MPA), all from Grand Valley State University. She is also a graduate and former class president ('15) of the Michigan Political Leadership Program, located in the Institute for Public Policy and Social Research (IPPSR) at Michigan State University's College of Social Science. Outside of academia, Adrienne creates and implements campaign strategies for future local politicians and maintains practice as a consultant for BlackTruck Media + Marketing.

ACKNOWLEDGMENTS

It is with immense gratitude that we thank the numerous business leaders, practitioners, and academic colleagues who generously contributed their expertise, time, and talent in the creation of this textbook. They enabled us to provide students with proven methods, practical applications through case studies, and firsthand accounts of the realities of our changing profession.

Our genuine thanks go to the Oxford University Press staff members who helped us bring this textbook to market successfully, realizing our ambition to bridge academics and business to improve the readiness of students entering the fields of public relations and marketing.

For our families and friends who have provided unwavering support and encouragement along the way, we are indebted and appreciate your patience and sacrifice.

Thank you to all of the practitioners, researchers, and educators who are on a quest to advance our profession and will be on the vanguard in leading the way by adopting and putting into practice the learning and skills gained from this collective work.

Digital Strategies

CHAPTER 1

An Era of Artificial Intelligence

KEY LEARNING OUTCOMES

Explain why industry professionals must build skills to formulate data-driven social strategies.

Understand how insights derived from social media are a key component in developing data-driven marketing and public relations strategies.

Differentiate between natural language processing, semantic analysis, machine learning, and artificial intelligence.

Assess the implications of artificial intelligence on public relations, marketing, and advertising industries.

Understand the role ethics plays in data and why it's important for PR and marketing.

Identify the implications surrounding the areas of paid media, earned media, owned media, and shared media.

THE EVOLVING PROFESSION

The disciplines of marketing and public relations (PR) continue to evolve at a rapid pace. Numerous job titles related to social media that never before existed within the industry have surfaced, including social media strategist, blogger, search engine optimization specialist, web copywriter, content strategist, influencer marketing manager, social customer care, brand ambassador, storyteller, analytics manager, and data scientist. Within most organizational structures, roles such as these typically ladder up to the C-suite; specifically, to the chief communication officer, chief experience officer, chief marketing officer, or chief digital officer. A quick glance at an organizational chart illustrates that no two companies share the same structure when it comes to staffing and aligning talent within these disciplines. For these reasons, we will use the terms "public relations and marketing" and "practitioners" throughout the text to reference the various types of people intended to read and benefit from this book, including those studying public relations, advertising, social media, and marketing.

ADJUSTMENTS IN PUBLIC RELATIONS, MARKETING, AND ADVERTISING

What does all of this mean for the industry practitioner? In a word—convergence. Researchers from the USC Annenberg Center for Public Relations and the Holmes Report note the continued convergence of marketing and public relations. In fact, 47 percent of PR professionals believe their area will become more closely aligned with marketing over the next five years.[1] This further illustrates the point that marketing, public relations, advertising, and social media are becoming more strategic and aligned.

Over the past decade, the fields of **marketing**, **public relations**, and **advertising** have changed. Social media was the first disruptor between the trifecta. We saw advances in planning and the incorporation of what was once a new strategy that integrated social platforms such as Twitter, Facebook, or Instagram. However, today, our focus must shift. As organizations continue to invest heavily in harnessing insights from the social web using social listening and advanced analytics, an entirely new industry has been born comprised of emerging technologies rooted in natural language processing, semantic analysis, machine learning, and artificial intelligence (AI). These evolving technologies equip marketing and public relations professionals with the ability to analyze and mine online conversations across social networks, in nearly any language, around the globe. As practitioners, we must turn our attention to the power of data-driven decision making and embrace the vast opportunity it beholds. For

---

According to Wendy Marx of Marx Public Relations, AI helps practitioners perform tasks that typically require human intelligence, such as the following:[1]

- researching data-driven stories using search functions;
- monitoring social media channels to help predict everything from crisis to product shortages;
- managing crises in the social sphere;
- transcribing audio into text; and
- creating strategic, customer-centric, targeted campaigns.

---

[1] Wendy Marx, "Artificial Intelligence and PR: What You Need to Know," Marx Communications, December 4, 2017, http://b2bprblog.marxand public relations.com/b2bpr/artificial-intelligence-and-pr.

these reasons, throughout the text we will use the term "social sphere" to represent the broad nature of how insights can be mined, analyzed, and utilized to develop data-driven strategies. Considered unstructured data from the social web, such data is most commonly sourced from opinion and social interactions shared publicly through social networking.

CUSTOMER EXPECTATIONS

Customers increasingly expect brands to deliver consistent and personalized experiences. **Social media** provides unprecedented opportunities to tap into public dialogue, from customer ratings and reviews to conversations shared on social networks. Marketing and public relations professionals now have the ability to tap into publicly shared opinion and commentary on social networks and use analytics to execute data-driven strategies to deliver personalized consumer experiences. **Social networks** also allow industry professionals to evaluate overlapping ecosystems and better understand relationships between individuals, open social network communities and groups, and members within private online communities. Studying consumer dialogue and behaviors both within and across associated social networks can offer clarity when it comes to identifying

- the context, purpose, and location of online conversations;
- which social networks, groups, and channels are being utilized most frequently;
- what is being said; and
- the voices that are most prominent within the conversations.

Each element can provide vital insights and aid in identifying areas to engage, drive influence, and earn trust.

Studies published by Converseon, a leading social intelligence digital consultancy, highlights that the appetite for applying social media data insights has increased within the broader industry. This expansion is creating a high level of demand for new data-driven skill sets, which are essential in applying data-driven strategies that drive business outcomes. A key factor in the report notes that "uses of social data expanding across the enterprise now include category/need state analysis, **social CRM, audience analytics/segmentation**, innovation, product development, **brand tracking**, customer journey/experience, **marketing mix modeling**, advocacy analysis, **reputation management, influencer identification, content/ linguistic analysis**, and more. . . . Insights teams can apply social data to a wide range of needs, including brand tracking, post segmentation, market mixed modeling, trend forecasting and more for fast and actionable results. Sales teams can plumb social media for new leads."[2]

As a result, a new push for leaders in marketing and public relations disciplines exists to appropriately resource and equip their teams with data-driven discipline skills and technologies.

SOCIAL INSIGHTS ACROSS AN ENTERPRISE—WHAT USERS WANT

As a leader in strategic research, Forrester is realizing increased demand to aid organizations gather insights from social platforms as a supplement to traditional business intelligence. The evolution of **business-to-consumer (B2C) marketing** is now expanding to include social listening providers for enhanced brand protection, conducting competitive intelligence analyses, and tracking trends. The future of social intelligence is in the enterprise, not just marketing. With a history in this space, Forrester previously established that the true value of social intelligence is its ability to provide consumer insights across diverse business units including marketing, customer service, market research, product development, risk and reputation management, human resources, creative development, media planning, and many others. According to the Converseon Effective Social Listening report "this technology can be defined as: Social listening platforms manage and analyze customer data from social sources and use that data to activate, measure, and recalibrate marketing and business programs."[3] Furthermore, an online Forrester survey revealed that brands predominantly combine insights derived from social data with other marketing findings.[4]

EXPLORING THE INTERDEPENDENCE OF FOUR FUNDAMENTAL TECHNOLOGIES

There are four distinct categories that establish the foundation of emerging social listening technologies: **natural language processing (NLP)**, **semantic analysis**, **machine learning**, and **artificial intelligence (AI)**. These capabilities have been advancing and evolving with increasing sophistication and precision.

The accompanying image presents the interrelationship of each. The base concept of natural language processing is that it provides a foundation for each subsequent area to build upon. Each level carries valuable information and understandings available for business intelligence purposes.[5]

How Natural Language Processing, Semantic Analysis,
Machine Learning, and Artificial Intelligence are interrelated

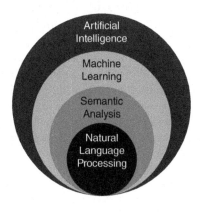

- Artificial Intelligence (AI) teaches systems to perform tasks based on ML and NLP such as: speech recognition, decision-making, translation between languages, visual perception

- Machine Learning (ML) Computers learn from pattern recognition

- Semantic Analysis: Evaluation of Tone, Sentiment, and Emotion

- Natural Language Processing (NLP): Text analysis, Summarization, Extraction and Retrieval

This figure illustrates the relationship between natural language processing, machine learning, and artificial intelligence.

Natural Language Processing

At its core, natural language processing (NLP) provides fundamental support to semantic analysis, machine learning, and artificial intelligence. Ehud Reiter, a researcher and professor at the University of Aberdeen in Britain, states that natural language processing is divided between speech and text or written language.[6] Gobinda Chowdhury, from the University of Strathclyde, Glasgow, defines NLP as an "application that explores how computers can be used to understand and manipulate natural language text or speech to do useful things."[7] This simply means that machines gather information based on how people understand and use language. With this information, computer systems can create tools, such as Alexa or Google Home, that can assist with tasks. For example, when we give the command "Hey Google, how do you say shirt in Spanish?" or "Alexa, let's play Mad Libs," these tools have been trained to understand human language patterns in order to search the web and respond with an answer.[8]

The linguistic science of natural language processing is rooted in text and language analytics, allowing for a basis of understanding the meanings of words in any language as well as the context in which these words and/or phrases are used, evoking sentiment and emotion.[9]

Semantics

Leveraging insights from sentiment analysis is essential to the development of data-driven social media strategies. Katie Delahaye Paine and William T. Paarlberg, authors of *Measure What Matters*, note that semantics allows a deeper understanding of metrics. This may include customer satisfaction ratings, comments, retweets, shares on social media channels, and conversions that lead to sales, as well as authentic engagements with consumers.[10]

Maria Ogneva, director of social media at Biz360 notes, "Automated sentiment analysis is the process of training a computer to identify sentiment within content through Natural Language Processing (NLP). Various sentiment measurement platforms employ different techniques and statistical methodologies to evaluate sentiment across the web. Some rely 100% on automated sentiment, some employ humans to analyze sentiment, and some use a hybrid system."[11] Psycholinguistics, or analysis of word choice, for example, allows us to build personality graphs to better understand the optimal language to use when creating personalized customer experiences.

Tools such as the IBM Watson Tone Analyzer can detect emotion and linguistic tones within all types of written text, including emails, comments on blogs and social media channels, and online surveys. Emma, the free email-mood-analyzer app from Microsoft AppSource, is promoted as an expert in sentiment analysis and text mining. The app alerts the writer if an email is positive or negative, detects irony within the written language, and can support English, French, and Spanish.[12] Tools such as these enable a company to better understand their customer base and the way in which marketing and public relations messages are perceived and received by a specific target audience. Armed with this information, practitioners are then able to adjust the tone of messaging. Organizations can also use the platform to learn the tone of their customers' written interactions on social channels. This allows a company to respond appropriately to individual customers in an effort to improve customer relations.[13]

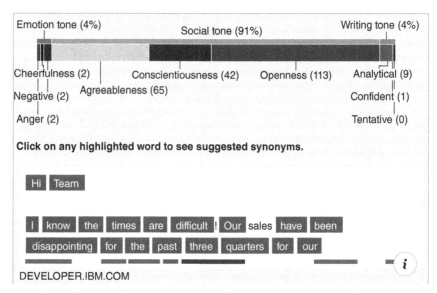

IBM Watson
August 31, 2015.

Happy? Angry? Curious what tone your writing conveys? Try Watson Tone Analyzer for insight: http://ibm.co/1GqcB0N

Emotion tone (4%)   Social tone (91%)   Writing tone (4%)

Cheerfulness (2)   Conscientiousness (42)   Openness (113)   Analytical (9)
Negative (2)   Agreeableness (65)   Confident (1)
Anger (2)   Tentative (0)

Click on any highlighted word to see suggested synonyms.

Hi Team

I know the times are difficult ! Our sales have been
disappointing for the past three quarters for our

DEVELOPER.IBM.COM

Machine Learning

Without being explicitly programmed, machine learning is a form of artificial intelligence that allows computers to learn. When exposed to new data, machines can essentially teach themselves programs.[14] Technically, machine learning is a subcategory of artificial intelligence, which deals more specifically with pattern recognition, natural language processing, and neural networks. Machine learning builds off of predictive analytics, adding increased monitoring and feedback capabilities. This is the "learning" within machine learning.

The last decade has given rise to predictive analytics capabilities, whereby organizations use historical data to look for patterns, create models from these patterns, and then use what is found to predict future actions. Many organizations have been collecting and analyzing analytics for years. These capabilities make it possible for marketing and public relations professionals to leverage data and analytics to provide insights into how a particular program or campaign performed historically, and subsequently adjust goals, strategies, or key performance indicators to allow real-time analyses into the performance of a company. With this type of analytics, decision makers can take advantage of continuous learning and intelligence, which yields refined models, improved accuracy of predictions, stronger insights, and greater responsiveness. Throughout the text, we will reference the above initiatives as "campaigns" and consider strategic data-driven decision making to be foundational to campaign development.

Artificial Intelligence

Combining elements of both machine learning and AI make it possible to make sense of what is often referred to as "dark data," or the unknown or previously untapped data across an organization, generated usually by systems, devices, and interactions.[15]

In *The State of Dark Data* report[1]—which surveyed more than 1,300 global business managers and leaders about how organizations collect, manage, and use data within the workplace—results show that while the current state of data is top of mind, action is often far behind:

- Seventy-six percent of respondents agree that "the organization that has the most data is going to win."
- Eighty-two percent say humans are and will always be at the heart of AI.
- Business leaders say their top three obstacles to recovering dark data is the volume of data, followed by the lack of necessary skill sets and resources.

However, looking to the future, AI is believed to be the next frontier for data-savvy organizations and will provide a multitude of opportunities for career paths and career growth:

Globally, respondents believe AI will generally augment opportunities, rather than replace people. While the survey revealed that few organizations are using AI right now, a majority see its vast potential. For example, in a series of use cases including operational efficiency, strategic decision making, HR and customer experience, only 10 to 15 percent say their organizations are

(continued)

deploying AI for these use cases while roughly two-thirds see the potential value.

- A majority of respondents (71 percent) saw potential in employing AI to analyze data.
- 73 percent think AI can make up for the skills gaps in IT.
- Only 12 percent are using AI to guide business strategy and 61 percent expect their organization to increase its use of AI this way over the next five years.[2]

---

[1] *The State of Dark Data*, Splunk, last modified April 30, 2019, accessed January 12, 2020, https://www.splunk.com/en_us/form/the-state-of-dark-data.html?utm_expid=.2 _hRnUDzTeW1wOabtuBwqg.0&utm_referrer=.

[2] Ibid.

Companies can unlock structured and unstructured formats by marrying up the appropriate algorithms and data to create systems that continually improve the customers' experiences. Systems driven by AI can perform tasks that normally require human intelligence, such as speech recognition, image recognition, visual perception, language translation, and decision making. As a result, the commercialization of AI is changing not only customer experiences, but also, and perhaps more importantly, consumer expectations. Innovations across industries are seen in almost every sector, with the most notable change to everyday citizens being the unprecedented adoption and comfort level that people have with voice recognition devices, such as Google Home, Apple's Siri or Amazon's Alexa. In a few short years it is predicted that customers will manage 85 percent of their relationship with a company without ever interacting with a human being.[16]

The Practical Guide: For Applying Effective Machine Learning to Social Listening Analysis

by Rob Key of Converseon

Organizations are awash in untapped, insight-rich unstructured data. Customer feedback and unprompted opinion through social media, product reviews, long-form survey verbatims, call center transcripts and more are veritable goldmines of insight for those customer-obsessed companies that can effectively harness, filter, process, and understand this massive, messy data set. Computer World magazine forecasts that unstructured information might account for more than 70 percent–80 percent of all data in organizations.

Yet organizations today face a conundrum: even as this data set grows exponentially, most brands are processing and using only a small portion of it— Forrester Research says most organizations are processing less than 21 percent of this unstructured data. And with some good reason: this unprompted "language data" is complex. Implicit meaning, sarcasm, slang context and much more make it challenging to separate the signals from the noise and make the data actionable in a time span needed for competitive advantage.

Today, however, a growing number of organizations are leveraging advanced natural language processing and text analytics solutions powered by artificial intelligence that are proving to be game-changers and allowing these firms to begin to fully leverage the long untapped value of this data set. But doing so requires a thoughtful and clear methodology and approach that builds on the latest data science, machine learning validation and processes.

What Can Social Intelligence Models Tell Us?

Is the conversation positive toward your brand, negative, or neutral? Sentiment models are designed to answer that question correctly.

EMOTION. Certainly, anger and sadness both convey a negative sentiment, but they might warrant different responses to the customers experiencing them. Plutchik's Wheel of Emotions is one common way of categorizing emotions, while other social scientists have defined alternative models.

INTENSITY. The strength of the passion behind an opinion can itself be measured. "It had a slight buttery off-note" is not as strong as "That is the worst-tasting $^#% I have ever tasted."

TRUST. Brand trust reflects a customer's expectation that a product or service (and sometimes corporate behavior) reflect the promises of the brand. Trust is a key quality of any relationship where customers make a purchase, yet brand trust sometimes fluctuates significantly over time. Identifying comments that exhibit brand trust can be challenging, as in the example, "I would be reluctant to use a different brand of shampoo on my infant's hair."

INNOVATION. In high tech, consumer electronics, and many other industries, a brand's reputation for innovation is a critical part of the buyer's decision making.

Finding the right conversations that reflect innovation is also not easy, because people often comment on things that are new, but not all of them are innovative.

VALUES. Brands today are expected to have a social purpose to benefit society more broadly. Consumers, especially millennials, are requiring brands to take stands on important "lightning rod" issues. By applying machine learning models to the social conversation, brands can better understand the risks, costs and benefits of engaging in the values discussions and help improve the perceptions of their CSR (Corporate Social Responsibility) efforts.

SOURCE: iabrahamsen, "The Practical Guide: For Applying Effective Machine Learning to Social Listening Analysis," Converseon, November 21, 2019, https://converseon.com/blog/the-practical-guide/. Reprinted with permission.

SERVING UP WHAT CUSTOMERS WANT, EVEN IF THEY DON'T REALIZE THEY WANT IT

The unparalleled progress of predictive analytic capabilities provides marketing and public relations professionals the necessary business intelligence to equip their organization with the ability to *predict desires and intent*. This capability makes it possible to build strategies that *proactively* serve the needs of consumers. Skilled marketing and public relations professionals who embrace these capabilities benefit through the development of novel strategies and subsequent successful execution, reinforced by data that delight consumers and frustrate competitors. Anticipating customer needs paves the way for opportunities to heighten responsiveness by delivering personalized experiences and improved customer experience in real time.

For example, a strategy in which brands provide personalized mobile coupons to patrons shopping in a store is not only timely but drives dramatically higher redemptions compared to print.[17]

Customized Content

In leveraging AI, professionals can modify messaging for specific audiences. This means that optimizing paid media in real time, specific to an individual consumer, may lead to an increase in favorable behaviors due to appropriately targeted messaging. With concurrent data in hand as an asset, today's professionals are able to provide their audiences with content they desire, rather than content that is useless.[18] AI can take customized content creation to the next level, as content directed toward customers will be hypertargeted and personalized.

FunMobility: A Lesson in User Experience

FunMobility, an organization specializing in creating an exciting experience for customers, was able to optimize the shopping experience of Ace Hardware patrons, leading to increased sales using featured content including themed mobile or email-based coupons redeemable at **point of sale (POS)** locations. To enhance engagement and interaction between customers and in-store marketing materials, Ace Hardware retailers partnered with FunMobility to launch a specific app-centric, mobile-based coupon and promotions program.[19] As a result, Ace Hardware dealers reported a six-fold increase in the average sales versus the industry standards. Linda Roarke, CEO of Pete's Ace Hardware located in Castro Valley, California, noted that this experience "has worked out really well for us. It's easy, our customers like it. This lets them know that this is the place to shop."[20] Brands such as Chiquita and Burger King have also seen success utilizing similar strategies with FunMobility.

In relation to online shopping, patrons commonly experience these suggestive selling techniques on e-commerce retail sites such as Amazon, that leverage a process known as **collaborative filtering**: providing recommendations even before customers begin searching for individual items. Product suggestions are based on products frequently purchased together and what shoppers buying similar products purchased. Amazon provides a clear explanation of the process on its recommendations FAQ page: "We determine your interests by examining the items you've purchased, items you've told us you own items you've rated, and items you've told us you like. We then compare your activity on our site with that of other customers, and using this comparison, are able to recommend other items that may interest you."[21] This may be easier for Amazon than other online retailers. Typical Amazon customers spend more time on Amazon's site than other sites they purchase products from. This means that Amazon can leverage the data they receive from customers spending extra time on their pages and propose even more accurate suggestions to users by asking them questions about the recommended products. Amazon could ask whether or not a customer likes the product, if the customer owns the product, or if the customer is willing to recommend the product to others. The more the data that a company has about what customers truly want, the more targeted search results can be.[22]

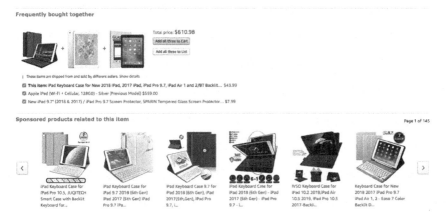

An example of Amazon's collaborative filtering abilities.

Additional items are often highlighted as "You may also like," or "Others also viewed," or "This item is commonly purchased with" and are often accompanied by bundled discounts at checkout. While retail may have been the first to adopt this method, the evolving customer experience continues to be paramount for nearly every online retailer across business categories.

SMARTER AND MORE STRATEGIC WITH ARTIFICIAL INTELLIGENCE

A recent Forrester Research Study notes that AI is transforming all areas of communications, including public relations, marketing, and advertising. Some of the traditional processes in place for today's professionals are resource intensive. However, AI has the power to change that through automation. AI-delivered tasks can be used to discover and analyze more combinations of data to provide deeper, more reliable, and actionable insights. Forrester's research noted that 79 percent of professionals believe that AI-powered marketing will create more strategic outcomes because communications teams will be more efficient and effective due to automated workflows.[23]

In Salesforce's annual state of marketing research study, the company predicted continued growth in AI. In fact, their study reported that AI is projected to increase 53 percent over the next few years, dominating the marketplace. When applied to strategic planning and program execution, data-driven insights gleaned from social intelligence research allow practitioners to develop robust, personalized engagement and community-focused strategies. Social media content strategies are also enhanced when informed by language patterns, topics of interest, and various other outputs. These capabilities allow for the development of digital experiences that resonate and motivate action more effectively than ever before.

AI already provides an organization with the ability to process data rapidly, meaning that brands can better anticipate the wants and needs of their customers. The power of leveraging data-driven insights allows for stronger and more direct messaging. Some of the most impactful changes to the marketing and public relations industry are due to the advances within AI, which include customized content and obvious implications for the **PESO model** (paid media, earned media, shared media, and owned media).

Paid Media

Paid advertising on social media outlets is no longer enough to support a successful outcome. Practitioners must understand nuances. For example, professionals must know how Facebook pixel works to create custom audiences or understand implementation of native advertising and the best publications to test within. They must learn to connect email marketing efforts to the growth of the organization. In today's landscape, practitioners must test theories and ideas and be willing to take risks.

Earned Media

The relationship between journalists and public relations professionals existed as a delicate symbiotic dance for decades, each function understanding the role the other plays in developing content that the public consumes. In 2006, SHIFT public relations released its first-ever social media press release, revolutionizing the industry.[24] AI is the next step in the evolution of this industry: it can allow practitioners to create media lists and more successfully develop copy that specifically targets a desired audience. For example, appropriate data interpretation can help practitioners create the most compelling headlines, identify proper social channels, categorize facts that will resonate best with specific journalists, and pinpoint which journalists, influencers, and bloggers to pitch. Columbia University's professor of mechanical engineering Hod Lipson noted, "Data is the fuel and the algorithm is the engine. We used to program computers. Now it is machine learning, we just feed it with data."[25]

Shared Media

Public relations and marketing professionals should be ready to use data to open a dialogue with senior leadership. Practitioners need to have a keen understanding of the data supporting the social platforms that their organizations have selected in order to promote an intelligent conversation about how the data affects the organization. For example, if you spend copious resources on Snapchat and an influencer encourages people to drop the social network, it is important to understand how this news may affect the company's Snapchat strategy.

Owned Media

Practitioners create sophisticated, resonating content to maximize an organizations owned channels, including corporate sponsored websites, blogs, and podcasts. Additionally, the use of predictive analytics should drive and inform organizational decisions. Therefore, it is imperative that practitioners embrace, rather than shy away from, analytics, as analytics drive decisions.

NIKE INNOVATION DRIVEN BY ALGORITHMS

Over the past few years Nike has devoted substantial resources in computational design to develop some of the most cutting-edge, high-performance sportswear available on the market today. Data, algorithms, and machines have changed the way that brands think about apparel, and Nike is leading the way.

Shelly-Ann Fraser-Pryce, the Jamaican Olympic runner, donned the latest pair of Nike running shoes at the Rio Olympics, aptly named the Zoom Superfly Elites. Rather than soles with the traditional screw-in spikes, her shoe soles were molded into a single, specialized plate. The shoes were specifically designed for her and developed to cut running time, in part, due to their incredible light weight.

According to Matt Burgess, tech writer for Wired, the trainers were some of the first designed using Nike's data leveraging algorithms. Computational design—which involves converting data into structural patterns and communicating those outcomes to the molding and manufacturing systems—played a critical role in the development process.[26] Burgess explained that computers have the advantage of being able to conceive and execute designs that the human brain has difficulty visualizing. This concept of computational assistance takes designing apparel to the next level.

Nike also leverages computational design to develop various other types of apparel, including shirts. According to Kurt Parker, Nike's VP of apparel design, "In apparel design, we have forever been combining multiple materials, depending on the problem we are solving, often resulting in the build-up of seams and complexity. Sometimes this creates a new problem as we are solving another. Over time, our understanding of the body in motion and new manufacturing techniques have started to converge."[27] It is this convergence of manufacturing and human kinetics that support a new paradigm in the apparel industry—specifically, utilization of computational design to convert data into advanced patterns. Outputs of this data-driven approach allow for a greater level of detail to be incorporated within the apparel. "It takes us to a completely different place," Parker confirms. "Instead of having to cut and sew multiple materials, we could just program the knitting machine to do it all at one moment, using one material instead of many."[28] As a result, the shirts in NikeLab NIKE A.A.E. 1.0 were developed using computational designs based on body map images. By connecting the data with apparel manufacturing, Nike has fundamentally changed the conventional T-shirt making process.

Not surprisingly, the integration of computational design is not unique to apparel design and is prevalent across numerous industries. Manufacturing using this technique often leads to a reduction of material weight, promotes the development of novel complex structures, and can ultimately reduce overall production time. As research into computational design was introduced in the 1960s by Carnegie Mellon University, this field is not new. The recent rise in renewed popularity is commonly tied to rapid manufacturing capabilities, increased reliability of machine learning systems, heightened processing power, and increased access to larger volumes of interpretable data.

You can bet that data, algorithms, and computational design are playing a larger, more influential role in what consumers are wearing.

THE ETHICS OF DATA

This chapter has focused a great deal on the importance of data, analytics, and artificial intelligence in the practice of marketing and public relations. Keeping in mind that although AI may be doing the heavy lifting, it's likely that humans will always be at the heart of AI,[29] working in sync with the data, so it's important that practitioners take responsibility of leading with ethical frameworks in mind. As such, professional codes or statement of ethics serve as norms and established standards of conduct to be maintained by practitioners serving in marketing and public relations aspects of business. With guidance from the Public Relations Society of America (PRSA), the American Marketing Association (AMA), and the American Advertising Federation (AAF), United States–based practitioners can utilize these standards to embrace high professional ethical norms and values guided by the responsibility required by various stakeholders at appropriate times of engagement. The International Public Relations Association (IPRA), International Institute of Marketing Professionals (IIMP), and International Advertising Association (IAA) assist common interests of the same disciplines globally and can provide similar guidance for the professions. The evolution of such codes is now beginning to include and consider disclosure of information and data-driven sections in order to aid consideration of ethical matters in each area.

PRSA Code of Ethics

The PRSA Code of Ethics applies to PRSA members. The Code is designed to be a useful guide for PRSA members as they carry out their ethical responsibilities. This document is designed to anticipate and accommodate, by precedent, ethical challenges that may arise. The scenarios outlined in the Code provision are actual examples of misconduct. More will be added as experience with the Code occurs.

The Public Relations Society of America (PRSA) is committed to ethical practices. The level of public trust PRSA members seek, as we serve the public good, means we have taken on a special obligation to operate ethically.

The value of member reputation depends upon the ethical conduct of everyone affiliated with the PRSA. Each of us sets an example for each other—as well as other professionals—by our pursuit of excellence with powerful standards of performance, professionalism, and ethical conduct.

Emphasis on enforcement of the Code has been eliminated. But, the PRSA Board of Directors retains the right to bar from membership or expel from the Society any individual who has been or is sanctioned by a government agency or convicted in a court of law of an action that fails to comply with the Code.

Ethical practice is the most important obligation of a PRSA member. We view the Member Code of Ethics as a model for other professions, organizations, and professionals.

PRSA Member Statement of Professional Values

This statement presents the core values of PRSA members and, more broadly, of the public relations profession. These values provide the foundation for the Member Code of Ethics and set the industry standard for the professional practice of public relations. These values are the fundamental beliefs that guide our behaviors and decision-making process. We believe our professional values are vital to the integrity of the profession as a whole.

Advocacy
We serve the public interest by acting as responsible advocates for those we represent. We provide a voice in the marketplace of ideas, facts, and viewpoints to aid informed public debate.

Honesty
We adhere to the highest standards of accuracy and truth in advancing the interests of those we represent and in communicating with the public.

Expertise
We acquire and responsibly use specialized knowledge and experience. We advance the profession through continued professional development, research, and education. We build mutual understanding, credibility, and relationships among a wide array of institutions and audiences.

Independence
We provide objective counsel to those we represent. We are accountable for our actions.

Loyalty
We are faithful to those we represent, while honoring our obligation to serve the public interest.

Fairness
We deal fairly with clients, employers, competitors, peers, vendors, the media, and the general public. We respect all opinions and support the right of free expression.

PRSA Code Provisions of Conduct

FREE FLOW OF INFORMATION Core Principle Protecting and advancing the free flow of accurate and truthful information is essential to serving the public interest and contributing to informed decision making in a democratic society.

INTENT:

- To maintain the integrity of relationships with the media, government officials, and the public.
- To aid informed decision-making.

GUIDELINES: A member shall:

- Preserve the integrity of the process of communication.
- Be honest and accurate in all communications.
- Act promptly to correct erroneous communications for which the practitioner is responsible.
- Preserve the free flow of unprejudiced information when giving or receiving gifts by ensuring that gifts are nominal, legal, and infrequent.

EXAMPLES OF IMPROPER CONDUCT UNDER THIS PROVISION:

- A member representing a ski manufacturer gives a pair of expensive racing skis to a sports magazine columnist, to influence the columnist to write favorable articles about the product.

(continued)

- A member entertains a government official beyond legal limits and/or in violation of government reporting requirements.

Competition
Core Principle Promoting healthy and fair competition among professionals preserves an ethical climate while fostering a robust business environment.

INTENT:

- To promote respect and fair competition among public relations professionals.
- To serve the public interest by providing the widest choice of practitioner options.

GUIDELINES: A member shall:

- Follow ethical hiring practices designed to respect free and open competition without deliberately undermining a competitor.
- Preserve intellectual property rights in the marketplace.

EXAMPLES OF IMPROPER CONDUCT UNDER THIS PROVISION:

- A member employed by a "client organization" shares helpful information with a counseling firm that is competing with others for the organization's business.
- A member spreads malicious and unfounded rumors about a competitor in order to alienate the competitor's clients and employees in a ploy to recruit people and business.

Disclosure of Information
Core Principle Open communication fosters informed decision making in a democratic society.

INTENT: To build trust with the public by revealing all information needed for responsible decision making.

GUIDELINES: A member shall:

- Be honest and accurate in all communications.
- Act promptly to correct erroneous communications for which the member is responsible.
- Investigate the truthfulness and accuracy of information released on behalf of those represented.
- Reveal the sponsors for causes and interests represented.
- Disclose financial interest (such as stock ownership) in a client's organization.
- Avoid deceptive practices.

EXAMPLES OF IMPROPER CONDUCT UNDER THIS PROVISION:

- Front groups: A member implements "grass roots" campaigns or letter-writing campaigns to legislators on behalf of undisclosed interest groups.
- Lying by omission: A practitioner for a corporation knowingly fails to release financial information, giving a misleading impression of the corporation's performance.
- A member discovers inaccurate information disseminated via a website or media kit and does not correct the information.

- A member deceives the public by employing people to pose as volunteers to speak at public hearings and participate in "grass roots" campaigns.

Safeguarding Confidences

Core Principle Client trust requires appropriate protection of confidential and private information.

INTENT: To protect the privacy rights of clients, organizations, and individuals by safeguarding confidential information.

GUIDELINES:

- A member shall: Safeguard the confidences and privacy rights of present, former, and prospective clients and employees.
- Protect privileged, confidential, or insider information gained from a client or organization.
- Immediately advise an appropriate authority if a member discovers that confidential information is being divulged by an employee of a client company or organization.

EXAMPLES OF IMPROPER CONDUCT UNDER THIS PROVISION:

- A member changes jobs, takes confidential information, and uses that information in the new position to the detriment of the former employer.
- A member intentionally leaks proprietary information to the detriment of some other party.

Conflicts of Interest

Core Principle Avoiding real, potential or perceived conflicts of interest builds the trust of clients, employers, and the publics.

INTENT:

- To earn trust and mutual respect with clients or employers.
- To build trust with the public by avoiding or ending situations that put one's personal or professional interests in conflict with society's interests.

GUIDELINES: A member shall:

- Act in the best interests of the client or employer, even subordinating the member's personal interests.
- Avoid actions and circumstances that may appear to compromise good business judgment or create a conflict between personal and professional interests.
- Disclose promptly any existing or potential conflict of interest to affected clients or organizations.
- Encourage clients and customers to determine if a conflict exists after notifying all affected parties.

EXAMPLES OF IMPROPER CONDUCT UNDER THIS PROVISION:

- The member fails to disclose that he or she has a strong financial interest in a client's chief competitor.

(continued)

- The member represents a "competitor company" or a "conflicting interest" without informing a prospective client.

Enhancing the Profession
Core Principle Public relations professionals work constantly to strengthen the public's trust in the profession.

INTENT:

- To build respect and credibility with the public for the profession of public relations.

- To improve, adapt and expand professional practices.

GUIDELINES: A member shall:

- Acknowledge that there is an obligation to protect and enhance the profession.

- Keep informed and educated about practices in the profession to ensure ethical conduct.

- Actively pursue personal professional development.

- Decline representation of clients or organizations that urge or require actions contrary to this Code.

- Accurately define what public relations activities can accomplish.

- Counsel subordinates in proper ethical decision making.

- Require that subordinates adhere to the ethical requirements of the Code.

- Report practices that fail to comply with the Code, whether committed by PRSA members or not, to the appropriate authority.

EXAMPLES OF IMPROPER CONDUCT UNDER THIS PROVISION:

- A PRSA member declares publicly that a product the client sells is safe, without disclosing evidence to the contrary.

- A member initially assigns some questionable client work to a non-member practitioner to avoid the ethical obligation of PRSA membership.

PRSA, "Code of Ethics," Public Relations Society of America, accessed January 12, 2020, https://www.prsa.org/about/ethics/prsa-code-of-ethics.

A review of blogs, books, and research studies highlight several areas to be conscious of when developing and implementing elements of AI. We've made it simple—brands should be accountable, act responsibly, and protect users. Let's take a closer look at each section.

Be Accountable
Because humans are developing and designing algorithms, bias inevitably seeps into their work. This is called **algorithmic bias**, which is a systematic and repeatable error found in computer systems that creates unfair outcomes privileging some user groups over others.[30] According to researchers at MIT, there are a number of ways that bias is introduced, including during the creation of a dataset or when

data is collected, digitized, adapted, and entered into a database or cataloged.[31] Search engine results and social media platforms are among the most prevalent areas where we see this type of bias. When this appears, it reinforces social biases of race, ethnicity, gender, sexuality, and even privacy rights.

To embrace an atmosphere of accountability, organizations should develop clear policies surrounding the development of any technologies or campaigns using AI. It is suggested that detailed records are kept and best practices are created.[32]

Act Responsibly

If your company has an ethics policy, then be sure to review and enforce the policy among team members. Ethics policies should align naturally with company accountability. The International Trade Association defines ethic as "responsible business conduct."[33] While this definition may seem oversimplified, it has merit. Acting responsibly should be aligned with company values because the company culture plays an integral role in relation to data mining, privacy, and the application of AI principles. Having set policies in place helps employees understand acceptable and reasonable actions across the entire company. From research and development to human resources, to something as simple as travel procedures or as complex as data collection, a company's ethics policy should be enforced. It's best for marketing and public relations professionals to keep these policies top of mind when developing data-powered campaigns.

Protect Users

The ease with which customers understand how data and AI are being implemented is important for all brands. Companies should be explicit and transparent when using a person's data. Critical to this conversation is **general data protection (GDPR)** regulation. Approved and adopted by the European Union (EU) in April 2016, and fully implemented in May 2018, GDPR helps users take control of their data. Sara Jodka, from the law offices of Dickinson Wright, notes that "personal data" under GDPR includes

> information related to an identified or identifiable natural person. This means that, if you can use any piece of information to learn or otherwise identify a natural person, the information is 'personal data' under the GDPR, and the processing of that data is protected by the GDPR. This type of information includes an individual's name, ID number, location data, online identifier or other factors specific to the physical, physiological, genetic, mental, economic, cultural or social identity of that person. It also includes, religion, trade union association, ethnicity, marital status, IP addresses, cookie strings, social media posts, online contacts, and mobile device IDs.[34]

While implemented in the EU, any multinational brand is impacted. Thus, being explicit and transparent is paramount for brands.

The ethical implications of data and AI should be top of mind for all practitioners. As society continues to depend on these technologies, brands must respond accordingly. And that means being ethical with their practices and uses.

IMPACT OF AI

Artificial intelligence is an integral part of our lives and as such will continue to flourish over the next several years. It's up to marketing and public relations professionals to understand their customers to provide customized campaigns.

Emerging technologies are here to stay. These capabilities are helping today's marketing and PR professionals become increasingly strategic, leveraging data-driven insights to develop incredibly sophisticated and engaging customer experiences. The presence of artificial intelligence within the broader industry presents massive opportunities to develop personalized content and offers, or present emotional triggers that inspire engaging topical conversions. Additionally, these capabilities can deliver measurable efficiency and effectiveness gains—for example, by implementing chatbots within the customer service realm to assist in sales, enhance effectiveness of campaigns, and ultimately drive improvements in expense-to-revenue ratios.

Although there are concerns about whether robots are taking over human jobs, individuals who invest in understanding how AI can be integral to data-driven strategies will set themselves apart by engaging customers better than before. You may not be a data scientist; however, there may be a time in the not-so-distant future when it will be commonplace for you to team up with one to mine and apply insights discerned from social media analytics. Businesses of all types need marketing and public relations leaders who understand the data and can apply the business intelligence to data-driven marketing and public relations strategy, optimizing techniques across paid, earned, earned, and shared engagement methods.

DISCUSSION QUESTIONS AND EXERCISES

1. To practice marketing and public relations in today's ever-changing environment, what skills must a professional possess?
2. Identify and explain the differences between natural language processing, semantic analysis, machine learning, and artificial intelligence.

3. What are the ethical implications of AI, and what role should practitioners play?

4. How should marketing and public relations practitioners incorporate ethics into their campaign strategy—particularly one that relies on data?

5. The debate surrounding human power versus machine power existed long before artificial intelligence was developed. Argue in favor or against the validity of this point. Provide concrete examples.

6. The chapter highlighted a campaign by Ace Hardware and other brands using mobile and email promotions from FunMobility. Look up and identify other programs that capitalize on the customer experience. Are they impactful? Do you participate in similar programs? If so, why?

7. *Small group exercise:* Assess how brands like Nike are leading the way in data, algorithmic decision making, and the incorporation of machines to think about the development of their products and services. Choose your favorite brand and formulate a strategy utilizing what you have learned with regard to artificial intelligence, natural language processing, semantic analysis, machine learning, and ethical considerations.

KEY TERMS

advertising
algorithmic bias
artificial intelligence (AI)
audience analytics
audience segmentation
brand tracking
business-to-consumer
  (B2C) marketing
collaborative filtering
content analysis

general data protection
  (GDPR)
influencer identification
linguistic analysis
machine learning
marketing
marketing mix modeling
natural language
  processing
PESO model

point of sale (POS)
public relations
reputation management
semantic analysis
social CRM
social media
social networks

NOTES

1. Fred Cook, *Global and Public Relations Report 2017*, Journalism and Public Relations, USC Annenberg School for Communication and Journalism, April 6, 2017, https://annenberg.usc.edu/sites/default/files/KOS_2017_GCP_April6.pdf.

2. "Converseon Effective Social Listening in 2017 Embracing New End-to-End Language Technologies to Unlock Social Data's Full Potential."

3. Jessica Liu and Arleen Chien, *The Forrester Wave™: Social Listening Platforms, Q3 2018; The 10 Providers That Matter Most and How They Stack Up*, August 21, 2018.

4. Forrester, "Global Social Listening Platforms Forrester Wave™ Customer Reference Online Survey, Q2 2018." https://www.forrester.com/report/The+Forrester+Wave+Social+Listening+Platforms+Q3+2018/-/E-RES137843

5. Gohar F. Khan, "Seven Layers of Social Media Analytics: Mining Business Insights from Social Media; Text, Actions, Networks, Hyperlinks, Apps, Search Engine, and Location Data" (self-pub., Createspace, 2015).

6. Ehud Reiter, "Natural Language Generation," in *The Handbook of Computational Linguistics and Natural Language Processing*, ed. Alexander Clark, Chris Fox, and Shalom Lappin (Chichester, UK: Wiley, 2010), 574–98, https://doi:10.1002/9781444324044.ch20.

7. Gobinda G. Chowdhury, "Natural Language Processing," *Annual Review of Information Science and Technology* 37, no. 1 (2005): 51–89, https://doi:10.1002/aris.1440370103.

8. C. J. F. Waaijer, C. A. van Bochove, and N. J. van Eck, "On the Map: *Nature* and *Science* Editorials," *Scientometrics* 86 (2011), 99–112, https://doi:10.1007/s11192-010-0205-9.

9. C. L. Sanchez Bocanegra, J. L. Sevillano Ramos, C. Rizo, et al., "HealthRecSys: A Semantic Content-Based Recommender System to Complement Health Videos," *BMC Medical Informatics and Decision Making* 17, no. 63 (2017), https://doi:10.1186/s12911-017-0431-7.

10. Katie Delahaye Paine and William T. Paarlberg, *Measure What Matters: Online Tools for Understanding Customers, Social Media, Engagement, and Key Relationships* (Hoboken, NJ: Wiley, 2011).

11. Maria Ogneva, "How Companies Can Use Sentiment Analysis to Improve Their Business," Mashable, April 19, 2010, https://mashable.com/2010/04/19/sentiment-analysis/#_Xj6X_ozC5qL.

12. Microsoft, "E-Mail-Mood-Analyzer," Microsoft Apps, accessed December 20, 2019, https://appsource.microsoft.com/en-us/product/office/WA104379982?tab=Overview.

13. "IBM Cloud," IBM Cloud Docs, https://console.bluemix.net/docs/services/tone-analyzer/index.html#about.

14. Alex Smola and S. V. N. Vishwanathan, *Introduction to Machine Learning* (Cambridge: Cambridge University Press, 2008), http://alex.smola.org/drafts/thebook.pdf.

15. Tim Tully, "Dark Data Has Huge Potential, but Not if We Keep Ignoring It," Splunk, last modified April 30, 2019, accessed January 12, 2020, https://www.splunk.com/en_us/blog/leadership/dark-data-has-huge-potential-but-not-if-we-keep-ignoring-it.html.

16. *Gartner C 360 Summit*, Gartner, 2011, https://www.gartner.com/imagesrv/summits/docs/na/customer-360/C360_2011_brochure_FINAL.pdf.

17. FunMobility, "The Agile Marketer's Guide to Mobile Coupons," LinkedIn SlideShare, January 28, 2016, http://www.slideshare.net/FunMobility/the-agile-marketers-guide-to-mobile-coupons.

18. Abbi Whitaker, "How Advancements in Artificial Intelligence Will Impact Public Relations," *Forbes*, March 20, 2017, https://www.forbes.com/sites/theyec/2017/03/20/how-advancements-in-artificial-intelligence-will-impact-public-relations/.

19. FunMobility, "FunMobility Announces Mobile Shopper Marketing Program for Retailers," FunMobility, January 14, 2015, https://www.funmobility.com/about-us/press-releases/funmobility-shopper-marketing-program-for-retailers/.

20. FunMobility, "The Agile Marketer's Guide to Mobile Coupons" LinkedIn SlideShare, January 28, 2016, http://www.slideshare.net/FunMobility/the-agile-marketers-guide-to-mobile-coupons.

21. Amazon, "About Recommendations," Amazon.ca: Computer and Video Games, accessed July 12, 2018, https://www.amazon.ca/gp/help/customer/display.html?nodeId=201,930,010.

22. Derrick Harris, "You Might Also Like. . . to Know How Online Recommendations Work," Gigaom, January 29, 2013, https://gigaom.com/2013/01/29/you-might-also-like-to-know-how-online-recommendations-work/.

23. Commissioned by Emarsys, *Building Trust and Confidence: AI Marketing Readiness in Retail and Ecommerce*, Forrester, 2017, https://www.emarsys.com/app/uploads/2018/01/Emarsys-Forrester-AI-Marketing-Readiness11Jul17.pdf.

24. Regina Luttrell, *Social Media How to Engage, Share, and Connect*, 3rd ed. (Lanham, MD: Rowman & Littlefield, 2016).

25. Abbi Whitaker, "How Advancements in Artificial Intelligence Will Impact Public Relations," *Forbes*, March 20, 2017, https://www.forbes.com/sites/theyec/2017/03/20/how-advancements-in-artificial-intelligence-will-impact-public-relations/.

26. Matt Burgess, "How Nike Used Algorithms to Help Design Its Latest Running Shoe," Wired, January 26, 2018, http://www.wired.co.uk/article/nike-epic-react-flyknit-price-new-shoe.

27. Marie O'Mahoney, "The Importance of Size and Fit," Industrial Fabrics Association International, accessed January 2, 2020, https://advancedtextilessource.com/2017/10/23/it-only-works-if-you-wear-it.

28. "A Glimpse into the Future by Way of a T-Shirt," Nike News, August 31, 2017, https://news.nike.com/news/nikelab-advanced-apparel-exploration-aae-1.

29. *The State of Dark Data*, Splunk, last modified April 30, 2019, accessed January 12, 2020, https://www.splunk.com/en_us/form/the-state-of-dark-data.html?utm_expid=.2_hRnUDzTeW1wOabtuBwqg.0&utm_referrer=.

30. Nicol Turner Lee, Paul Resnick, and Genie Barton, "Algorithmic Bias Detection and Mitigation: Best Practices and Policies to Reduce Consumer Harms," Brookings, last modified May 22, 2019, accessed January 12, 2020, https://www.brookings.edu/research/algorithmic-bias-detection-and-mitigation-best-practices-and-policies-to-reduce-consumer-harms/.

31. Tarleton Gillespie, Pablo Boczkowski, and Kristin Foot, *Media Technologies* (Cambridge, MA: MIT Press, 2014), pp. 1–30.

32. Nicholas Diakopoulos, "Algorithmic Accountability: On the Investigation of Black Boxes," Tow Center for Digital Journalism, accessed November 19, 2017, https://towcenter.columbia.edu/news/algorithmic-accountability-reporting-investigation-black-boxes.

33. Jennifer Williams, "Business Ethics Policies & Procedures," *Chron* (blog), accessed November 18, 2019, https://smallbusiness.chron.com/business-ethics-policies-procedures-2728.html.

34. Sara Jodka, "What US-Based Companies Need to Know about the GDPR, and Why," *Dickenson Wright* (blog), March 2018, https://www.dickinson-wright.com/news-alerts/what-usbased-companies-need-to-know. See also "Art. 4 GDPR: Definitions," GDPR, May 25, 2018, accessed January 2, 2020, https://gdpr-info.eu/art-4-gdpr/.

CHAPTER 2

LUPE Model—Developing Data-Driven Campaigns

KEY LEARNING OUTCOMES

Understand that planning is the first component in developing a data-driven strategy.

Recognize why research is fundamental to planning.

Learn the differences between objectives, strategies, and tactics.

Evaluate the role data plays in the planning process.

Learn how to utilize the LUPE model—*Listen and Learn, Understand, Plan, Execute and Evaluate*—to create sound strategies.

Recognize the framework of how each step is connected to develop sound data-driven decisions.

PLAN FIRST, AND THEN MEASURE

Developing a strategic plan is a fundamental task of every public relations, marketing, and advertising practitioners. In fact, these plans often serve as an organized framework to help guide practitioners. Practitioners rely on strategic planning methods as the foundation for designing and implementing sound programs. The technological advancements discussed in Chapter 1 have made gathering social intelligence from public discourse shared across the social web possible. Social listening and monitoring capabilities, also referred to as conversation mining, allow practitioners to listen and learn. Utilizing social media research as a means for understanding and keeping pace with market dynamics, competition, consumer behavior, key issues, topical trending themes, threats, opportunities, and much more adds a powerful ingredient to the strategic planning recipe. In the quest to formulate the optimal implementation for tactical execution, practitioners begin planning well in advance to ensure that there will be

Teams develop strategic programs through proactive, deliberate, tactical planning.

adequate time to conduct such foundational market research. This stage guides strategy and goal setting relative to market discovery and definition, competitive trends, predictive insights, or even latent opportunity identification. The development of strategic programs requires proactive, deliberate, tactical planning. Practitioners should connect the public relations and marketing plan to the company's overall strategic goals. Using a company's annual goals as a guide, practitioners can then formulate individual plans, campaigns, and strategies around what the organization values most. In their book *A Framework for Marketing Management*, Phillip Kotler and Kevin Lane describe the essential role of strategic planning as a "critical component in achieving a successful outcome; therefore, understanding how to establish a plan aligned to the company's goals and implement a plan effectively is of the utmost importance. Market-oriented strategic planning is the managerial processes of developing and maintaining a viable fit between the organization's objectives, skills, and resources and its changing market opportunities."[1] Generally speaking, most public relations, marketing, and advertising practitioners recognize the opportunity and use insights gleaned from social intelligence to inform data-driven decisions and improve strategic planning.

LUPE Model

The **LUPE model**—*Listen and Learn, Understand, Plan, Execute and Evaluate*—is introduced in this chapter and highlighted throughout the text via case studies that provide sound examples. Grounded in **research** through evaluation, this model provides a planning method that integrates social listening and optimization from beginning to end. Whether you are a marketing or advertising practitioner, public relations practitioner, or a social media strategist, the steps used in the LUPE model are applicable across a variety of disciplines and can be applied across industries. This framework encourages organizational alignment in establishing a set of clear goals and **objectives** supported by an interconnected

strategy, tactical elements that will be implemented to accomplish the goals in a measurable way.

We recognize that there are many planning frameworks used within the fields of public relations and marketing. These include the four-step RACE and ROPE models, the Public Relations Society of America's RPIE model, the seven Ps of the marketing mix, John and Torelli's BLIP model, Porter's five forces model, and even the PESTLE analysis. The LUPE model utilizes social intelligence to address the analytical and data-driven aspects of developing a public relations and marketing program and campaigns to harness the power of applying data-driven insights to planning and execution while also incorporating traditional communications principles. Leading with research, planning enables public relations, marketing, and advertising practitioners to build a solid foundation by which practitioners can achieve their company's goals and objectives. This model offers a step-by-step framework to support data-driven insights and planning.

As illustrated in the Accreditation in Public Relations (APR) study guide, practitioners must initially conduct **formative research** when embarking upon any program or campaign plan. This type of research provides the appropriate background that allows for effective understanding of the **target audience** consumer behaviors, market opportunity, competitive landscape, which is then applied to planning as well as identifying areas for adjustments in program implementation.[2] Typically in the research phase, market and audience analysis is conducted through social media research, social listening and monitoring, and primary and/or secondary market research to learn about, validate, or further examine trends, attitudes, and public opinion; and a deep dive into the challenges and opportunities the organization faces. From here, the organization can begin to focus on proper development and implementation of the strategic plan. Here is where practitioners ensure the strategies developed are in line with the executable **tactics**. In the final step of planning, **summative research** occurs. This is where practitioners execute, assess, and evaluate outcomes by analyzing performance data. They evaluate opportunities to improve outcomes through refinement and optimization while measuring progress against the established benchmarks. This approach has many benefits. Fundamentally, it puts the customer in the center and allows the strategic planning process to be grounded in the understanding of the customers, their pain points, buying decision processes, and consumption habits. It also establishes a "test and learn" approach to measuring progress with a focus on iterative improvement. As a result, practitioners are using data-driven decision making throughout the process, harnessing insights to determine priorities and inform choices. As Peter Drucker, the well-known management scholar, stated, "Marketing is the whole business seen from the point of view of its final result, that is, from the customer's point of view."[3]

This chapter is concise by design, allowing readers to see and understand each area of the LUPE model. The following sections will provide a breakdown of the framework.

Listen and Learn

Research Goals: Develop a sentence that outlines the opportunity or problem. Rank the most significant aspect of the campaign and how social media research as well as other market research will support it. Formulate the questions that the research will answer, and define what success looks like and what could possibly impede accomplishments. This step translates into establishing clear research objectives. Teams must identify the problem/opportunity to be addressed by the research project (stated in terms of key decisions that will subsequently be made using the research's results).	**Prioritize Requirements:** Determine priorities for effective research—for example, understanding what kind of data will be required to conduct these analyses; what social networks and/or channels will be evaluated; what information must appear in the final report; and what types of analyses are required to develop the content of this final report.	**Field the Research:** Conduct social media listening and monitoring, and primary and secondary research. Survey external audiences, competitors, social dialogue, social sentiment, and market trends to examine opinion, behaviors, and attitudes.

Listen and Learn, the initial step of the LUPE model, is grounded in social media research. Here practitioners listen and learn by tapping into social listening and monitoring capabilities, in addition to gathering input from their stakeholders across the organizations, to build out a comprehensive research plan to support data-driven decisions necessary for the program or campaign. For example, using social listening and monitoring tools, practitioners listen and learn from online conversation, and identify influencers, social venues of importance, competitive standing, sentiment, and natural language conveyed in social dialogue and much more. Essential within this first step is research, which can be defined as "the systematic gathering of information to describe and understand a situation, check assumptions about publics and perceptions, and determine the public relations consequences. Research is the foundation for effective strategic public relations planning. Research helps define the problem and publics."[4] Practitioners should research, leverage, and understand areas where common threads exist in order to better anticipate and plan for successful outcomes. Here are some examples:

- Social listening, monitoring: Social media channels may be used to monitor conversation relevant to a brand, a competitor, or customer experiences. This may include any relevant topic of interest that provides insights on sentiment and tone of dialogue shared across social networks. There are numerous social listening tools, including Social Studio from Salesforce; Meltwater; Crimson Hexagon, which is now part of Brandwatch; and Cyfe.

- Influencer discovery: Social graph analysis provides data visualization of relationship-level ecosystems, individual connectivity, reach, degree of prominence, authority, and level of engagement. These insights can be applied to influencer program strategy and tiered based on prioritization of influencers within a program. Gephi and NodeXL are tools that can be used to create social graphs.
- Media planning and buying: Analysis of customer behaviors, understanding context, and identifying which social networks a target audience most often engages can be utilized to optimize strategies, leading to increased efficiency and effectiveness across paid media across channels.
- Customer experience: This information allows brands to recognize and act on direct customer feedback about their experiences and expectations of the product or service.
- Employee engagement: This information allows brands to understand and respond to employee experience feedback to address and improve workforce optimization goals.

Understand

Analyze: Conduct analysis to determine key findings and insights from social listening and monitoring, and conduct the primary and secondary research. Determine if additional research is necessary to better understand audiences or trends. This is accomplished by conducting additional market analysis, to further examine opinion, behaviors, and attitudes. Insights derived from the analysis guide the development of goals and objectives.	Goals: Develop a simple statement that summarizes the results necessary to achieve the opportunity or solve the problem. Include key insights from the research and analysis that establish a benchmark from which to measure progress.	Objectives: Write down objectives. Statements that emerge from an organization's goals are considered objectives. Practitioners write SMART objectives: specific, measurable, attainable, results-oriented, and timebound.[a]

In step 2 of the LUPE model, practitioners begin to understand and use insights from the research analysis to develop data-driven strategies, set goals, identify publics, outline **SMART objectives**, and articulate strategies. This data-driven understanding guides decisions and priorities necessary when determining specific tactics and approaches to accomplish the defined goals and objectives. In this phase, practitioners frequently analyze and evaluate the following:

- Target audience: Practitioners should obtain information on decision makers; these could be a mix of consumers, current customers, prospective customers, and influencers.
- Segmentation: **Market segmentation** is the process of dividing a group of potential consumers into different clusters based on characteristics. What a company is then left with are sets of consumers that should respond similarly

to **marketing** strategies. These segments tend to share traits, including needs, interests, and geographic location.[5] The more consumers require personalization, the more brands must develop accurate segmentation. Using AI algorithms, practitioners can examine and analyze the habits, likes/dislikes, and previous activities of their targeted audience, leading to heightened levels of personalization and engagement.

- Personalized content planning: A Demand Metric study indicated that 80 percent of marketers agree that personalized content is more effective than any other type of content.[6] To reinforce loyalty and a sense of appreciation, personalized content often results in consumer action. You will see several examples of this throughout the book. For public relations, marketing, and advertising practitioners, using data can better segment target audiences while also optimizing campaigns across all channels.
- Search query: Practitioners should focus on building content that matches their customers' search queries through **search engine optimization (SEO)** and **social media optimization (SMO)**. This can be achieved by leveraging insights identified using customers' most frequently searched keywords or phrases.
- Ad targeting: Targeted advertising helps public relations, marketing, and advertising practitioners isolate their audience with acute accuracy.

Plan

Plan

Target Audience: Using your understanding of the natural language expressed in social dialogue, attributes, behaviors, and buying patterns of target audience ascertained from the previous *learn* and *understand* phases, identify the specific target audience(s) that must be reached to achieve the plan's goal and objectives. Each target audience will have specific messaging, strategies, channel, and communications preferences that must be considered and applied to the tactics developed. You may develop primary messages or secondary messages for each audience.	Tactics: Establish *tactics*, the tangible aspects of the plan. These are creative elements such as social media posts, videos, images, websites, events, publicity, or blogs developed for specific channels.	Timeline and Budget: Create a timeline and budget, which are essential to the planning process. Timelines highlight when a tactic begins and ends. Gantt charts are often used in planning. To project overall costs of each tactic, develop a budget to stay on task.

In this third phase of the LUPE model, practitioners will determine the optimal tactics to execute the strategic approach by create timelines that correlate to the implementation strategy.[7] The execution plan defines which social networks the target audience participates in and should be prioritized for building relationships with target publics. This could be customers, key influencers, extended communities. Timing is everything; therefore, it is suggested that practitioners should consider the following when conducting this step of the process:[8]

- Identifying the channels that will be used to reach their target audience;
- Size of the overall target audience;
- Plan to reach each segment through customization;
- What is necessary to achieve the overall plan objectives;
- A plan to ensure each person on the campaign understands who is responsible for each portion, what is due when, the budget, the timeline, and
- Metrics to be considered—the best way to evaluate and monitor results.[9]

Execute and Evaluate

Execute and Evaluate

Content: Evaluate the tactical execution of tactics to determine content performance in terms of the content types and the channels in which the content was distributed, will determine which channels reached the target audience more effectively and once reached which content forms attained higher engagement and re-sharing.	Empower Advocates: Evaluate the effectiveness of the execution and engagement led by influencers, employees, and brand advocates who were equipped to share information across all channels.	Harvest Results: Determine a cadence for analysis and reporting. Create a summary of elements that clearly articulate the performance and help stakeholders understand results.
Metrics that would guide the evaluation stage are reach, engagement, advocacy and conversion. Evaluating the content and channels best able to influence consumer behavior, achieve goals and drive advocacy across all social media driven channels Messaging via PESO channels will be analyzed to glean data.		

The last component of the LUPE model allows the practitioner to measure and evaluate the effectiveness of the program execution against the defined objectives. During the execution and evaluation stage, practitioners must establish a measurement framework with key performance indicators and determine cadence for analyzing and reporting. According to Robert Wynne, an executive from Wynne PR, measurement matters because industry practitioners are continually asked to justify their contributions and impact—particularly in the competitive landscape for resources, clients, money, and respect.[10] In general, outcome objectives call for modifications in awareness or opinions. Applicable customer behavioral change, however, is the ultimate sign of public relations effectiveness. Additionally, traditional financial analysis of programs occurs during this phase, identifying any realized revenue impacts, cost implications, or recognition of efficiency/productivity gains.

Practitioners should always enhance the campaign strategies and tactics by **optimizing** to improve efficiency and effectiveness. By making data-driven public relations and marketing decisions, practitioners can execute changes by using insights from ongoing social media listening to adjust and optimize content and engagement to drive business outcomes.

THE IMPORTANCE OF CREATING AN EXECUTABLE PLAN

Developing a public relations and marketing plan is an essential component of the profession. All plans need rigorous research and a dose of creativity. A strategic plan can lead to sound decisions, backed by data, that flourish into a comprehensive campaign.

DISCUSSION QUESTIONS AND EXERCISES

1. Explain why having a plan is important for public relations, marketing, and advertising practitioners.
2. Deconstruct the elements of the LUPE model. What makes this model so effective when planning a campaign?
3. Discuss each area of the LUPE model, and explain how a how a cohesive plan is formed.
4. The advantage of data-driven insights comes from listening and analysis. Identify a brand that used the LUPE model to build a successful campaign. Conversely, identify a campaign that failed to effectively use data to make informed decisions and discuss how data-driven decisions could have improved their campaign.
5. What does it mean to empower advocates and harness results?
6. *Small group exercise:* Now that you have learned the components of the LUPE model, build a comprehensive strategy for responding to a national public health crisis. Be sure to consider each area when making decisions.

KEY TERMS

formative research	research	strategy
LUPE model	SMART Objectives	summative research
market segmentation	search engine	tactic
marketing	optimization (SEO)	target audience
objective	social media optimization	
optimizing	(SMO)	

NOTES

1. Philip Kotler and Kevin Lane Keller, *A Framework for Marketing Management* (Pearson Education, 2016).
2. "APR Study Guide," Study Guide for the Examination for Accreditation in Public Relations, Public Relations Society of America, 2017, http://www.praccreditation.org/resources/documents/apr-study-guide.pdf.

3. Franklin S. Houston, "The Marketing Concept, What It Is and What It Is Not," *Journal of Marketing* 37, no. 50 (1986): 81–87. Brenner, Michael, Eric Wittlake, Zoe Callista, Tiffany Brown, and John Fox, "Marketing IS Business: The Wisdom of Peter Drucker," Marketing Insider Group, September 14, 2019, https://marketinginsidergroup.com/strategy/marketing-is-business-the-wisdom-of-peter-drucker.

4. Brenner et al., "Marketing IS Business."

5. Regina M. Luttrell and Luke W. Capizzo, *The PR Agency Handbook* (Thousand Oaks, CA: SAGE, 2018).mentation/.

6. Dillon Baker, "How Personalization Is Changing Content Marketing," Contently, accessed January 2, 2020, https://contently.com/2017/03/31/personalization-changing-content-marketing.

7. Regina M. Luttrell and Luke W. Capizzo, *The PR Agency Handbook* (Thousand Oaks, CA: SAGE, 2018).

8. "APR Study Guide," Study Guide for the Examination for Accreditation in Public Relations, Public Relations Society of America, 2017, http://www.praccreditation.org/resources/documents/apr-study-guide.pdf.

9. Ibid.

10. Robert Wynne, "Explaining PR's Barcelona Principles," *Forbes*, February 1, 2016, accessed June 6, 2018, https://www.forbes.com/sites/robertwynne/2016/02/01/explaining-the-barcelona-principles/.

CHAPTER 3

Anything Can Be Measured; Measure What Counts

KEY LEARNING OUTCOMES

Recognize the value and importance of planning and measurement.

Understand the elements of selecting and implementing a measurement strategy.

Recognize where PESO—paid media, earned media, shared media, and owned media—fit within measurement.

Envision measurement framework during planning to track progress against goals from the outset of program execution.

Differentiate between three types of analytics: prescriptive, descriptive, and predictive.

THE VALUE OF MEASUREMENT

A compelling digital campaign has the power to engage, inspire, and boost brand awareness. The first step in establishing how to best optimize and measure the success of improvements is to set a clear public relations and marketing strategy.

This chapter sets the stage for the numerous complexities related to data and measurement to provide students with the foundation for understanding the various methods available to measure digitally driven campaigns, programs, and initiatives. The most common mistake practitioners make is to set loose or undefined goals, not clearly tied to the desired output. The most important questions a practitioner should be asking their self is, what does success look like, and how will it be measured? In addition, and of equal importance, is having the wherewithal to determine the appropriate tools necessary for measuring progress—how each metric will be tracked and used to report the information to stakeholders.

Today's Digital Landscape

Before exploring the topic of measurement, it is essential to understand the rapidly evolving role of today's public relations, marketing, and advertising practitioners. Although the historically visible divisions between the fields of public relations (PR), marketing, and advertising are waning, it does not mean that harmony now exists among the three. On the contrary, these professions are continually under pressure to demonstrate measurable value, especially related to their digital activities. In essence, programs must demonstrate quantifiable means of achieving business goals.

The last decade has seen consumers make a clear shift toward consuming digital media. This preference has made it increasingly difficult to attract and retain customers using traditional PR and marketing efforts.[1] This evolution in behaviors is where the immense value of data gathered from interactions taking place within social media, social networks, and online communities becomes incredibly important. This change in consumer preference has prompted practitioners to complement their core skill sets by learning how to apply insights collected from social intelligence, develop well-thought-out data-driven strategies, and adopt analytically based decision-making processes to achieve organizational objectives.[2]

However, a long-standing, fundamental question remains across the public relations and marketing disciplines: which business role owns *social media*? The assumption behind this simple yet complex query is that the true owner of *social* can influence trust and behaviors, develop authentic relationships, and create meaningful conversations within the social sphere. Additionally, insights garnered from social listening research and social media analytics are both leveraged as social intelligence and applied to the development of data-driven strategies; the notion of distinctly defining *ownership* becomes increasingly restrictive and limiting. As such, pioneering social organizations consider *social* a foundational and essential skill practiced across business functions, not limited to PR or marketing. Simply by letting *social* exist over various functions, the idea of *ownership* becomes irrelevant. Functions within an organization can all benefit from social intelligence when defined and strategically developed appropriately.

As a best practice, practitioners should reference and follow available guidelines when evaluating the success of a campaign or program. The **Barcelona Principles** were developed to offer practitioners a set of standards by which they could effectively measure outcomes. According to the writers, these seven principles serve as a structure for practitioners to incorporate the evolution of the media landscape into a transparent, reliable, and consistent framework.[1] Some consider the Barcelona Principles foundational because they provide clarity to programs while emphasizing the importance of measurement. Here are the seven principles as outlined during the Annual European Summit on Measurement in Barcelona:[2]

---

[1] Ben Levine, "Barcelona Principles 3.0," PR News, accessed January 7, 2021, https://amecorg .com/2020/07/barcelona-principles-3-0/.

[2] Ibid.

Principle 1: Setting goals is an absolute prerequisite to communications planning, measurement, and evaluation. Be sure objectives are SMART—specific, measurable, achievable, realistic, and timebound.[3]

Principle 2: Measurement and evaluation should identify outputs, outcomes, and potential impact. Stephanie Loudee from Agility PR explains the three this way:[4] Outputs are qualitative and quantitative metrics that can be derived from measurement through paid, earned, shared, and owned media endeavors. Outtakes measure if your message was received, and outcomes are grounded in results such as click-throughs, website traffic, coupon code usage, or app downloads.

Principle 3: Outcomes and impact should be identified for stakeholders, society, and the organization.

Principle 4: Communication measurement and evaluation should include both qualitative and quantitative analysis. Measurement should also include negative, neutral, and positive progress of the campaign or program.

Principle 5: Advertising Value Equivalents (AVEs) are not the value of communication. Instead, practitioners should measure the quality of media coverage in order to understand effectiveness.

Principle 6: Holistic communication measurement and evaluation includes all relevant online and offline channels.

Principle 7: Communication measurement and evaluation are rooted in integrity and transparency to drive learning and insights. Awareness and avoidance of biasing related to the broader societal context, or within the analysis itself, is paramount to accurate measurement.

---

[3] CDC, "Evaluation Briefs: Writing SMART Objectives," updated August 2018, https://www.cdc.gov/healthyyouth/evaluation/pdf/brief3b.pdf.

[4] Stephanie Luedee, "The AMEC Framework and Standardizing PR Measurement," Agility PR Solutions, December 13, 2019, https://www.agilitypr.com/pr-news/pr-tools/the-amec-framework-and-standardizing-pr-measurement/.

MEASUREMENT IS ESSENTIAL

The evolving digital landscape demands a combination of creative and analytical approaches to justify and support decisions and strategies. Digital **analytics** has emerged as a useful technology for tackling measurability challenges by improving the traceability of customer behavior and automating the collection of associated data. This technological advancement provides public relations, marketing, and advertising practitioners with tremendous insights into the effects of customer behavior. However, this information is useful only when practitioners understand *how* to apply the findings appropriately to actionable strategies. Given the general skill misalignment between data interpretation and applicability, most public relations and marketing departments do not have the necessary organizational support for the successful implementation of digital analytics within a campaign.[3] Therefore, it is imperative that practitioners become adept at establishing measurement frameworks that allow identification of optimal data sources, implementation of tracking processes, and attribution methodologies to correlate program execution results with organizational goals. It is important to understand the three prominent types of analytics necessary to implement and develop data-driven strategies: descriptive, predictive, prescriptive.

Descriptive Analytics

Focused on gathering and describing data in the form of reports, visual outputs, and clustering, **descriptive analytics** allows users to condense large amounts of data into smaller, targeted information. Descriptive analytics, the most basic form of analytics, is the process of gathering intelligence and mining data. Ninety percent of organizations today use this type of analytics, leveraging data to evolve strategies for the future.[4] Descriptive analytics provides answers to questions related to actual events. Algorithmic outcomes—such as number of replies per post, page views, and response times—are informative.[5] Organizations can collect and analyze descriptive analytics using a variety of services, one being Google Analytics. Outputs from these tools help practitioners understand the data associated with historical events and can validate whether a campaign or program achieved success.

Predictive Analytics

Utilizing **predictive analytics** allows practitioners to examine large amounts of data to better predict future actions or events. Organizations most commonly use predictive analytics to identify the best time frame for a promotion and coordinate the appropriate customer base with the best offer that will fulfill the larger objectives. This type of analytics is one of the easiest and most straightforward ways to optimize campaigns and quantify return on investment (ROI). As noted in Chapter 1, predictive analytics affords business leaders the necessary intelligence to better predict desires and intent, creating a path toward data-driven strategies that meet the needs of the customer.

Prescriptive Analytics

A method of applying mathematical and computational sciences to support decision options falls within **prescriptive analytics**. The goal of this type of analytics is to leverage the results of descriptive and predictive analytics, not only anticipating when and what will happen, but also why a particular outcome may occur.

Data-driven strategies provide new opportunities in understanding customer dynamics. The data associated with customer interactions across various social media channels inform public relations, marketing, and advertising practitioners and lead to a direct measure of the effects of strategic activities. Researcher Joel Järvinen notes that these insightful capabilities are a direct result of the advancements of digital analytics. By collecting data on customer behaviors, brands can identify patterns such as preferences, purchasing decisions, messaging, and audience perceptions.[6] With so much information available about today's customer, organizations would be wise to adopt data-driven decision-making processes and strategies based on insights obtained across their numerous media channels.

FOUNDATIONAL MEASUREMENT FRAMEWORKS

Depending on the organization's goals and objectives, measurement can range from simple to highly complex. Public relations, marketing, and advertising practitioners use numerous measurement models; however, they often struggle to decipher which types of measurements are comprehensive, sound, and rigorous. The **Association for Measurement and Evaluation of Communication (AMEC)** developed the Integrated Evaluation Framework, one of the first digital measurement frameworks implemented today.[7]

Measuring Communication Efforts with AMEC

Occasionally, the need to update measurement guidelines arises as industries adopt new models, methods, or metrics. To answer the need for a robust set of standards, AMEC developed the Integrated Evaluation Framework. This measurement framework includes evaluation spanning multiple disciplines—including marketing, public relations, advertising, performance management, public administration, and organizational development. By including other disciplines, fields of practice, and social psychology, the AMEC framework utilized some of the most common and best practices of measurement. Drawing from a solid foundation of theory and applied strategic planning, AMEC developed the Integrated Evaluation Framework using models based on logic and found within many disciplines.[8] The premise is that the model is an integration of best practices from other fields and disciplines, ultimately bringing about greater consistency, rigor, and validity. The AMEC Integrated Evaluation Framework combines the PESO model with the elements of exposure, engagement, influence, impact, and advocacy across all social media–driven channels. The framework provides an excellent instrument for measurement and evaluation.

The Framework at First Glance

The AMEC framework provides an easy-to-use, online interface, allowing practitioners to input information related to an organization's campaign. The seven areas that are important to document with the appropriate information include the following:

1. Objectives—align campaign objectives with organizational objectives. *Objectives measure impact.*
2. Inputs—define the target audience, describe the situational analysis, and highlight the budget and resources necessary to execute the campaign.
3. Activity—capture the activities. For example, what research was conducted? Practitioners can input action items specific to the campaign and the areas within the **PESO model**.
4. Outputs—analyze what is measured across PESO. For example, study number of retweets, unique visits to a website, or number of downloads for a case study.
5. Outtakes—measure the action taken by the target audience.
6. Outcomes—assess the effect of the communications on the target audience.
7. Impact—examine the impact of the campaign. For example, see whether there was an increase in sales, policy change, or maximum achievement of donations for a specific project.

This framework not only provides a very practical guide to measuring campaigns but also works well with the LUPE model. By simplifying the process, AMEC has enabled practitioners to easily identify the appropriate tools and measures that connect business outcomes with campaign outcomes. The tactical elements within the AMEC framework are the tangible elements found within the PESO model.

PESO: A Model for All

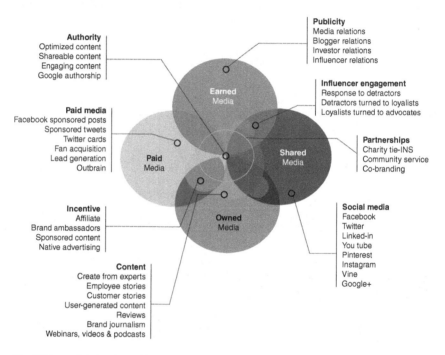

The PESO model, developed by Gini Dietrich, Illustrates convergence in overlapping areas of paid, earned, shared and owned media.

The adoption of digital strategies has further blurred the lines between the disciplines of marketing, advertising, and public relations. With every new digital campaign using areas from the **PESO model**, differentiators are becoming more unclear.[9]

The PESO model was developed in 2014 by Gini Dietrich, founder and CEO of Arment Dietrich, an integrated marketing communication firm, and author of *Spin Sucks*. Dietrich notes that the four areas within media—paid media, earned media, shared media, and owned media—overlap and can be implemented in concert with the others. The success of a campaign utilizing PESO demands crossover between each area. Earned media can, at times, cross into shared media, while owned media can become earned media. Dietrich provides a rationale for how each area of the model is utilized most effectively:[10]

Paid Media. Paid media includes traditional advertising, sponsored content on social platforms, and e-marketing initiatives. Advertising such as Facebook ads, LinkedIn videos, and Outbrain promotions are used for content amplification.

Earned Media. Earned media is often understood as media relations or publicity. Having a newspaper or trade publication include an article on your brand, appearing on the local news to discuss an initiative by your organization, or chatting about your company on a podcast are all examples of earned media. Earned media can also include influencer relations or even search engine optimization.

Shared Media. The largest component within this area is social media. Although organizations initially used social media for customer service and marketing, they have started to use it—both internally and externally—as their main source of communication. Brands curate content, use live video, or create captivating stories. Shared media is returning to its original purpose by creating engagement and community.

Owned Media. Owned media is the content that a brand owns. This content is part of a branded website, blog, or podcast. Brands control the messaging and develop their narratives in the way that they want the story told. It is important not to confuse this with hosting content on other platforms; rather, an organization owns the content as well as the platform it lives on.

Dietrich points out that when the PESO model is working optimally, it elevates businesses to the level of thought leaders and authorities.[11] Following its debut, both public relations and marketing practitioners have widely adopted and incorporated the PESO model into their practices, each in a distinct way that connects back to the roots of the profession. As noted previously, PR practitioners have traditionally been the communicators, writers, and storytellers, while marketing practitioners are driven primarily by the bottom-line metrics. Today, that is changing. Public relations people are more closely paying attention to the value and importance of data-driven outcomes, while those in marketing are beginning to understand the value of storytelling and connecting with their audience on a personal level. As a result, the importance of measurement cannot be understated across these evolving professions.

Grasping the Connection between PESO and AMEC

By Gini Dietrich

[In this essay, which originally appeared on *Spin Sucks*, Dietrich provides examples of how to measure each area of media—paid, earned, owned, and shared—using the framework.]

Metrics in Paid Media
Landing pages: That landing page is where an organization can collect email addresses from the users who want to receive content from an organization. Those

(continued)

individuals become what are called "warm leads." These leads can then be nurtured and eventually turned into customers.

Social media marketing ad conversions: Using data from Facebook, Twitter, LinkedIn, and Google AdWords, an organization can easily drive new leads to their website and measurement activities from it. Facebook, hands down, is one of the best ways to convert from social media. Are people clicking on your ad? What are they doing once on your website? An organization will want to see a correlation between people clicking and people buying. Track this accordingly.

Email database: There is almost nothing better for lead generation, nurturing, and conversion than email marketing. This is not necessarily a monthly newsletter that is distributed and highlights the latest and greatest products or projects. That's not effective. Customers want to know what the organization can do for them. By changing your perspective on email marketing and offering content that puts your prospect in the driver's seat, organizations will find it far more effective. When an organization sets up its own tracking dashboard, they will not only want to see an increase in the number of email addresses in the database, they will also want to see an increase in the number of people who click on links in the company's emails. An organization should set up their measurement program to include unique URLs so they can track what's the most effective. Using this campaign URL Builder tool can help: https://ga-dev-tools.appspot.com/campaign-url-builder/

Leads and conversions: With Google Analytics, and a customer relationship management tool (CRM), it is incredibly easy today to know if the campaigns are working. For instance, with analytics, an organization should be able to figure out the impacts on many key objectives.

Metrics in Earned Media

Web performance: Orbit Media Studio conducted a survey among 1,300 bloggers and found that nearly half only occasionally or never review their analytics.[1] But there's so much data in that free tool! Get it. Play with it. Understand it. And create your PR measurement. Pay attention to how much new traffic a specific story, blog post, tweet or Facebook mention brings to the organization. Is the web traffic qualified traffic? Do they visit other pages? Is the bounce rate low? Do they spend some significant time on your site? Each of these insights will tell an organization how valuable that third-party influencer is to your campaign and will help with scoring in the future.

New audiences: At the top of the public relations and marketing pyramid live the audiences and loyal fans—the people who are becoming aware of the brand via its entire means of communication. These audiences come from the markets that a brand can serve. It is the job of practitioners to build those audiences and to identify and cultivate the loyal fans of a brand. Track any new audiences through the number of unique visitors to your website and quantify their value. Once your audience value is quantified, you can compute the ROI of your in real dollars and cents.

Media, blogger and influencer scoring: Consider this . . . does the *Puxatoomie News Herald* have as high a score as the *New York Times*? Does an influencer with 10,000 followers have the same score as someone with 1,000 followers? It could very well be that the person with 1,000 followers can incentivize purchase with 10 percent of his followers, while the person with 10,000 followers can incentivize

---

[1] Andy Crestodina, "Blogging Statistics and Trends: The 2017 Survey of 1000 Bloggers," Orbit Media Studios, April 9, 2018, Accessed June 6, 2018, https://www.orbitmedia.com/blog/blogging-statistics/.

purchase with only one percent. When an organization sets up their PR campaign to focus on the third-party influencers who truly help the business, do not get caught up in the ego-driven results. Focus on the *Puxatoomie News Herald* if they bring you better results than the *New York Times*.

Metrics in Shared Media

Social media advertising: Think particularly about Facebook and LinkedIn advertising. Both have the potential to drive leads *and* conversions. LinkedIn advertising is more expensive, and it does not reach as wide an audience, but if you are in a service or B2B organization, it could be the right tool. Social media advertising should drive new email subscribers, which generates qualified leads and converts them to sales. Every industry has different metrics, when it comes to cost per lead and percentage conversion but try to aim for less than $1.00 per lead and one to three percent conversion.

Rating system: Just like an organization can score earned media, the company can do the same for social media updates and shares. Assign a point system to your efforts. For instance, likes are one point, comments are five points, and shares are 10 points. Then assign points to each social network. On Twitter, you can use five points for a tweet and 10 points for a retweet. The point here is that you very quickly learn which campaigns worked well and which fell flat on their face.

Unique stuff: By "stuff," it means unique identifiers such as with tracking parameters including URLs, landing pages, coupons, discount codes or even telephone numbers. The only place these unique identifiers should be used is in social media. An organization can have different identifiers for the other media types to measure their effectiveness in a larger campaign. This allows an organization to easily point to the success of one tactic or marketing platform. In Google Analytics, track how many people are using your unique stuff assigned to your shared media updates. To develop your own unique URLs simply use https://support.google.com/analytics/answer/1033867?hl=en

Metrics in Owned Media

Email marketing: If an organization has a structured owned media program, the company is likely distributing information through email marketing. When integrating content with this paid media tactic, track items such as downloads and shares. Do people download the content? Do they read or watch or listen to it once it's been downloaded? Is it so good they can't help but share it with their communities? Are they bringing you new website visitors—which correlate to new leads—because you've provided so much value?

Social media shares: Social media shares matter. Ever been to a site where you've read a piece of content, thought it brilliant, and then noticed there are no social shares? Your immediate thought is not, "Oh this content must be crap" (though that does enter your mind). Your immediate thought is, "What's wrong with me that I thought this so brilliant?" Social shares matter because they provide social proof.[2]

Community: There is much of debate about what a community can do, both for your vanity metrics and your social shares. Having built a community and

---

[2] Pamela Vaughan, "10 Ways to Instantly Amplify the Social Proof of Your Marketing," HubSpot Blog, accessed June 6, 2018, https://blog.hubspot.com/blog/tabid/6307/bid/32418/10-Ways-to-Instantly-Amplify-the-Social-Proof-of-Your-Marketing.aspx.

(continued)

replicating that same success for clients, I can tell you—hands down—an engaged community drives sales. Track the effectiveness of your community through sales, speaking engagement recommendations, client referrals, or paid webinar attendees. Build your community! In some cases, it will integrate with your influencer relations and brand ambassadors.

Sales: Any public relations campaign that does not include sales as a metric is doing it wrong. Start at the top with things such as website traffic and social media referrals. Move to the middle with attribution and lead generation.[3] Then move to the bottom with conversions and sales. The goal is cold, hard cash and your PR campaign can get you there.

---

[3] Raj Sathyamurthi, "The How and Why of PR Attribution," AirPR, July 13, 2017, accessed June 6, 2018, https://airpr.com/blog/pr-attribution/.
Reprinted with permission from Gini Dietrich.

THE REALITY OF MEASUREMENT

On the journey toward measurement excellence, organizations have discovered the value of accurate measurement. Practitioners can alert teams to unexpected incidents that may require immediate attention or illustrate predictable peaks and valleys that may be managed with appropriate forms of action.[12] Decisions driven by metrics and data help ensure campaigns are moving in the right direction.

To thrive in this rapidly evolving, increasingly intelligent world, public relations, marketing, and advertising practitioners must invest in building their skills to effectively create data-driven social media strategies by applying insights from social media analytics. It is essential for today's practitioners to have a foundational understanding of measurement frameworks to evaluate data-driven results.

DISCUSSION QUESTIONS AND EXERCISES

1. Discuss the value and importance of measurement within the fields of public relations and marketing. Provide specific examples of how brands have utilized data to make decisions and develop campaigns.
2. This chapter discussed prescriptive, descriptive, and predictive analytics. What are the differences between these three types, and how do they each play a role in measurement?
3. Describe the elements of selecting and developing a measurement strategy. How does the AMEC model play a role in measurement?
4. Knowing what you have learned about the Barcelona Principles, identify the impact these guidelines have had on practitioners within public relations and marketing.
5. How can public relations and marketing team harness the data found within paid media, earned media, shared media, and owned media channels?
6. *Small group exercise:* Compare the PESO model along with the AMEC model then see how the two work with the LUPE model to develop a strategy whereby the three work and intersect.

KEY TERMS

analytics
Association for
  Measurement
  and Evaluation of

Communication
  (AMEC)
Barcelona Principles
descriptive analytics

PESO model
predictive analytics
prescriptive analytics

NOTES

1. James G. Webster and Thomas B. Ksiazek, "The Dynamics of Audience Fragmentation: Public Attention in an Age of Digital Media," *Journal of Communication* 62, no. 1 (2012): 39–56, doi:10.1111/j.1460-2466.2011.01616.x.

2. Ibid. See also Y.-R. Lin, B. Keegan, D. Margolin, and D. Lazer, "Rising Tides or Rising Stars? Dynamics of Shared Attention on Twitter during Media Events," *PLoS ONE* 9, no. 5 (2014): e94093, https://doi.org/10.1371/journal.pone.0094093.

3. S. Lavalle, E. Lesser, R. Shockley, M. S. Hopkins, and N. Kruschwitz, "Big Data, Analytics and the Path from Insights to Value," *MIT Sloan Management Review* 52, no. 2 (2011): 21–31.

4. Binny Matthews, "Types of Analytics: Descriptive, Predictive, Prescriptive Analytics," DeZyre, January 22, 2018, https://www.dezyre.com/article/types-of-analytics-descriptive-predictive-prescriptive-analytics/209.

5. Ibid., accessed January 2, 2020.

6. Joel Järvinen, "The Use of Digital Analytics for Measuring and Optimizing Digital Marketing Performance," University of Jyväskylä, 2016, https://jyx.jyu.fi/dspace/bitstream/handle/123456789/51512/978-951-39-6777-2_vaitos21102016.pdf?sequence=1.

7. "AMEC Integrated Evaluation Framework," Arthur W. Page Society, July 27, 2016, https://page.org/blog/amec-integrated-evaluation-framework.

8. *The New AMEC Integrated Evaluation Framework: A Collection of Coverage from The Measurement Standard*, Carma, 2016, http://www.themeasurementstandard.com/wp-content/uploads/2016/09/AMEC-Framework-Ebook-CARMA.pdf.

9. Gini Dietrich, "PESO MODEL," Arment Dietrich, 2014, https://armentdietrich.com/peso-model/.

10. Gini Dietrich, "What Is the PESO Model?," PRSA Content Connection, March 14, 2018, https://contentconnection.prsa.org/resources/articles/what-is-the-peso-model.

11. Ibid.

12. Carolyn Pexton, "Perception Versus Reality: Importance of Measurement," IsixSigma, accessed June 7, 2018, https://www.isixsigma.com/tools-templates/measurement-systems-analysis-msa-gage-rr/perception-versus-reality-importance-measurement/.

CHAPTER 4

Convergence of Social Media, Search, and Content Marketing

KEY LEARNING OUTCOMES

Recognize the attributes of convergence between search engine
optimization (SEO) and social media optimization (SMO).

Explain how SEO and SMO play a critical role in the
development of web content.

Explain how to optimize branded content for driving
consumer behavior in a measured way.

Describe how utilizing insights from search plays a critical role in
writing content for the web and social media.

Apply insights from SEO and SMO to develop content
optimization techniques.

Explain the key factors that social media has on a brands search.

A CONVERGING WORLD

Search engine optimization (SEO) plays a critical role in developing content
for the web and social media. Done well, SEO informs using keywords that have
a high degree of relevance to the search query. Professionals that understand
SEO, as well as the importance of keyword insights, will have an advantage
when developing content. Search engine algorithms utilize contextually relevant
words and phrases to present optimal content matching a user's search query,
producing content in rank order on **search engine results pages (SERPs)**
through **natural language processing (NLP)**.[1] NLP is a process that helps
practitioners identify and understand the natural language that consumers use
throughout the stages of the buying cycle, or what we refer to in marketing
as "user journey." Gone are the days of writing content optimized for just the
robots; now content must be pleasing to both robots (algorithms) *and* humans
(users). That's where NLP comes in. Constructing better content through NLP,
by connecting user questions to answers through your owned content, helps

match the user journey and bring the user to your site more often, with higher relevance, and actually satisfies the user by making them more likely to trust and return to your content.[2]

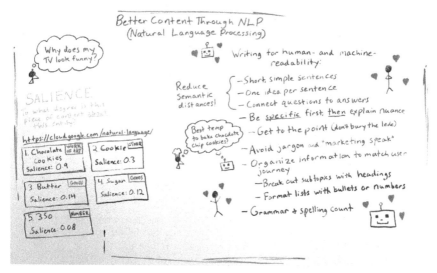

Ideation of better content through Natural Language Processing (NLP)
SOURCE: Ruth Burr Reedy, "Better Content through NLP (Natural Language Processing) Whiteboard Friday," Moz, November 22, 2019, https://moz.com/blog/better-content-through-natural-language-processing.

This chapter will explore the fundamentals of search and social convergence. Readers will learn how research and analytics are related to keyword search and apply them to content optimization.

Global Internet Usage

A Statista search engine report revealed that over the past 12 months, 46.8 percent of the global population actively accessed the Internet, with little indication that the trend will slow down. On the contrary, projections indicate that this number will swell to 53.7 percent over the next few years.[3]

The utilization of Internet search engines continues to increase year over year at a rate that is difficult to accurately track. The forecast metrics presented in Statista's 2018 Market Share chart, coupled with the data available from the website Internet Life Stats, indicate that there are 3.5 billion daily searches using Google's search engine. This equates to 1.28 trillion searches annually worldwide.[4] Net Market Share, a market share statistics for Internet technologies company, notes that Google is the favorite search engine used by consumers, averaging a net share of 75 percent. For comparison, competing search engines such as Yahoo!, Bing, and Baidu average between 5 to 10 percent of the Internet search audience.[5] Commercial SEO analyst Jason Kaye noted that algorithms developed and used by Google are known to be updated up to 600 times a year.[6] This is largely due to Google's ability to analyze user queries and provide the most appropriate web pages.

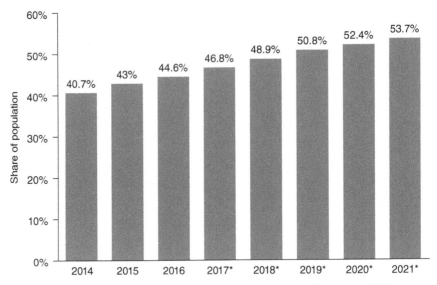

This image illustrates Internet use beginning in 2014 and projected through to 2021.
SOURCE: "Global Internet User Penetration 2021 | Statistic." Statista, www.statista.com/statistics/325706/global-Internet-user-penetration/.

From a historical perspective, 2015 marked a tipping point wherein online search engines became more trusted than traditional media.[7]

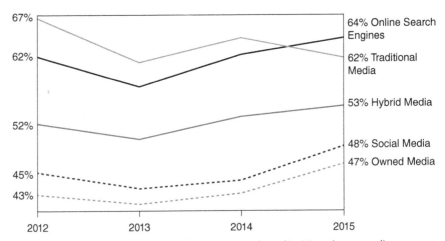

The Edelman Trust Barometer is an online survey conducted in 28 markets, sampling over 34,000 respondents, measuring public trust.

However, it is important to point out that the notion of search has expanded well beyond Google, with marketers from various organizations and industries now considering alternative search channels. This was intended to describe how practitioners are using search findings to inform content creation, optimization, social engagement and promotion. This shift toward diversifying search provides an opportunity for brands and public relations, marketing, and advertising practitioners to engage in strategic planning that spans multiple disciplines. To meet organizational needs for customer engagement in an always-on digital world, the convergence of search, social media, content, and public relations is now inevitable and essential.

At the same time, customer expectations are also evolving. Brands need to react appropriately and expect more than just presentations about product features or calls to action. In fact, nearly 90 percent of buying decisions occur following online research, with consumers weighing numerous information sources before finalizing a purchase. For marketing communications practitioners, more is not always better. In a converging world, relevance, timeliness, and ease of sharing is rapidly becoming a preferred model. This means that it is critical to increase visibility in every location where the potential to influence a consumer exists. Additionally, brands need to meet or exceed changing customer expectations, delivering a better experience in brand and customer interactions.

The convergence of social media and search engines is now an important element of brand survival, because customers want to connect with the brand, other consumers, and the larger online social sphere on numerous levels. Convergence allows a brand to highlight itself at times and locations where the probability of influence is greatest. Keran Smith, from Lyfe Marketing, offers up some best practices when applying a convergence strategy:[8]

- writing high quality content;
- developing a simple sharing method;
- updating social media profiles, images, and videos;
- initiating and taking part in conversations happening on owned channels, and throughout the social sphere; and
- measuring and evaluating performance.

As a result, Smith notes that a brands social media may benefit from any of the following:

- refining link quality,
- building a stronger audience,
- increasing the number of searches,
- understanding what a brand's target audience wants and needs, and
- improving local search.[9]

When individuals or organizations utilize **search engines**, they are doing so with specific intent to locate contextually relevant information. While motivations for search can range from identifying the best shopping deal to finding clinically valid medical information, users provide numerous keywords, phrases, or questions related to the information sought. As search engine **algorithms** improve, their precision also follows suit, identifying and providing the most relevant information to satisfy the query. As a result, users have become so accustomed to locating what they are looking for using search engines that these platforms have become the go-to source for gathering intelligence. From a business perspective, this reliance on search is critical and provides keen insights into how to best identify and facilitate interactions more directly with customers. It should not come as a surprise that the start of social engagement with any consumer begins, in many cases, prior to the point of purchase.

The Cycle of Convergence: Search, Social, and Content Marketing

By Arnie Kuenn

[Author and executive Arnie Kuenn proposes an eight-stage interdependent cycle of convergence for search, social, and content marketing in a book titled *Content Marketing Works: 8 Steps to Transform Your Business*.]

A graphical representation of Kuenn's cycle of search, social media, and content marketing as a continuous eight-step process. Vertical Measures, "ICC12 Convergence of Search Social and Content," LinkedIn SlideShare, February 23, 2012, www.slideshare.net/verticalmeasures/icc12-convergence-of-search-social-and-content.

Each step in the cycle is important and supports adjacent areas to provide a more comprehensive picture.

1. Strategy Development: Establish Strategic Goals

To track content success and guide your campaign, a strategy with specific objectives is paramount. By developing and implementing goals, a practitioner can understand what is working, and even make changes along the way to uncover the most effective formula. Begin by considering the following questions:[1]

- Why are you creating this content?
- Who is your audience and who are you?

---

[1] Julia McCoy, "A Data-Driven Answer on Where to Publish Content (& Where Not To)," Express Writers, March 15, 2017, https://expresswriters.com/data-driven-answer-on-where-to-publish-content/.

- Where do you plan to publish your content?
- What will you measure?
- What may be different a year from now?

2. Research: Start with Keyword Research

Before heading down the ideation and research path, it is important to understand the keywords and phrases that are key to your business. Keep in mind that this is not the same type of keyword research you might conduct for an advertising campaign. This research is for content ideation. In a traditional sense, the goal of keyword research for advertising is to identify as many keyword combinations as possible to load into your ad campaign. With ideation, the focus is on the longer phrases that users are searching to further build out content. The resulting set of "ideas" is an excellent way to identify new keyword combinations. By entering a single term, you get hundreds of variations, with useful data generated for each listed term. With keyword research as your foundation, pinpoint the most relevant keyword phrases that your customers use with the greatest frequency.

3. Content Creation: Take Inventory of Current Content

It is critical to take inventory of all current content housed on your site and your social channels. It can be a daunting task for larger sites, but crucial to understanding a starting point. Inherently, when conducting inventories of website content, it is quite common to discover pages that have old, inaccurate information presented on them. Some pages may need to be eliminated. Existing content can provide a lot of information regarding awareness of the subtleties in the ways that customers phrase search requests, content they respond to and what invites user engagement. When you get to know the dynamics in your potential customers' conversations, it is easier to develop rich answers to their most pressing questions, delivering those answers in terms that make sense to them.

- Consider your audience needs
- Develop content that satisfies needs
- Use insights from research to build content using keywords that will resonate with searcher's intent

After taking time to brainstorm various topics that can answer popular questions and provide value to the targeted audience, consider moving toward the process of quality content creation.

4. Content Optimization: Continuous Process of Monitoring and Implementing Improvement

A big part of any content marketing strategy is implementing new ideas. It is not about trial and error; rather, it is about trial and testing. When trying a new idea, measure the impact and success. Every time new content is created, follow up with measurement, which allows you to understand what works for your target audience, so you can continue to create and optimize content that works.

(continued)

5. Content Promotion: Put the "Marketing" in Content Marketing

Promotion is about communicating the value of your content to the individuals who will be able to share it with their expanded networks. Proactively finding ways to spread content outside of an immediate sphere of influence allows you to draw a wider audience to your site and grow the existing base of followers. Developing quality content is only half the battle, with the other being maximizing content exposure. Remember, the best content in the world is only as valuable as your ability to make it visible.

6. Content Distribution: Give Content Wings

Distribution goes hand in hand with promotion, so naturally it follows as the next step. To increase the chances of success, select the distribution vehicles that will work best for your organization. In other words, distribute to the places where much of your audience resides. Repurposing content is a fantastic way to capitalize on a successful piece of media, or to take a fabulous idea that may not be so hot in its current form and work to improve it. Starting with the goals of your content, seek out other avenues to use the piece to reach a wider audience. If the current content resonates with the targeted demographic, consider repurposing it for distribution on a different channel that attracts a similar audience.

7. Link Building: Attach Links

Defined objectives depend heavily on search engine rankings and exposure through links from other pages to your own. A major contributor to search engine rankings is the number of links to your website, and links from reputable sites help increase traffic to your site.

- Identify low hanging fruit: internal links and blog & forum participation
- Targeted links: Competitive research for similar content; use search operators to find opportunities
- Ask your clients & suppliers for links

8. Measurement: ROI

Everyone wants to know that their efforts bring back the best return possible. More importantly, measurement and tracking using benchmarks and goals helps support the content marketing **return on investment (ROI)**. Metrics that track content marketing shape, and lend efficiency to, future content development efforts.

[For a convergence strategy to be successful, Kuenn notes that practicing all eight steps makes a difference.]

Reprinted with permissions granted by Arnie Kuenn.

THEN AND NOW

So much has changed since 1998. Even the layout of search results pages has radically changed since the establishment of Google. One thing that has not changed is the basis for Google's search mechanism: organic (unpaid), algorithmically generated search results. However, these fundamentals now present a variety of ancillary information, specifically relevant to the search, and may include promotional advertisements.

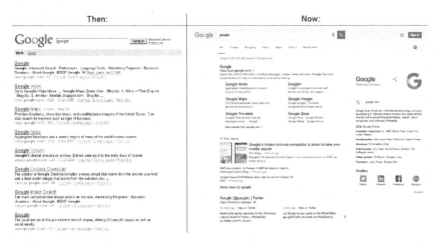

A Google search for the term "Google" highlights the "then" and "now" of search and social convergence.

The accompanying figure illustrates that although search result pages originally consisted of a simple identifiable list of corresponding search outcomes (left "Then"), Google added increased functionality in 2016. Take, for example, the search term "Google." This search reveals a News Box, a Knowledge Graph, social media integration, social sharing, and even a social content ranking in the search results (right "Now"). These elements represent the convergence of search and social, resulting from the integration of these corresponding disciplines.

How does this apply to business? Leading brands invest heavily in optimizing their social media strategy by capitalizing on the convergence of indexing social content. It is important to note that convergent strategies leverage preexisting content, often leading to alternative search channels.[10] For example, Google includes popular social media updates at the top of the search engine results page (SERP), or the web page displayed when a user conducts a search. The important outputs of the SERP are the results identified as close matches to a keyword or phrase-based query, including paid media placements (advertisements). By setting appropriate convergent strategies, brands can seize opportunities when available. Using such tactics can help search engines realize that organizational content is quality content and achieve increased value if discovered in more searches. Public relations, marketing, and advertising practitioners can use this information to refine their strategies by leveraging search-ranking tools, leading to an increased position within the organic search engine listing.

Historically speaking, SEO has stood as a subset within the marketing discipline; focused on growing visibility in organic, or non-paid, search engine results. Today, public relations, marketing, and advertising practitioners must successfully develop and implement SEO strategies for their clients or organizations. SEO is both technical and creative with the intent of improving website rankings, driving traffic, and increasing brand visibility. Additionally, the idea of SEO may seem complex if not understood properly. Words found on a page, the ways that other websites link to a company's pages, appropriate structure, and ranking all impact searchability and indexing to serve up contextually relevant content. Based on the construct of each element, search engines perform evaluations of websites using complex algorithms.

CONTENT MARKETING TRIANGLE

The web is continuously evolving to keep pace with new, innovative platforms. The days of linear information flow are long gone. Increasingly, content artifacts shared via the social web benefit from the advancement of multidirectional flow across a variety of platforms, formats, and devices. Couple this with the unprecedented mass adoption of the Internet, and it is evident that social networking and the mobile web have revolutionized our ability to access, share, and publish information at scale.

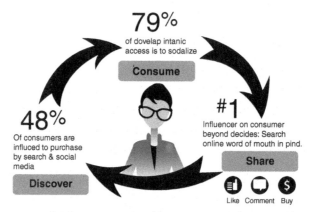

The cycle of consumer optimization of discovering and sharing content and information via social media.
SOURCE: Lee Odden, Optimize: How to Attract and Engage More Customers by Integrating SEO, Social Media, and Content Marketing (Hoboken, NJ: Wiley, 2012).

Optimizing Search

The evolving landscapes of marketing, public relations, and communications has made it clear that results-oriented public relations, marketing, and advertising practitioners *need* to understand and monitor both the front- and back-end land-scapes of search to maintain a competitive advantage. Organizational disciplines need to eliminate the idea of functional silos within communications so that the larger, cross-functional collaborative groups can better understand, create, and deliver optimal customer experiences and preferences with everyone leveraging search and social media. Achieving both requires data-driven decision making that constantly evaluates what works and adapts the most critical aspects of content and social media engagement using an optimized mind set.[11]

For example, Google informs users that the mission of the company is to "organize the world's information and make it universally accessible and useful."[12] Public relations and marketing professionals need to understand and embrace the idea of approaching search engine optimization holistically with an awareness that whatever can be searched could also be optimized.

The Challenge of Optimized Integration

Integrating optimization techniques can be a challenge for organizations that operate under a stand-alone functional department siloed wherein, for example, marketing "owns" SEO, public relations manages the social media efforts, and content creation is shared across multiple areas. This operational setup presents optimization in isolation, where one function may be duplicating or conflicting with another unintentionally. As public relations, marketing, and advertising practitioners learn more about the dynamic nature of search and social convergence, they can adjust their practices and processes and adopt dynamically shared responsibilities. However, organizational change like this requires leadership to support common goals and the ability to identify the best integration optimization strategies. Investment in training, process, tools, and technology enable these practices as well as enhance collaboration and skills transfer.

Unfortunately, many organizations struggle to drive the change necessary to integrate the disciplines of public relations and marketing. To understand how a shift toward optimization strategies fits within an organization, consider starting with a small-scale pilot wherein teams identify a lower visibility project and are tasked to collaborate closely and openly share progress both upstream and horizontally. It is important to understand how to best flatten silos and foster increased collaboration while experimenting with social media integration, SEO, and other necessary objectives.

Within the larger context of organizational communication efforts, it should not come as a surprise that social media continues to play an increasingly important role in the public relations and marketing strategies of every brand. Elements of social need to be connected to various other functional areas and incorporated into the broader digital strategy of the organization. Planning for a social strategy requires an understanding of how the tactics will support the larger communications, marketing, public relations, and business goals. Taking the appropriate time to plan aids in framing a strategic approach and establishes measures for monitoring progress, performance, and success.

Organizations should not simply view social media as just another communication channel available to push out content to a desired audience; rather, it provides an outlet to connect internal branding teams with these important target audiences. Social is critical in developing and establishing long-term relationships with the public and an essential element of many marketing and communication-supporting functions.[13]

USE AN OPTIMIZATION FRAMEWORK THAT INTRINSICALLY LINKS SEARCH AND SOCIAL

Competition plays an important part in driving business growth, further supporting the importance for marketing communications professionals to evolve their practices to capitalize fully on the many optimization opportunities created by the convergence of search and social. While industry analysts and pundits advocate prioritizing strategy, it is often difficult to do so in a comprehensive and practical way, especially as it relates to specializations including content marketing and social media.[14]

Public relations and marketing professionals can adopt adaptive approaches to observe overall direction and simultaneously measure short-term impact. An increasing number of search engine marketing experts recommend integration of both social media and content marketing endeavors to better support SEO and social media optimization (SMO) objectives. The content marketing optimization framework presented by Lee Odden provides an example of a customer-centric approach that takes into consideration both SEO and SMO. He calls this the content marketing trilogy: discovery, consumption, and engagement.[15] This organized and comprehensive approach presents a framework that is applicable for any online content produced by an organization, built on the principle of maintaining both customers and keywords at the center of any strategy.

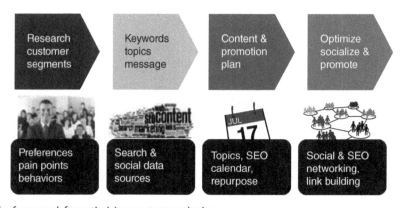

The framework for optimizing content marketing.

Customer Relevance

Many organizations grapple with priorities when formulating their social and content marketing strategies. It is common to question whether the selection and evaluation of optimization techniques should focus on what is best for the organization or the keyword-centered customers. This may boil down to simple semantics; however, these concepts cannot be mutually exclusive regarding targeted audiences and keyword searches. The key for public relations and social media professionals, as well as online marketers, is to identify relevant keywords associated with their desired product or service before focusing on issues like customer behaviors, pain points, and location within the overall buying cycle.

In the initial stages of planning a social strategy, organizations and professionals alike need to remember the importance of customer relevance. Understanding how a preferred target audience uses social media and their preferred avenues for engagement is imperative. Identifying these factors early aids an organization in generating value using one platform over another and ensures that the larger strategy remains on track. The most effective way to research factors important to a target audience is by implementing the practice of continuous social listening, which informs and supports the broader social outreach strategy. Organizations that commit to this practice benefit by more precisely identifying their targeted audience.

When evaluating customer preferences, behaviors, and pain points, businesses need to utilize these insights and apply them to any social engagement planning. So how exactly do organizations find the appropriate audience for their product or service? Historically, research supporting social outreach endeavors have been completed using market segmentation techniques. However, the widespread adoption of today's evolving digital landscape requires a heightened level of thought and planning as it relates to targeted audiences, including the most appropriate platforms or avenues for engagement and connections. When defining a target audience, consider any of the following:

- Specifically, who is it that the organization is truly looking to connect with?
- What process is necessary to identify the desired audience(s)?
- What are the demographics of this audience?
- Within the online community, where does the target audience prefer to participate?
- What drives this audience, and what are they passionate about?
- What is the status of the audience/organizational relationship?
- Regarding the larger brand, are the opinions of the desired audience negative, positive, or neutral?
- What are the audience's pain points or other interests?

Proper identification and investigation of these considerations provide an organization with the opportunity to rank each with an associated value or importance to the larger brand, ideally kick-starting efforts to build a contextually relevant social engagement strategy. When done correctly, the more time that organizations set aside up front for target audience planning, the smoother the implementation and execution of their integrated outreach plan.[16]

Practitioners are empowered to tailor each campaign to specific customer needs, realizing increased influence and laying the groundwork for audiences to follow through on the desired action. Including keyword optimization to a thoughtful SEO and SMO strategy is a powerful concept. Content public relations and marketing professionals may consider the following when identifying audience-exclusive keywords:[17]

- Find out what consumers care about. This aids in the identification of customer segments.
- Evaluate and understand pain points and relevant information that consumers need throughout the buying cycle. Depending on the product/service, the buying cycle may comprise multiple stages, especially in business-to-business transactions when purchasing involves multiple stakeholders.
- Identify and select motivations that inspire purchase and social interactions when formulating priorities.

Keywords

The more an organization understands the habits of their customers, the more important content optimization for search and social becomes. There is no better time to connect with a targeted audience than when they are using a search engine to query for a specific service or product. To satisfy a customer's search query appropriately, an organization should build a relevant keyword list that connects customers directly with their interests. As noted previously, this is accomplished by optimizing content based on keywords or phrases.

Additionally, when emphasizing search **keywords** for digital content, consider the appropriate method of including these terms/phrases cross-functionally to achieve continuity across content forms. The algorithmic exchange bridging social and search platforms has become more and more sophisticated as search engines advance machine learning. These technological developments allow search engines to recognize actions and navigational patterns of buyers during their investigation of online informational resources.

For example, when entering the keyword phrase "IBM Social Business" in a web browser, the following search engine results page (SERP) output demonstrates the interplay and convergence of paid and organic SEO and SMO.

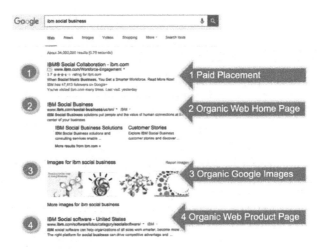

SERP results for "IBM Social Business."

Achieving this type of result leverages many of the following strategies:

- Use tools such as Google Search Console, Google Ads Keyword Tool, Google Trends, AnswerThePublic, Moz, SEMRush, SpyFu, and Wordtracker to analyze keywords.[18]
- Implement one or more tools—such as Brandwatch, Crimson Hexagon, Meltwater, or Hootsuite—to monitor and gauge social media for related topic clusters relevant to your search keywords.
- Develop a running/dynamic glossary of pertinent search keywords and social topics when creating original content for the social sphere.

Furthermore, incorporating social listening techniques into the evaluation of natural language expressed during social conversations related to the phrase "Social Business" reveals numerous adjacencies and other pertinent topics (see accompanying image).

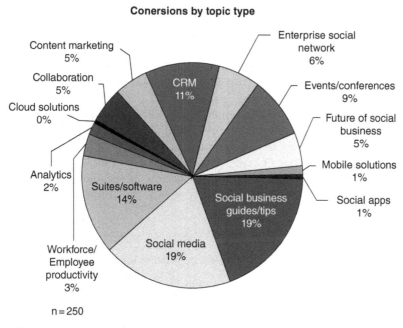

Social listening topics related to and associated with "Social Business."

Lastly, conducting a simple keyword examination for "Social Business" reveals comparative search volume demand and related terms (see accompanying image).

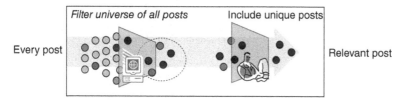

Created in collaboration with IBM Market Insights, Social Insights Practice.

Keyword Research

Researching and selecting appropriate keywords to support social listening is vital to the implementation of strategies resulting from these insights. In a world that continues to expand technologically, with more and more people able to connect to the social web, it is not surprising that the number of new digital imprints and messages continues to expand at a dramatic pace as well. Although many of these digital footprints are not likely related or relevant to a specific brand or product/service, it is still critical for an organization to identify an appropriate library of keywords that align with any online conversation of interest.

Keyword Identification

Appropriately understanding which keywords are important to operational success allows an organization to pinpoint rapidly only the most related conversation relevant to the desired objectives. Fundamentally, this process works like a series of screens that sift or sort for specific sizes of stones or baking flour particles.

Start by determining the inclusion criteria within the sample of interest and identifying any keywords of interest related to the signal. Taking time up front to ensure that the terms are not too broad is essential to eliminating, as much as possible, any inclusion of extraneous information within the data. However, on the contrary, if the keywords are too narrow or specific, an organization may miss important and pertinent conversations, often leading to inaccurate conclusions.

Refining Keywords

The practice of mining online conversations often requires numerous "strings":

- The "category" string is necessary to identify relevant discussions specific to power-type servers. A resulting **Boolean keyword string** is comprised of phrases or terms related to the areas of interest that occur most frequently,[19] pinpointing the relevant terminology that consumers use to capture the appropriate conversations.
- The "branded" string is necessary to filter all mentions of keywords contained within the broader conversations investigated by power-type servers and is most commonly applied to branded terms or products.

String utilization and **topic hierarchy** example: IBM Power Systems:

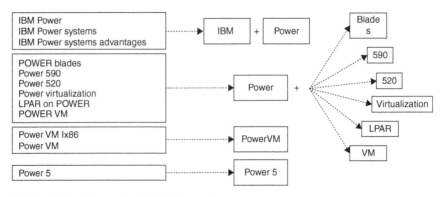

IBM Market Insights and social insights practice.

Consider any of the following when identifying relevant keywords or phrases while researching social listening:

1. Review any and all available product or brand-specific messaging.
2. Review competitors' key messaging.
3. Develop a topical hierarchy to categorize and organize keywords.
4. If appropriate, add additional information, including a topic name.
5. Identify alternative meanings that any keyword may have within the industry as a whole.
6. Define terms or phrases that should be considered irrelevant.
7. Define and qualify all acronyms.
8. Ensure keywords are defined by their proximity to other keywords.
9. Validate keywords using search engines, Twitter, and other social platforms.

IMPORTANCE OF CONTENT

Author and content marketing consultant Pam Didner shares that "Content—is King and Creativity is Queen," noting that while **content marketing** is a burgeoning practice, soon it will become mainstream, and not everyone will create content well. Embracing research and establishing a foundation of data-driven decision making based on customer insights, analytics, and creativity will set apart the efforts of better online public relations and marketing professionals.[20]

The responsibility of researching keywords and topics relevant to search query phrases falls squarely on the professional practitioners. This practice alone often results in content creation that resonates with and successfully satisfies a consumer's interests and needs. Data-driven insights have quickly become a fundamental contributor to the content development, publishing, and optimization processes. Adopting these methodologies supports improvements in editorial planning, timing of content delivery, optimization focus, and performance evaluation. Teams should be afforded ample opportunities to create content spontaneously and to capitalize on unanticipated opportunities revealed through research insights. Dynamic reactions to SEO and SMO intelligence allow teams to be nimble and take advantage of real-time opportunities, current events, and emerging topics with high interest. It is critical to stay focused on organizational goals and target audience needs by adopting best practices into SEO and SMO optimization processes:

- Content planning should be rooted in addressing the needs of customer segments while utilizing keywords and topically relevant phrases that are most closely associated with the service and/or product offering.
- Continuity and consistency is critical when using keywords to optimize content across websites, blogs, and through social media channels.
- **Content creation** practices that produce content flexible enough for multiuse applications extend the utility and reach of the content. Content reuse, also commonly described as content repurposing or evergreen content, allows for future use, often extending its life.

OPTIMIZE AND SOCIALIZE

Implementing a convergent approach to SEO and SMO best practices often result in a heightened degree of content discoverability by those who seek it. Developing an appropriate keyword index, an organizationally relevant content plan, and better insights into the customer preferences provides the necessary components to support future actions and executable tasks. With public relations and marketing teams working collaboratively and trained on SEO and SMO best practices, content will more directly resonate with the targeted audiences. Utilizing social listening and any associated analytics can present real-time opportunities for optimization refinement, and, when operationalized, the organizational investment in optimized search and social convergence should lead to a measurable outcome.

Finally, **link building** occurs when optimized and highly relevant content are presented to individuals across social networks, which in turn inspires sharing, which drives traffic and engagement with links. Incorporating social and web page links into your content provides search engines with the necessary associations used by algorithms to rank and present helpful information in search results, leading customers to share. It is important for organizations to continue to invest in the training of marketing communications professionals, especially on the intrinsic link between search and social, and how each can capitalize on convergence. The strategies, goals, and methodologies of measurement will vary according to the organization's overall strategic plan; however, the frameworks presented here can apply to all forms of online content slated for publishing. In a converged search and social sphere, Odden summarizes the importance of the social: "There is no *optimize* without a smart dose of *socialize*."[21]

Using Analytics to Inform Holiday Facebook Ad Campaigns for Small Business

By Karen Sutherland, Ph.D., University of the Sunshine Coast

Introduction

With social media user numbers predicted to reach 3.02 billion by 2021, the widespread use of the technology has impacted many facets of society, particularly in the world of small business.[1] Like never before, business owners have access to a rich supply of data generated by social media users that can provide in-depth insights into social media performance, brand mentions and target audiences.[2] Analyzing social media data can assist small business owners in the ongoing improvement of their social media activities and presence and provide information on how to best connect with customers to meet business goals. Before social media, small businesses were required to conduct their own market research or employ the services of a market research company to gather customer insights,

---

[1]"Number of Social Media Users Worldwide from 2010 to 2021 (in Billions)," Statista, last modified 2019, accessed March 13, 2019, https://www.statista.com/statistics/278414/number-of-worldwide-social-network-users/.

[2]Emmanouil Perakakis, George Mastorakis, and Ioannis Kopanakis, "Social Media Monitoring: An Innovative Intelligent Approach," *Designs* 3, no. 2 (2019): 24.

processes that could often be time consuming and expensive. Today, social media platforms such as Facebook and Instagram and applications such as Google Analytics generate comprehensive audience and customer data in real time that can be analyzed to inform fundamental business decisions.[3] This data is easy to access and cost-free, which has provided small business owners who use social media with considerable power in the form of knowledge. Rather than relying on guesswork or running on instinct, business owners have access to digital evidence detailing the characteristics, preferences and online activities of their current and prospective customers.

However, the value of using social media analytics to inform decision making is not always understood by some small business owners and digital marketing and public relations professionals alike. The pure volume of data generated by social media may seem too overwhelming to navigate or analysis may seem like a task that is too time-consuming. Whatever the reason, misguided social media tactics may result in missed opportunities to connect with audiences because data were not used to underpin their development and implementation. It is this phenomenon that is explored throughout this chapter.

The case study presented in this chapter compares the performance metrics and online sales generated from two Facebook advertising campaigns for an online gift store. The goal of each campaign was to increase sales during the two most important holiday periods for this business: Christmas and Mother's Day. However, there were two distinct differences in the planning and implementation of each Facebook advertising campaign.

Firstly, staff at a digital marketing agency managed the Christmas Facebook advertising campaign without analyzing existing data to inform decisions regarding the campaign's structure and implementation.

Toward the end of the Christmas campaign, the business owner regained control of their social media channels from the digital marketing firm, analyzed existing user data and performance metrics using Facebook Insights and Google Analytics and used these insights to plan and implement the Mother's Day Facebook advertising campaign.

Using the LUPE model, this case study will detail the data analysis conducted by the business owner to plan and implement the Mother's Day Facebook advertising campaign and present results from each campaign as a comparative analysis. The aim of this case study is to present differences in the results of a Facebook advertising when one has been informed by data and the other has not.

Listen and Learn

In this initial stage, research and gathering as much information as possible from and about key stakeholders and then analyzing this data to inform decisions is paramount. This was a step completely missed by the digital marketing firm in the Christmas campaign. Agency staff did not consult with the business owner before or during the campaign and neglected to analyze any existing Facebook data in relation to user demographics or previous advertising data for the business.

---

[3] Javier Vidal-Garcia, Marta Vidal, and Rafael Hernandez Barros, "Computational Business Intelligence, Big Data, and Their Role in Business Decisions in the Age of the Internet of Things," in *The Internet of Things in the Modern Business Environment*, ed. In Lee (Hershey, IL: Business Science Reference, 2017), 1047–67.

(*continued*)

Table 1   Data Analyses before Each Facebook Advertising Campaign

PRE-CHRISTMAS	PRE-MOTHER'S DAY
Data was not analyzed.	Demographic from Facebook Insights (Age, Gender, Location, Language, Content generating greatest engagement)
	Christmas advertising performance data

In contrast, as detailed in Table 1, the business owner analyzed the following metrics and used this information to develop the Mother's Day campaign.

Completing this stage of analysis was essential for the business owner to understand

- the characteristics of their existing followers and customers,
- when this group are most likely online, and
- the type of content in terms of images, video, visual branding, and written copy that most resonates with this group.

With this knowledge, the business owner was able to construct audience personas (profiles of their average customer) to help them to better understand the people that they were trying to connect with throughout their Mother's Day Facebook advertising campaign and create relevant content to resonate with that audience.[4]

From the data gathered and analyzed throughout the *Listen and Learn* stage, the business owner found that 99 percent of their 46k Facebook followers were women and 42 percent were aged between 35 and 44 (Figure 1). Furthermore, 43k of those followers lived in Australia where the business is based, and they engaged

Figure 1   Facebook Insights through business manager illustrating post type, average reach, and engagement.

---

[4]Lee-Ann Kastman Breuch, *Involving the Audience: A Rhetorical Perspective on Using Social Media to Improve Websites* (New York: Routledge, 2019), e-book.

Figure 2 The success of different post types in relation to audience engagement.

most with photo-based content (Figures 1 and 2). With this knowledge, the business owner could move onto the next stage of the LUPE model: *Understand*.

Understand

In the *Understand* stage, insights gathered from the previous stage are used to develop strategies and articulate their necessary components such as goals and SMART objectives. Drawing from the audience demographic data from Facebook Insights, the business owner developed the following goals and SMART objectives.

Goal: To increase Mother's Day 2019 online sales in comparison to Christmas 2018 online sales.

Objective 1: To increase traffic from Facebook to our website by an average 10 percent in the 28 days before Mother's Day in comparison to the 25 agency-managed days before Christmas.

Objective 2: To increase sales in our online store by 5 percent in the 28 days before Mother's Day in comparison to the 40 days before Christmas.

With these strategic components in place, the business owner could move on to the next stage of the LUPE model: *Plan* to develop a Facebook advertising campaign to support the achievement of the goals and objectives identified in the *Understand* phase.

Plan

The key components of the *Plan* stage as identified by the authors, are Target Audience, Tactics, Timeline, and Budget. Drawing on the previously gathered data from Facebook Insights and from Facebook Business Manager relating to the Christmas advertising campaign, the business owner used this information to guide their decisions in the further development of their Mother's Day campaign. Table 2 details the specific components that were decided for each campaign in relation to Target Audience, Tactics, Timeline, and Budget.

As demonstrated in Table 2, there were many differences between the two campaigns. Based on their analysis of the demographic data (Figure 1), the

(continued)

Table 2 Comparison of Target Audience, Tactics, and Budget Used in the Christmas and Mother's Day Campaigns

CHRISTMAS FACEBOOK ADVERTISING CAMPAIGN (NOT INFORMED BY DATA)	MOTHER'S DAY FACEBOOK ADVERTISING CAMPAIGN (INFORMED BY DATA)
Target Audience: Men and Women 18–65	**Target Audience:** Women 25–59
Tactics: *37 Different Advertisements.* These advertisements were very ad hoc. It was more of a scattergun approach (Osborne, 2018), 5.	**Tactics:** *14 Different Advertisements applying the AIDA model* (attention, interest, desire, action) to ease current and prospective customers through the purchasing journey (Barry & Howard, 1990), 6.
Timeline: 15th November 2018–25 December 2018	**Timeline:** 15 April–12 May 2019
Budget: $22,800	**Budget:** $12,700

business owner decided to target women only in the age ranges with the greatest representation (25–59). Furthermore, they simplified the approach that was used for the Christmas campaign that targeted a wider and more diverse audience and used 37 different advertisements to do so. This approach could best be described as a "scattergun approach" that draws on quantity over quality in an attempt to reach as many potential customers as possible.[5]

The audience targeted in the Christmas campaign also included men and a much wider age range of 18–65 despite the business's audience insights demonstrating extremely low representation in these demographic categories. Furthermore, the business owner adopted a traditional marketing approach and used the AIDA model, which stands for Attention, Interest, Desire, Action.[6] Rather than creating a wide range of ads hoping that a few will work, the AIDA approach guides prospective customers through the stages of first learning about a product (Attention), creating relevance between the customer and the product, usually by explaining how it can solve a common problem (Interest), further increasing that relevance and connection so that it results in a prospective customer making the decision to purchase (Desire) and then providing an offer the prospective customer cannot refuse, resulting in a purchase (Action).[7] The business owner developed their Facebook audience categories and Mother's Day advertisements around these four stages of the customer purchasing journey, targeting both new and existing customers.

Finally, the timeframes were also different. The Christmas campaign began in early November, whereas the Mother's Day campaign began 28 days before Mother's Day. The decision for this was based on Google Analytics data that indicated sales in the online store did not increase until two to three weeks before a holiday event and reached their greatest volume the few days before the final

---

[5]Marcus Osborne, *Stop Advertising, Start Branding: How to Build the Brand That Will Build Your Business* (Kibworth Beauchamp, Leicestershire: Matador, 2016).

[6]Thomas E. Barry and Daniel J. Howard, "A Review and Critique of the Hierarchy of Effects in Advertising," *International Journal of Advertising* 9, no. 2 (1990): 121–35.

[7]Ibid.

delivery deadline (when orders can be processed and sent out in time for the particular holiday). Therefore, the decision was made for the Mother's Day campaign to concentrate the advertising spend to the time period where the data indicated that people are more likely to purchase in a bid to maximize sales during this period. With the planning stage in place, the business owner moved on to the next phase of the LUPE model, *Execute and Evaluate*.

Execute and Evaluate

With the strategic decision formulated through data analysis in the *Understand* and *Plan* phases, the business owner created a range of relevant audiences and advertising content based on their findings. Table 3 contains the parameters used for each Facebook campaign.

Table 3 Facebook Advertising Parameters for Christmas and Mother's Day Campaigns

PRE-CHRISTMAS (NOT INFORMED BY DATA)	PRE-MOTHER'S DAY (INFORMED BY DATA)
Number of ads: 37	**Number of ads:** 15
Types of ads: Image and text	**Types of ads:** Images with Text|Videos with Text
Number of audiences: 37	
The Facebook Ad Set names:	Various under the Facebook Ad categories in line with the AIDA model (Barry & Howard, 1990), 10:
• Lookalike Audience Purchases—180 days—Men & Women	• Awareness,
• Remarketing—180 days—Website Visitor or FB post engagement (no add to cart)—Women	• Consideration, and
	• Conversion.
• Remarketing—180 days—Abandoned Carts—Women	**Number of audiences:** 14
• Demographic B—34- to 55-year-old Moms of kids 13 to 18 years old	**The Facebook Ad Set names:**
• Demographic A—24- to 55-year-old Moms of kids 6–12 years old	• Mother's Day—Remarketing early bird postage offer
• Lookalike 2% to 3% (Likes of FoF) w Demographics	• AU—29–59
• Teachers	• Traffic—Early bird postage
• Remarketing—Add to Cart—30 Days—Copy	• AU—25–55
• Post: "FREE THIS WEEK ONLY. Christmas is about family ..."	• AU—25–58
• Demographic C—50- to 64-year-old Moms of adult children 18+	• Simply Said Messages
	• Video traffic
• Remarketing—180 days—Made a purchase—Men and Women	• AU—26–59
	• Traffic How-to Video
• Remarketing—180 days—Loyalty made Purchase—Women	• Free Shipping_Cassie
	• Brand Awareness video
	• Mothers_Day_Comp
	• AU—25–56
	• Product awareness

(*continued*)

Table 3 (Continued)

PRE-CHRISTMAS (NOT INFORMED BY DATA)	PRE-MOTHER'S DAY (INFORMED BY DATA)
• Lookalike Audience Purchases 180 days—Men and Women—Optimized for Add to Cart	
• Demographic—24–50-year-old Moms of kids 0–5 years old—Optimized for Add to Cart	
• Demographic—24–50-year-old Moms of kids 6–12 years old—Optimized for Add to Cart	
• Post: "Order now and we would love to give you a custom . . ."	
• Post: "These gifts are about love and saying thank you . . ."	
• Lookalike 1% (Made a Purchase)—Women Only	
• 25-Nov-18	
• Offer Ads Only—Lookalike Audience Purchases 180 days—Men and Women	
• Offer Ads Only—Demographic—24- to 50-year-old Moms of kids 6–12 years old	
• Offer Ads Only—Demographic—36- to 64-year-old Moms of kids 18+ years old	
• Remarketing—180 days—Abandoned Carts—Men	
• Demographic—24- to 50-year-old Moms of kids 0–5 years old—Optimized for Add to Cart	
• Demographic—24- to 50-year-old Moms of kids 6–12 years old—Optimized for Add to Cart	
• Post: "Have you subscribed to our news-letter yet? . . ."	
• Remarketing—180 days—Website Visitor or FB post engagement (no add to cart)—Women	
• Lookalike Audience Purchases—180 days—Men and Women—Optimized for Add to Cart	
• Demographic—24- to 50-year-old Moms of kids 0–5 years old	
• Lookalike Audience Purchases—180 days—Men and Women	

Table 3 (Continued)

PRE-CHRISTMAS (NOT INFORMED BY DATA)	PRE-MOTHER'S DAY (INFORMED BY DATA)
• Demographic – 24–50-year-old Moms of kids 6–12 years old	
• Remarketing—180 days— Abandoned Carts—Women	
• Remarketing—180 days—Website Visitor or FB post engagement (no add to cart)—Men	

Evident in Table 3 is the sheer volume of advertisements and audiences created and executed by the digital marketing firm for the Christmas Facebook advertising campaign in comparison with the Mother's Day campaign. Also, the Christmas campaign included advertisements targeted directly at men, even though the data did not indicate men to be the primary purchasers of products from this business. It must be noted that the business owner regained control of their Facebook Advertising campaign during the Christmas campaign on the 9th of December, and the 17th of December was the final day that products could be mailed to reach customers in time for the Christmas holiday.

Figure 3 denotes the website traffic directed to the online store throughout the Christmas Facebook advertising campaign. The peak during the last phase of the campaign could be due to people panic buying to meet the postage deadline and/or the impact of the business owner taking back control of their Facebook ads. However, traffic did not reach above the 1000-person mark until after the time that the business owner regained control of the advertising campaign.

Figure 4 closely examines the period from when the business owner regained control of the Facebook advertising to the deadline delivery date. It is interesting to note that traffic steadily increased with a slight dip on the 12th of December before hitting the peak of the Christmas campaign on the 14th of December. This peak resulted in more than double the traffic driven to the site while the digital agency had control of the Christmas campaign.

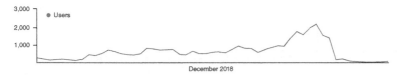

Figure 3 Website traffic throughout the Christmas Facebook advertising campaign, November 9 to December 25, 2018.

(continued)

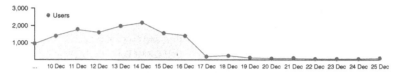

Figure 4 Website traffic throughout the Christmas Facebook advertising campaign, December 9 to December 25, 2018.

Figure 5 Website traffic throughout the Mother's Day Facebook advertising campaign, April 12 to May 12, 2019.

Figure 5 displays website traffic during the four-week Mother's Day Facebook advertising campaign. Throughout this campaign the business owner had complete control and used data analysis to inform the structure and content of the Facebook advertisements implemented. Throughout the four-week Mother's Day campaign, traffic dipped below 1000 at three points. However, in comparison, the traffic during the Christmas campaign reached above 1000 users when the business owner regained control of their Facebook advertisements from the digital agency.

The business owner using data analysis to inform their decisions in developing and implementing the Facebook advertising campaigns for the final days of the Christmas campaign and the entire Mother's Day campaign seems to have increased the amount of website traffic driven to their online store, in comparison with traffic rates achieved by the digital marketing agency.

However, while an increase in traffic is in line with one of the SMART objectives, the business owner was then required to complete the final stage of the LUPE model, *Evaluate*, to assess if they met their specific objective of a 10 percent increase in traffic and a 5 percent increase in sales. It was also important during the Evaluate phase to measure the performance of different metrics associated with the campaign to analyze whether components should be replicated or omitted in the future.

The *Evaluation* stage of the LUPE model, introduced in Chapter 2, involved first assessing whether the Mother's Day campaign met its overall goal and SMART objectives, then evaluating other metrics to assess the campaign's performance in relation to the Christmas campaign when the digital agency had control. Please note that the results presented in this section have been calculated to demonstrate the average of the total divided by the number of days in each campaign. The Christmas campaign has been divided into two sections. The first denotes when the digital marketing agency has control, and the second details when the business owner regained management of the campaign. The business owner was responsible for the entire Mother's Day Facebook advertising campaign; therefore, only one set of results is presented.

Table 4 Evaluation of Results in Meeting the Goal

Goal: To increase Mother's Day 2019 online sales in comparison to Christmas 2018 online sales.

Christmas Campaign with Digital Marketing Firm in Control (25 days)	Christmas Campaign with Business Owner in Control (15 days)	Mother's Day Campaign (28 days)
Overall online sales = $76,009.00	Overall online sales = $56,552.24	Overall online sales = $40,557.35
Average daily online sales = $3040.36	Average daily online sales = $3770.15	Average daily online sales = $1448.48
Overall Return on Investment = $61,759.00	**Overall Return on Investment = $48,002.24**	**Overall Return on Investment = $27,857.35**
Overall sales generated via Facebook = $30,792.10	Overall sales generated via Facebook = $27,550.50	Overall sales generated via Facebook = $19,147.10
Average daily sales generated by Facebook = $1231.65	Average daily sales generated by Facebook = $1836.70	Average daily sales generated by Facebook = $683.25
Overall, return on Investment of Facebook Advertising Spend = $16,542.10	**Overall, Return on Investment of Facebook Advertising Spend = $19,000.50**	**Overall, Return on Investment of Facebook Advertising Spend = $6447.19**
Daily Average Return on Investment of Facebook Advertising Spend = $661.69	**Daily Average Return on Investment of Facebook Advertising Spend = $1266.70**	**Daily Average Return on Investment of Facebook Advertising Spend = $230.26**

Overall result: The overall goal of increasing sales during the Mother's Day campaign compared to the Christmas campaign was not achieved. However, it is important to note the significant increase in performance when the business owner regained control of their Facebook advertising within the final weeks of the Christmas campaign, more than doubling the average return on investment of Facebook advertising spend compared with the performance of the digital agency.

There may be several external factors contributing to the decline of sales during the Mother's Day campaign such as website issues, Easter and school holidays falling very closely to Mother's Day, and a federal election dominating Facebook advertising. Furthermore, reducing the advertising spend and campaign duration may have also impacted performance.

Table 5 Evaluation of Results in Meeting Objective 1

Objective 1: *To increase traffic from Facebook to our website by an average 10 percent in the 28 days before Mother's Day in comparison to the 25 agency-managed days before Christmas.*

Christmas Campaign with Digital Marketing Firm in Control (25 days)	Christmas Campaign with Business Owner in Control (15 days)	Mother's Day Campaign (28 days)
Website traffic overall = 17,473 people	Website traffic overall = 12,672 people	Website traffic overall = 25,667

(continued)

Table 5 (Continued)

Average number of people visiting per day = 699	Average number of people visiting per day = 845	Average number of people visiting per day = 917
	Percentage increase between the Christmas campaign averages of the business owner's results and agency results: 21 percent	Percentage increase between the averages of business owner's Mother's Day results and agency's Christmas results: 31 percent

Overall result: Website traffic increased by 31 percent in the specified time period.

This SMART objective was exceeded. However, after comparing the Mother's Day website traffic results with the online sales figures generated from the Facebook advertisements during the same period, an issue becomes apparent. The Mother's Day Facebook advertisements have been effective in driving traffic to the online store; however, this traffic is not converting into sales once it gets there.

This business employed the digital marketing firm to overhaul their website in the lead-up to the Christmas Facebook advertising campaign and were still experiencing issues leading into the Mother's Day advertising period. This lack of conversion on the website suggests that something was causing prospective customers not to purchase from the online store, and this requires much deeper analysis to rectify these issues.

Objective 2: To increase sales in our online store by 5 percent in the 28 days before Mother's Day in comparison to the 40 days before Christmas.

Overall result: As highlighted previously, this SMART objective was not achieved. Greater numbers of people were visiting the online store, but these visits were not converting into sales. Further analysis is required to gain a deeper insight into what changed on the website between Christmas and Mother's Day to reduce sales despite greater numbers of people on average visiting the online store. Without the analysis undertaken in this chapter, it would have been challenging to pinpoint exactly why sales were so low throughout the Mother's Day period.

Table 6 contains further performance metrics relating to the business's website and online store that may provide further information relating to the decrease in sales during the Mother's Day campaign.

Table 6 further indicates that issues with the online store seemed to increase when the owner regained control of their Facebook advertisements. Firstly, the bounce rate increased once they regained control during the Christmas campaign and further increased throughout the Mother's Day campaign period. Bounce rate indicates the number of people that visit a website and leave soon after. Furthermore, while the average time that people spent in the store increased slightly toward the end of the Christmas advertising period, this decreased dramatically throughout Mother's Day. Deeper analysis of website usability data is required to understand why people are leaving the site so quickly without purchasing products. This research must determine if prospective customers are not finding what they

Table 6 Further Website Performance Metrics

CHRISTMAS	MOTHER'S DAY
Digital Marketing Firm Results (25 days)	**Business Owner Results (28 days)**
• *Main website traffic source:*	• *Main website traffic source:*
Facebook/cpc (cost per click) ad with link to website	m.facebook.com/ (clicking through to website via mobile device)
• *Bounce rate:* 32.74 percent	• *Bounce rate:* 45.88 percent
• *Average session duration*: 4 mins., 48 secs.	• *Average session duration:* 2 mins., 31 secs.
Business Owner Results (15 days)	
• *Main website traffic source:*	
m.facebook.com/ (clicking through to website via mobile device)	
• *Bounce rate:* 34.10 percent	
• *Average session duration*: 4 mins., 53 secs.	

are looking for, are arriving on a webpage that they are not expecting, or there are issues with the online shopping cart that are preventing the transaction process.

Also important to mention, the digital marketing agency targeted some Facebook advertisements specifically at men throughout the Christmas campaign even though males constituted only 1 percent of the business's Facebook followers. This targeting strategy resulted in only 1 purchase out of 525 total purchases made during the Christmas period and cost the business owner $133.51 in advertising spend, or a cost per link click (CPC) of $66.76, to achieve that one purchase. This is further evidence suggesting the importance of using data analysis to inform decision making, particularly when developing paid advertising campaigns.

Final Thoughts: Christmas and Mother's Day

This case study compared the performance metrics and online sales generated from two Facebook advertising campaigns for an online gift store. The goal of each campaign was to increase sales during the two most important holiday periods for this business: Christmas and Mother's Day. The Mother's Day campaign employed the LUPE model and used data analysis to inform its structure and implementation, whereas the mostly agency-led Christmas advertising campaign did not. While the Mother's Day campaign did not achieve its goal of increasing sales, it met its SMART objective of increasing traffic to its online store. Data analyzed during the *Evaluate* stage highlighted an issue with website traffic not converting into online sales, which highlighted a need for much deeper analysis. Overall, this chapter provided clear evidence of the insight that data analysis can provide to small business owners when using social media and other digital marketing tools to support their

(*continued*)

businesses and the losses that can occur or remain undetected when data analysis is neglected. With the use of in-house marketing resources increasing, it is essential for business owners to understand how to analyze social media performance data to support continuous improvement.[8]

[8]Will Burns, "As In-House Agencies Become the Norm, the Opportunities for Outside Agencies Evolve," *Forbes*, last modified September 12, 2018, accessed December 25, 2019, https://www.forbes.com/sites/willburns/2018/09/12/as-in-house-agencies-become-the-norm-the-opportunities-for-outside-agencies-evolve/#493383ad661c/.

CONCLUSION

If this chapter has revealed one idea, it is that data derived from a customer's online behavior powers today's promotional decisions. The motivations, desires, values, and necessities differ from one customer to the next. However, all customers demand personalization. A savvy brand understands that online behavior reveals advantageous insights about their brand, customers, and the relationship between the two.

DISCUSSION QUESTIONS AND EXERCISES

1. This chapter explored the importance of SEO, SMO, and search coming together. Interpret what a converged world means.
2. The fourth annual *State of Marketing* report from Salesforce reported that 52 percent of consumers are likely to switch brands if a company doesn't personalize communications.[22] Based on what you learned in this chapter, how can create a personalized experience?
3. This chapter revealed how to use data to reach customers. Do you think it is just as important to use data to determine which customers should be left alone? For example, if a customer has had a negative experience with your brand, should you offer that customer a discount? Ponder and discuss the pros and cons of this approach.
4. By utilizing insights from search, formulate a strategy for developing content for the web and social media. Illustrate the factors that play a role in the development of content for paid, earned, shared, and owned channels.
5. *Small group exercise:* Assumptions about individual customers must encompass more than an "audience persona" outlining likes, dislikes, demographics, or even characteristics.[23] Decisions about customers should be made based on their online behaviors. Take a moment to search for a product on Amazon or a streaming video on Hulu or Netflix—and then identify and discuss the keywords chosen and the options revealed. Do you see phrases such as "Because you watched" or "Customers who bought this item also bought"? What does this tell you about your online search habits and who you are as a customer?

KEY TERMS

algorithms

Boolean keyword string

content creation

content marketing

keywords

link building

natural language
  processing (NLP)

return on investment
  (ROI)

search engine

search engine
  optimization (SEO)

search engine results page
  (SERP)

string utilization

topical hierarchy

NOTES

1. R. Reedy, "Better Content through NLP (Natural Language Processing) Whiteboard Friday," created for MozCom2019, from Moz.com, accessed December 12, 2019, https://d2v4zi8pl64nxt.cloudfront.net/better-content-through-natural-language-proce ssing/5dd761b0c48413.04534027.jpg.

2. Ruth Burr Reedy, "Better Content through NLP (Natural Language Processing) Whiteboard Friday," Moz, November 22, 2019, https://moz.com/blog/better-content-through-natural-language-processing.

3. "Global Internet User Penetration 2021 | Statistic," Statista, www.statista.com/statistics/325706/global-Internet-user-penetration/.

4. Ibid.

5. "Search Engine Statistics 2018," *Smart Insights* (blog), January 30, 2018, www.smartinsights.com/search-engine-marketing/search-engine-statistics/. See also "Google vs. Bing vs. Yahoo Comparison & Review," Tech Help Canada, accessed January 2, 2020, https://www.techhelp.ca/google-bing-yahoo-compare.

6. Jason Kaye, "How Does Google Search Actually Work?," *Telegraph*, March 28, 2018, https://www.telegraph.co.uk/spark/marketing-guides/how-does-google-work/.

7. Edelman Inc., "2015 Edelman Trust Barometer," YouTube, January 21, 2015, www.youtube.com/watch?v=09eDlatXIB4#action=share.

8. "Social Media SEO: What You Need to Know to Grow Your Business," *Digital Marketing* (blog), LYFE Marketing, August 6, 2019, http://www.lyfemarketing.com/blog/social-media-seo/.

9. Ibid.

10. Jayson DeMers, "6 Social Media Practices That Boost SEO," *Forbes*, January 27, 2015, www.forbes.com/sites/jaysondemers/2015/01/27/6-social-media-practices-that-boost-seo/#e1467c33d171.

11. Lee Odden, *Optimize: How to Attract and Engage More Customers by Integrating SEO, Social Media, and Content Marketing* (Hoboken, NJ: Wiley, 2012).

12. Barbara Farfan, "Google Business Profile and Mission Statement," The Balance Small Business, March 29, 2018, accessed July 14, 2018. https://www.thebalancesmb.com/google-business-profile-2892814.

13. Susan Emerick, "Defining Your Social Strategy," February 6, 2013, http://susanemerick.com/defining-your-social-strategy/.

14. "Content Marketing Tactics—30 Examples," *TopRank* (blog), April 8, 2016, www.toprankblog.com/2011/06/content-marketing-definition-tactics/

15. Lee Odden, *Optimize: How to Attract and Engage More Customers by Integrating SEO, Social Media, and Content Marketing* (Hoboken, NJ: Wiley, 2012).

16. Susan Emerick, "Defining Your Social Strategy," February 6, 2013, http://susanemerick. com/defining-your-social-strategy/.

17. Lee Odden, *Optimize: How to Attract and Engage More Customers by Integrating SEO, Social Media, and Content Marketing* (Hoboken, NJ: Wiley, 2012).

18. PowerSuite, SEO, "8 Free Keyword Research Tools for SEO (That Beat Their Paid Alternatives)," Search Engine Land, December 18, 2019, https://searchengineland. com/8-free-keyword-research-tools-for-seo-that-beat-their-paid-alternatives-318091.

19. A Boolean keyword string is a set of keywords that employs Boolean logic to focus and return specific, relevant messages in search.

20. "International Content Marketing—Intel's Journey to Globalizing an Editorial Plan," *TopRank* (blog), September 8, 2011, www.toprankblog.com/2011/09/intel-globalize-editorial-planning/.

21. Lee Odden, *Optimize: How to Attract and Engage More Customers by Integrating SEO, Social Media, and Content Marketing* (Hoboken, NJ: Wiley, 2012).

22. *Fourth Annual State of Marketing Report*, Salesforce, 2017, https://a.sfdcstatic.com/ content/dam/www/ocms-backup/assets/pdf/datasheets/salesforce-research-fourth-annual-state-of-marketing.pdf.

23. Gary DeAsi, "How to Use Customer Behavior Data to Drive Revenue (Like Amazon, Netflix & Google)," Pointillist, August 14, 2018, accessed January 20, 2019, https:// www.pointillist.com/blog/customer-behavior-data/.

CHAPTER 5

Data-Driven Influencer Strategy

KEY LEARNING OUTCOMES

Explain how to apply business insights gained through social intelligence to understand buyer behavior.

Describe how brands use social intelligence to influence brand perception and how insights are leveraged to impact brand positioning.

Explain how brands leverage social media analytic techniques to understand trends in

Describe influence marketing and how brands can incorporate it in their marketing mix.

Understand the FTC implications for following guidelines.

Deconstruct and explain the FTC's influencer disclosure best practices.

INFLUENCE IN A DATA-DRIVEN WORLD

The emergence of social networks has provided an entirely new medium in which to build influence. Marketing and communications professionals must not only find the appropriate influencer, but also identify a platform to drive and measure the impact of influencer marketing in social media. While multiple variations of the term "influencer" exist, these individuals tend to exhibit many similar characteristics. This chapter explores these commonalities and provides readers with a framework for measuring and prioritizing influencers.

As the practice of influence marketing continues to evolve, so do the technologies and services that "track" the degree to which individuals are considered "influential." Therefore, data-driven public relations and marketing leaders need to understand how to create, manage, and measure brand influencers in social media marketing. This chapter will introduce two types of technologies, each of which is capable of supporting influence marketing to scale. The first uses social semantic analysis and machine learning to identify individuals who have the potential to influence, or who are already established as influencers, and includes a supporting scoring methodology. The second technology provides influencers and/or potential influencers with a platform to share content; this is known as an influencer marketing platform.

LAYING THE FOUNDATION: TYPES OF INFLUENCERS

Public relations, marketing, and advertising practitioners have targeted influential individuals for years. In fact, this is a common marketing and public relations practice. People are influenced by others in their life, including friends, family, co-workers, or even neighbors. Some people within these groups wield greater influence over others. Thus, public relations, marketing, and advertising practitioners tap into that influence to make an impact, increase exposure, create meaningful engagements, and develop brand **advocates**.

Unfortunately, practices of influencer relations often lack common language and a framework in which to develop influencer campaigns. To begin, it is probably best to specify what is meant by the terms 'influence,' 'influencer,' and 'influencer marketing.'

By definition, to *influence* something is to affect a particular trait or outcome, behavior, or opinion.[1] There are multiple levels of influence, but marketers would be best served to identify key **influencers** in their field of interest, those individuals or groups that possess a better than average ability to influence. Factors that contribute to the success of key influencers include their overall communication frequency, social network size, personal level of persuasiveness, and other attributes. Audiences that key influencers target, known as **influencees**, are those individuals whose opinions or behaviors change when introduced to new information. With this baseline understanding in hand, it should not come as a surprise that **influencer marketing** focuses on achieving specific business objectives by leveraging key influencer engagement with influencees. Marketers and communication professionals should focus their efforts and resources on key influencers with the greatest likelihood of influencing their community of influencees. Distinctive attributes of five categories of influencers are identified in the accompanying image.[2]

Advocate	Ambassador	Citizen	Professional occupational	Celebrity
An individual who shows support for, pleads the case of or defends a brand, cause, product or service while remaining formally unaffiliated with the brand and unremunerated	An individual remunerated by or otherwise 'allied' with a brand or cause; their actions are, in some manner, endorsed by the brand with an acknowledged and transparent affiliation that is mutually beneficial	The 'everyman' of influence. Citizen influencers are otherwise average people who have greater then average likelihood to influence though their social network	Individuals, who by definition of their job function, are in the position to influence others directly through their authoritative or instructive statements	An individuals whose name recognition commands a great deal of public fascination ('celebrity status') and has the ability to use their status to communicate with broad effect

WOMMA five categories of influencers defined.

USING SOCIAL MEDIA ANALYTICS TO UNDERSTAND BUYER BEHAVIOR

Advancements in natural language processing and semantic analysis have resulted from increasingly sophisticated machine learning innovations. As described in earlier chapters, these emerging technologies aid marketing and PR professionals by allowing them to make data-driven decisions. Application of insights collected from social intelligence provide a deeper level of strategic planning and program execution, allowing public relations, marketing, and advertising practitioners to understand brand perceptions, inform positioning, and create content that provides the highest value. More importantly, practitioners can further refine social media content optimization and engagement strategies, enabling improved performance over time.

These technologies also aid in the identification and evaluation of social networks through analysis and data visualization to better locate and understand relationship ecosystems. Information from these tools enables public relations, marketing, and advertising practitioners to concentrate on the development of more precise engagement strategies across a spectrum of channels including social networks, technical forums, and other online communities. The ideal outcome is to target engagement specifically where the audience of interest is seeking their information. Social network analysis empowers practitioners to discover and classify prominent individuals who possess the potential to influence, both of which are paramount to formulating successful engagement strategies and influencer marketing programs.

Influencer Marketing and Influencer Relations

Influencer marketing and influencer relations are forms of marketing and PR that focus on specific key individuals who have the ability to successfully sway opinions, influence decisions, and motivate behavior to drive action of key target publics.[3] By including social network analysis within a practitioner's everyday toolkit, such individuals are easier to identify. As noted previously, influencer marketing is not necessarily a new concept. Word-of-mouth, social influence, PR, and public affairs all tap into social intelligence and its advanced analytics, allowing influencer discovery and connectivity through data visualizations possible. This provides public relations, marketing, and advertising practitioners with another tool to develop highly targeted and measurable influencer marketing initiatives.

While influencers reside within an array of social spheres, they share an ability to persuade followers based on their credibility, prominence, and value. An influencer is an individual who

- has achieved a certain level of distinction within online and offline communities,
- has amassed a large reach,
- holds a certain level of expertise,
- is well respected among peers, and
- engages in a sustained way and interacts frequently within their community.

1-9-90 RULE

A well-known "rule," known in Internet culture and social networking as 1-9-90, relates to those individuals who make up an Internet community.[4] This tenet posits that approximately 1 percent of website users are active in new content creation,

---

The New Influential

Leading data science professor Wendy Moe, from the Robert H. Smith School of Business, University of Maryland, notes that in an offline environment, becoming influential requires a platform that has a large reach using mass communication. However, a myriad of social media platforms offer access to an exponentially larger population, providing the potential influencer with an even greater reach. Influencers in today's connected world do not necessarily need to be leaders or have fancy titles; rather, they simply require remote access with which to post videos, blogs, or comments using their social platforms. Moe also highlights that within this environment, influencers may establish themselves within their surrounding structure. People can deliberately curate a "presence" online which may not be the same as they appear face to face (for instance, in the public eye). More than likely, influencers are regular people who leverage a platform to shape the perspectives and opinions within their network.[1]

---

[1] Wendy W. Moe and David A. Schweidel, *Social Media Intelligence* (Cambridge: Cambridge University Press, 2014).

with the remaining 99 percent essentially playing the role of "lurker": individuals satisfied with observing and not necessarily contributing. This rule has implications for online influence because it highlights that the 1 percent of individuals identified as content contributors on the Internet represents the same proportion (1 percent) of those viewing it. Simply put, for a single post that appears on a forum, approximately 99 other visitors to the website are only viewing that content and not posting.

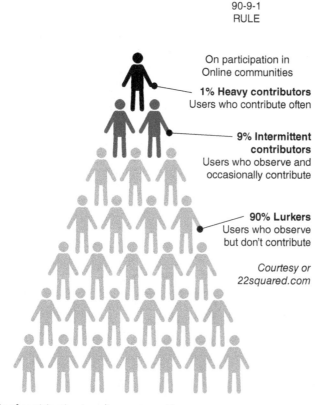

THE
90-9-1
RULE

On participation in
Online communities

1% Heavy contributors
Users who contribute often

**9% Intermittent
contributors**
Users who observe and
occasionally contribute

90% Lurkers
Users who observe
but don't contribute

*Courtesy or
22squared.com*

90-9-1 rule of participation in online communities.

A comparable version of this concept, known as the *90-9-1* rule, stresses the idea that in a collaborative website or social network, 90 percent of the community are there only to view content, while 9 percent of the participants edit content, and the remaining 1 percent are responsible for the curation of new content. Keep in mind that the breakdown of percentages can vary depending on the content subject. If entering a forum required individuals to play the role of contributor, the rate of participation would most certainly exceed 1 percent; however, new content will still originate from a fraction of the users.

Author, blogger, and marketing professional Sam Fiorella suggests that it would be beneficial for brands to leverage the 1:9:90 principle when identifying and engaging with influencers, as well as understand the ecosystem and help develop it.[5]

INFLUENCER ECOSYSTEM

The accompanying visualization depicts an influencer ecosystem. By completing such an analysis, practitioners can better navigate the vast network of influencers, understand how they are connected, and identify topics that they discuss most often. Key components to keep in mind regarding the interrelationships and connectivity within the graphic include the following:

- The circles indicate the grouping of influencers aligning with the two topics of interest—topic A and topic B.
- The diameter of the circle represents the degree of influence, with larger circles representing a broader/higher degree of influence.
- The connected lines highlight the connectivity of the individuals. The thickness of each line represents the degree to which it is connected and involved in the dialogue.
- The small dots within the circles identify company employees discovered during the analysis. These individuals built their degree of online influence by sharing their expertise in a sustained and committed way over time.

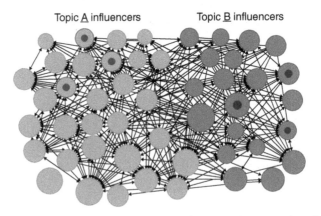

Topic A influencers   Topic B influencers

Visualization of two types of influencers as they overlap networks on social media.

However, the task of mapping an influencer ecosystem is only a contributing piece toward understanding the larger sphere of influence of the individual or group. Knowing something about the person or organization is equally important.

The text *The Most Powerful Brand on Earth* identifies six commonalities associated with successful influencers.[6] They

- possess an expertise, a heightened degree of passion for a topic, and recognize how to establish credibility and build trust within a network;
- effectively collaborate within a social environment and are comfortable posting comments and publishing content;
- understand how building relationships using digital media platforms can create value;
- actively engage (sustained activity) their communities using social media;
- continually evaluate and refine their skills and involvement to realize business/personal objectives; and
- actively listen to social media conversations and participate in brand-specific research with the goal of enhancing personal and professional connections.

The process of evaluating insights from social media analytics and applying them to an influencer's social footprint also requires establishing selection criteria to ensure that influencers align with the goals of the influencer-marketing program or campaign. Consider the following criteria questions:

- What degree of authority or credibility does the prospective influencer have on the topic related to your organizational goals?
- Which social networks do they participate on most actively?
- To what extent does the influencer publish original content?
- To what extent does the influencer share content written by others?

SOCIAL INSIGHTS ACROSS AN ENTERPRISE

As a leader in strategic research, Forrester is realizing increased demand to aid organizations gather insights from social platforms as a supplement to traditional business intelligence. The evolution of business to consumer (B2C) marketing is now expanding to include social listening providers for enhanced brand protection, competitive intelligence analyses, and trend tracking. However, enterprises are still not using social intelligence to its full potential. With a history in this space, Forrester previously established that the true value of social intelligence is its ability to provide consumer insights across diverse business units—including marketing, customer service, market research, product development, risk and reputation management, human resources, creative development, media planning, and many others.[7] "Social listening platforms manage and analyze customer data from social sources and use that data to activate, measure, and recalibrate marketing and business programs."[8]

A Forrester survey (see accompanying image) revealed that brands combine insights derived from social data with other marketing findings.

"Do you integrate and apply social data from your social listening platform to any of the following?"
(Multiple responses accepted; not all responses shown) (select all that apply)

Market research data sets (e.g., focus groups, ethnography)   56%
Audience segmentation   49%
Web analytics   47%
Digital ad targeting   40%
Voice of the customer data (e.g., customer feedback survey data)   35%
CRM data   19%
In-store data   16%
Traditional ad targetting   16%
Human resources data   9%
Call center transcripts   9%
Chat transcripts   7%

Base: 43 respondents

Sentiment analysis of publicly available content.

Harvesting Insights from the Social Web

Social listening and conducting sentiment analyses provide organizations with essential insights into both short-term trends and longer-term opportunities. Simply remaining alert and open to consumer passions demonstrates to an audience that the organization is listening and attentive to their needs. Furthermore, by being ever vigilant through social media monitoring, companies that invest will potentially avoid making costly mistakes as new campaigns and products are developed. Creating an optimal experience for consumers relies on combining social data insights with all other available data—including, but not limited to, customer relationship management (CRM), voice of the customer (VoC), commentary from ratings and reviews, and sentiment analysis—in order to support the right customer experience for each audience segment. The exercise of conducting a global-level competitive analysis is now possible. Brands can capitalize on evaluating publicly shared ratings and reviews to understand what consumers are specifically saying about a competitor's product or service. Functionally speaking, collecting and examining social analytics is an ongoing investment, allowing brands to follow relevant conversations in real time. Social media analytics provides brands a way to look back, stay current, and anticipate consumer needs proactively. With that in mind, brands must continually invest in social media analytics to be able to fuel the next strategy.[9]

Additionally, it is not enough anymore to merely collect data; practitioners also need appropriate training and tools to successfully navigate the noise to tease out information relevant to their organizational objectives. In today's connected environment, a tremendous number of messages are posted to the Internet on any given day, hour, or minute. Most of these posts are not necessarily attributable to any specific brand or topic. By studying customer behaviors, marketing and PR professionals gain an understanding as to what language these communities use and where these social conversations are taking place. These insights, when applied appropriately, can support engagement and optimization strategies, leveraging natural language and semantic analyses to narrow search outputs to only information deemed important. Like the screening process used when organizing a focus group, establishing inclusion criteria within a social listening sample is important to identify the appropriate conversations.

KEY STEPS TO COLLECT INSIGHTS

- *Define* keywords, phrases, or concepts: Using keyword research, define keywords and phrases that are topically relevant and satisfy the intent of a given user's search query.
- *Mine* publicly available social media data related to the keywords, phrases, or concepts based on relevance: Data mining involves analyzing content using analytics software.
- *Analyze* data to understand and classify relevant insights (the human component): Complete data analysis through market research, data, and/or business analysts. However, the advancements of social media analytics platforms make it possible for anyone to analyze and derive insights more readily.
- *Establish* benchmark metrics: Develop a set of standards by which measurement takes place. This involves setting an initial benchmark and then measuring against it on a defined frequency.
- *Evaluate* performance against benchmark: Conduct a comparative analysis that reveals insights on trends over time.

Examples of publicly available data sources, representing a spectrum of content types that are published across various social media channels, include social networks, microblogs (Twitter), social media news aggregators, blogs, photo and video sharing, wikis, forums/newsgroups, and online communities.

APPLYING BUSINESS INSIGHTS FROM SOCIAL INTELLIGENCE

Numerous aspects of data analysis exist that can help public relations, marketing, and advertising practitioners gain insights from social media. The following five elements provide a foundation for the practice:

1. *Volume*: Conversational volume will ebb and flow over time. The goal is to identify an overall increase, despite lapses and lulls in the discussion. The

accompanying example highlights how a brand monitored the volume of social media dialogue over a specific period of time, providing insights on the response to the launch of a social media optimization effort. Not surprisingly, online dialogue increased.

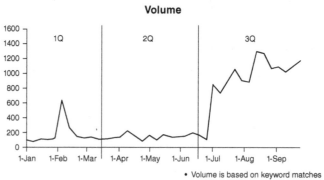

- Volume is based on keyword matches
- Volume is measured on the record level

Insights on the response to the launch of a social media optimization effort.

2. *Conversation volume by message type*: It is not only *how much* is being said, but also *why* people are creating a buzz. Brands now can continuously monitor a variety of discussion topics—from complaints to recommendations—and even track when information is shared.

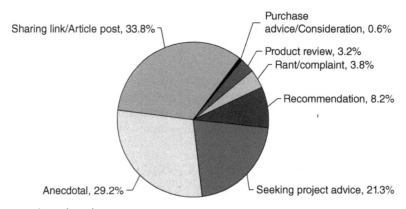

Conversation volume by message type.

3. *Conversation volume by venue*: Identifying the social platforms that consumers are most active on can help brands focus their engagement efforts. The accompanying example breaks down where the target audience conversations are occurring by measuring conversation volume by venue.

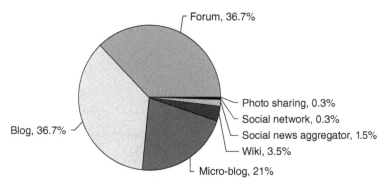

Conversation volume by venue.

4. *Voice*: Identifying who is contributing to the conversation is of critical importance when analyzing the online discussions. Segments, target audiences, and influencers offer different values to the longevity of the conversation, and they can be tracked over time to determine increase or decrease in engagement by role.

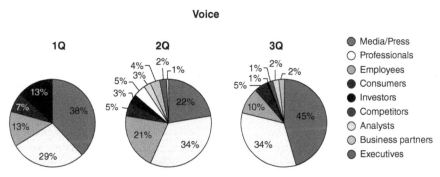

Conversation volume by voice.

5. *Conversation topic relationships, volume, and sentiment*: Valuable attributions, such as discussion tone—classified as positive, negative, or neutral sentiment—help marketers understand how conversational themes relate to one another (see top image, p. 86).

To thrive in this technologically based, machine-mediated world, marketers must begin to think well beyond just using keywords.[10] Contributing to search engine optimization (SEO), digital and social media optimization strategies are more informed when insights are applied using social media analytics. Marketers need to understand not only the context of each query, but also where online discussions are occurring to create content and engagement strategies that support buyer decisions. Leveraging insights with real-time and predictive systems allows marketers to nimbly pivot into action, by anticipating customers' needs and heightening responsiveness to drive an improved customer experience.[11]

Volume
Size of half circle

Sentiment
▨ Positive
░ Neutral
■ Negative

Relationship
Width of connecting line

User preference
Product W
Events
Interoperability
Cost/affordability
Industry news
announcements
Product T support
Security
Server B
performance
Product V
performance
Product C
Product migration
Scalability
Product B

Conversation topic relationships, volume, and sentiment.

INFLUENCER IDENTIFICATION AND THEIR POTENTIAL TO INFLUENCE

One of the most important requirements to remember when initiating an influencer evaluation program is that the passion and expertise of the individual/group must align with the overall program goals. Furthermore, prioritize those individuals with measurable market influence, especially for the target audiences that matter to the brand. These are the individuals most likely to drive results. Researching and recognizing the persona of these market influencers is also important as it can inform brand who the market influencer is, whether they should consider following them, and potentially pursue a relationship within support of the defined business goals.

The accompanying image highlights uses of specific influencer criteria to illustrate engagement within a defined community.

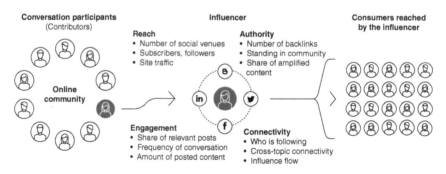

Influencer criteria and engagement within a defined community.

INFLUENCE—IT'S COMPLICATED

The combination of social media listening and supporting analytics undeniably represents the largest source of unsolicited public opinion. Organizations can gather important tactical and strategic insights by mining social media, which, when applied to pertinent areas of a business, can help drive business outcomes. Recognizing the importance of influence in supporting successful organizational initiatives, countless brands now invest substantial resources into developing and maintaining relationships with online influencers. The most successful influencer relationship programs spread their efforts across a range of influencers, while also investing in establishing their own employees as influencers.

Keep in mind that in the early days of social media, individuals and organizations alike mistakenly thought that successful outcomes from social media were achieved primarily by identifying the most influential people in online conversations and hoping that they did not say anything damaging about the brand.

Appropriately described in the book *Influence Marketing*, authors Sam Fiorella and Danny Brown note that "influence is the ability to generating action from a message or recommendation to a purchase and then measuring that. The trouble marketers have is, not only finding the right influencer, but also the ability to find a platform to drive and measure the effect of influencer marketing in social media."[12]

REGULATORY ISSUES FOR MARKETERS

As much as marketing, communication, and PR practitioners seem to be on top of leveraging technologies to support organizational goals and objectives, a large disconnect still exists between these same professionals and the content creators— specifically related to regulatory concerns about disclosure and transparency. As shocking as it may sound, 6 in 10 marketers are not aware of the U.S. **Federal Trade Commission (FTC)** disclosure guidelines, and 1 in 3 has asked a creator to disregard them intentionally. The FTC's function is to serve the best interests of consumers by preventing unfair and deceptive business practices, and to enable informed consumer choices and the public's understanding of fair competition.

The FTC is most concerned about truth in advertising when it comes to influencer marketing. The goal is for influencers to not mislead their followers, either purposefully or accidentally. Ensuring fluidity among consumers, brands, and influencers is key. Requirements from the FTC state that influencers must announce and publicly disclose relationships they have with brands. Truth and transparency are simple, and, according to the FTC, compensation received for content curation can be realized through money, free products or services, discounts and coupons, experiences, and any other type of special incentive. The rules are simple: if an individual or organization receives compensation for a post, the post is considered sponsored and therefore must be disclosed.

Knowing When to Disclose

A leader in influencer marketing and social media, IZEA Worldwide, developed a list of FTC disclosure best practices for its clients. Since most brands struggle with knowing when an influencer should disclose a relationship with a brand, IZEA set forth a simple guideline: disclose whenever there is a material relationship.[13] The FTC influencer disclosure best practices, "Disclosures 101 for Social Media Influencers," indicate that if an influencer is providing content about a product they personally purchased and were not in any way compensated for, then the need to disclose that the post is unnecessary. The experts at IZEA provide this example: *let's say you purchased a new pair of shoes and thought they were the most comfortable shoes ever. You are so excited and want everyone to know. You have zero connections to the brand, and you don't any employees at the company. You log onto your favorite social media account and share what you like about these shoes with your friends, family, and followers.*[14] In this, you are simply sharing your opinion about your new shoes.

However, the situation changes once there is an exchange of any kind. A relationship now exists. This means that as an influencer, you would now be obliged to disclose the connection to the brand with your friends, family, and followers. Money is not the sole determiner of whether an influencer needs to disclose their relationship. If a brand sends an influencer a product at no cost (free) or provides a free weekend getaway, the recipient's potential to influence others about an item or brand has occurred. The practice of disclosing free gifts has been common in public relations and journalism for years. Most organizations include guidelines in their corporate ethics policy on accepting gifts. A simple search on the Internet reveals ethics policies set in place by any number of corporations such as General Electric, Levi Strauss, Google, Ikea, or newspapers including the *New York Times* and the *Washington Post*.

Conspicuous Disclosure

Additionally, the FTC influencer disclosure best practices specify that individuals should not have to research whether an endorsement is really an ad. Any disclosure statement should be clearly visible, even among a sea of hashtags. If the content is a video, the FTC prefers that the disclosure appear in the video itself, rather than in the description of the video. Instagram posts need to clearly disclose within the first three lines without the reader having to click "more."

Sometimes conspicuous disclosure is not enough, however, particularly if the ad is misleading. The Advertising Standards Authority (ASA) filed a complaint against *Geordie Shore* star Sophie Kasaei. With her 1.5 million Instagram followers, she possesses quite a bit of influence. In a split-screen before-and-after style photograph, she is shown looking like she has an expanded belly while holding Flat Tummy Tea products. The caption reads, "Nothings [sic] gonna get you flat the same as this tea will. The excuses are in the past, much like the water weight I used to have." The ASA received a complaint that contested the claim that the tea could help with weight loss.[15] "The ASA noted that the post violated CAP Code rules that marketing containing nutrition or health claims 'must be supported by documentary evidence to show they meet the conditions of use associated with the relevant claim, as specified in the EU Register [of nutrition and health claims made on foods].'"[16]

Sophie Kasaei in the much disputed Instagram post.

Simplicity Matters

Keeping things simple is another best practice when disclosing relationships with influencers. Including "#ad" or "#promotion" is all that a brand really needs to be compliant. Influencers should be clear and direct; otherwise, an organization risks losing the trust of its audience. One example of an unclear and confusing disclosure is from Joy the Baker. On her blog, during the Kentucky Derby, she announced a giveaway while unveiling a new recipe. She wrote, "I've partnered with The Kentucky Derby to bring you an approachable at home Derby-inspired menu. **I'm inviting you to create your own Kentucky Derby inspired dish, share it with us and have the chance to WIN A TRIP TO THIS YEAR'S KENTUCKY DERBY!**"[17] In this example her language is unclear. What is her relationship with the Kentucky Derby? What is a "partner"? Did the Kentucky Derby give her something? Is she being paid? Did she also win a trip to the derby? The reader does not know from the way the text is written. More explicit, definitive language would make the partnership much clearer to the readers.

Monitoring Influencers

Brand should not assume influencers will follow disclosure rules and best practices. The FTC may not necessarily punish an organization for ignoring bad influencer practices out of the gate but will reach out at some point if there is a trail of influencers who continue to skip disclosures when a specific product is involved.

While it is not the responsibility of an organization to babysit influencers, it is common to confirm that these individuals are including appropriate disclosures. Monitoring influencers through social media analytics tools such as Cyfe, Social

Studio, or Crimson Hexagon allows practitioners to see what is being posted. This will help ensure that posts comply with the rules. On its surface, monitoring influencer disclosure can seem like a major effort; however, it is much easier to implement than to correct each time the FTC sends notice about an influencer.

Employee Influence Helps People Do Well

In taking influence marketing a step further, it is important to guide employees appropriately when building their personal online profiles as brand **ambassadors**. Proper development of relationships and engagement with key networks using social media are essential to increasing online influence. Outline and educate employees on the extent to which they should use social media to increase their position as an online influencer. The following represent a few simple ways to get started:

- Determine the degree to which employees already publish in social media in support of the brand.
- Identify criteria that employees should meet to be effectively empowered when using social media.
- Start a list of potential influencer candidates and verify their current skills. Additionally, make note of other proficiencies and those that may be important to learn.
- Assess capabilities for developing a training curriculum and certification program.
- Determine the online communities where employees or thought leaders have built an influential presence in social media, and decide how to increase their impact within that community.
- Review existing influencer activities, paying special attention to the number of influencers. Perhaps it will be important to expand the overall portfolio of influencers.
- Conduct research to understand where important brand influencers spend their time online. Determine whether you need to adjust the venues where engagement occurs.

SOURCE: Chris Boudreaux, and Susan F. Emerick, *The Most Powerful Brand on Earth: How to Transform Teams, Empower Employees, Integrate Partners and Mobilize Customers to Beat the Competition in Digital and Social Media* (Upper Saddle River, NJ: Prentice Hall, 2014).

Life Alive: Micro-Influencer Campaign Uses Data to Drive Results
By Adam Ritchie, APR, a Ritch Brand

Introduction

As social media emerged as a tool to facilitate communication, so too did a type of **celebrity**: regular people turned social media influencers climbed the ladder to fame, influence, and some even to fortune.[1] While celebrity influencers and

---

[1]S. Venus Jin and Aziz Muqaddam, "Product Placement 2.0: 'Do Brands Need Influencers, or Do Influencers Need Brands?,'" Journal of Brand Management 26, no. 5 (2019): 522–37; Seunga Venus Jin, "'Celebrity 2.0 and Beyond!' Effects of Facebook Profile Sources on Social Networking Advertising," Computers in Human Behavior 79 (2018): 154–68.

product placement are not new ideas in advertising, public relations, or public re-lations and marketing,[2] the medium in which these endorsements are present cre-ates a new celebrity playground and more opportunities for two-sided celebrity endorsements, which have shown since the 1980s to improve effectiveness rat-ings, elicit significantly higher credibility, and create higher brand loyalty overall.[3]

While not limited to *just* social media, influencers transcend digital media and often overlap into the blog space, photo-sharing networks, review networks, gaming, and other virtual worlds.[4] The most influential of those crossed these boundaries and transformed their personal networking to a full-fledged brand, sometimes incorporating their own products into the mix.[5] When influencers were first identified, brands were highly swayed by the idea of the macro-influencer, an influencer with a high follower count—somewhere between 10,000 and 1 million+ followers. But as time elapsed, the idea of engagement became more prevalent in this space, with follower count not holding the weight it once did. Now, power comes from the influencer's ability to impact their audience and inspire them to action, opening the door for micro-influencers with 500 to 10,000 followers.[6]

Make no mistake about it: the relationships between audience and influencers are real. And according to an influencer benchmark report by MediaKix, marketers are comfortable and confident about influencer marketing as a legitimate chan-nel for brand success, with 80 percent of marketers finding influencer marketing effective, 71 percent of them saying it even helps drive high-quality traffic and customers to the brand, and 89 percent saying that return on investment (ROI) is comparable to or better than other marketing channels.[7] However, the fame that comes with the influencer reputation is built solidly on the backs of those followers and how the social media efforts of the influencer are used to create engagement based on their personal brand. This is no happy accident. While proof of market-ing outcomes based on influencer contributions is something we are only now starting to see play out in the research, social media influencers are nonetheless considered a fundamental part of an integrated marketing strategy to solicit con-tribution to ideals like stronger brand recognition, favorable brand attitude, and

---

[2]B. Zafer Erdogan, "Celebrity Endorsement: A Literature Review," *Journal of Marketing Management* 15, no. 4 (1999): 291–314; Kathleen A. Farrell, Gordon V. Karels, Kenneth W. Montfort, and Christine A. McClatchey, "Celebrity Performance and Endorsement Value: The Case of Tiger Woods," *Managerial Finance* 26, no. 7 (2000): 1–15.

[3]Michael A. Kamins, Meribeth J. Brand, Stuart A. Hoeke, and John C. Moe, "Two-Sided versus One-Sided Celebrity Endorsements: The Impact on Advertising Effectiveness and Credibility," *Journal of Advertising* 18, no. 2 (1989): 4–10; Sejung Marina Choi, and Nora J. Rifon, "It Is a Match: The Impact of Congruence between Celebrity Image and Consumer Ideal Self on Endorsement Effectiveness," *Psychology & Marketing* 29, no. 9 (2012): 639–50; Sommer Kapitan and David H. Silvera, "From Digital Media Influencers to Celebrity Endorsers: Attributions Drive Endorser Effectiveness," *Marketing Letters* 27, no. 3 (2016): 553–67.

[4]Jin and Muqaddam, "Product Placement 2.0."

[5]Anne Martensen, Sofia Brockenhuus-Schack, and Anastasia Lauritsen Zahid, "How Citizen Influencers Persuade Their Followers," *Journal of Fashion Marketing and Management: An International Journal* 22, no. 3 (2018): 335–53.

[6]Shane Barker, "Micro vs. Macro Influencer Marketing: Know the Difference," *Shane Barker* (blog), April 25, 2019, accessed November 10, 2019, https://shanebarker.com/blog/macro-vs-micro-influencer-marketing-campaign/.

[7]"Influencer Marketing 2019 Industry Benchmarks," *MediaKix* (blog), January 1, 2019, accessed December 1, 2019, https://mediakix.com/influencer-marketing-resources/influencer-marketing-industry-statistics-survey-benchmarks/#instagram.

(continued)

raising awareness about events, product launches, and brand announcements. Another troubling finding of the benchmark report is that 61 percent of marketers agree that it is difficult to find the right influencers for a campaign and the primary concern in relationship to an influencer campaign is finding creative ways to measure ROI of a tactic that has the top three goals of brand awareness, reaching new untapped audiences, and generating sales or other conversions.[8]

So, how can a brick-and-mortar restaurant capture the attention of digital natives in a big city filled with distractions and options on an infinite scroll? Public relations can collect the right influencers, unite them into a cohort, and inspire them to join the brand on a journey to create new products. With a series of menu items conceived, developed, named after, and promoted by our social insiders, we put a café brand at the center of the city's food, healthy living and student scenes, tripled its social interactions, reached millions of consumers and drove sales while nourishing nonprofits.

Using the LUPE model, this chapter will detail the use of micro-influencers in a campaign designed by Adam Ritchie Brand Promotion for client Life Alive. The aim of this case study is to show how influencers can create effective return on investment for integrated campaigns when the client is flexible and the professional allows a firm to use primary research and creativity to solve complicated issues while using influencers online to drive traffic to a brick-and-mortar location.

Listen and Learn

The first step in the LUPE framework is *Listen and Learn*. In this beginning stage, a simple outline is made to address the opportunity or problem to draft the research agenda, establish what type of analysis is necessary, and create audience segmentation. From here, *Listen and Learn* sets the stage for strategic problem solving and helps to establish a framework for the campaign rooted in research. Without *Listen and Learn* it is not possible to accurately rank the aspects of the campaign that must be addressed nor even deduce what success *looks like* for the client.

Life Alive[9] quietly opened a flagship organic café near Boston University to highlight its new look and feel and offer uplifting communal experiences. But the café's soft opening went unnoticed by press months before public relations was first engaged and it was already considered old news. With restaurants popping up every day—hundreds each year—promoting the café would be a challenge.

The client requested outreach to food-focused, active and educated consumers of all genders, ages 18 to 38, in metro Boston and beyond, to drive awareness, engagement, demand and sales, solidify the brand as a top healthy eating destination, position the owner as a fast casual dining authority and establish the new location as an experimental concept hub—all by the end of the year (within five months from campaign launch).

Secondary research showed fast casual and vegetarian options were "exploding" in the market.[10] "Millennial food sophisticates" influenced our target

---

[8]Ibid.

[9]Home page, Life Alive, last modified 2018, accessed October 12, 2019, https://www.lifealive.com/.

[10]Devra First, "What to Expect from Restaurants in 2019," *Boston Globe* (blog), January 16, 2018, accessed November 17, 2019, https://www.bostonglobe.com/lifestyle/style/2018/01/15/what-expect-from-restaurants/CyA134D3wWtJlvs4qw7Pfl/story.html.

audience.[11] They believed food represented culture and saw it as "an expression of who they are."[12] They were especially interested in the story behind their food, wanted "behind the scenes" food prep content and preferred "small batch and artisanal."[13] Instagram was their social platform of choice.[14] And 81 percent of them believed they could have an impact on social issues by using social media.[15]

For primary research, a focus group was performed with Gen Z Instagrammers. Information collected consisted of their thoughts on the brand, the new space, companies in their feeds and what they considered post- and comment-worthy. Researchers observed which menu items caught their attention, and how they interacted with the food and with each other. Color, customization and community were actionable takeaways which would later be used to craft strategy.

If food was deeply personal, small batch was a preference, and presentation was as important as flavor, we would follow these insights somewhere new. A group of influencers from overlapping circles was handpicked and the agency worked with them to invent custom offerings from scratch and share them with the world through social media—this created need and later would lead to foot traffic to the café.

Completing this stage of analysis was essential for the agency to understand

- powerful social trends;
- niche industry trends with micro-influencers;
- use of influencers as a group or a team, instead of individually; and
- which social platforms to use, and which ones to let go.

Without the insights gathered in the *Listen and Learn* stage, the agency could not have tapped into a strong sentiment among the target audience. Nor would they have understood the alignment with pop culture elements at play, how those two would or could potentially intersect creating a campaign like no other. This research allowed for influencer discovery—or, in this case, creation: applied to media planning or programmatic media buying to optimize conversion and continue social listening and media monitoring to improve the campaign as it continued.

Without the impact of this knowledge, the agency could not have moved into the next stage of the LUPE model: *Understand*, where insight is turned into concepts.

---

[11]Laurie Demeritt, "Food Forward: Millennials and Gen Z Are Crafting Their Own Journey," *SmartBrief* (blog), June 15, 2016, accessed October 18, 2019, https://www.smartbrief.com/original/2016/06/food-forward-millennials-and-gen-z-are-crafting-their-own-journey-1.

[12]"Food for Thought—What Sets Gen Z Apart When It Comes to Food Preparation and Consumption," *NPD* (blog), October 2017, accessed November 17, 2019, https://www.npd.com/wps/portal/npd/us/news/thought-leadership/2018/what-sets-gen-z-apart-when-it-comes-to-food-preparation-and-consumption/.

[13]University Caterers Organisation, "TUCO Report 2016 Final," last modified 2016.

[14]Pew Research Center, "Social Media Fact Sheet," *Pew Research* (blog), June 12, 2019, accessed November 10, 2019, https://www.pewresearch.org/internet/fact-sheet/social-media/.

[15]"2017 Cone Gen Z CSR Study: How to Speak Z," *Cone* (blog), 2017, accessed November 16, 2019, https://www.conecomm.com/research-blog/2017-genz-csr-study.

(continued)

Understand

After dissecting the research and consulting with one of the city's most respected Instagrammers, we identified and recruited nine other micro-influencers spanning three categories: food, healthy living and student life. The criteria included thousands of authentic followers leaving substantive comments, ethnic/gender diversity to represent the openness of the brand, and trust within their communities by regularly participating in panels and events.

The *Understanding* stage in the LUPE model takes insights from the *Listen and Learn* stage and uses them to develop deep empathy and insights, which are then used to create SMART objectives. It is at this point that it is also determined whether enough research has been collected in step 1.

Goal: To increase awareness and generate foot traffic through unique creative experience that go beyond promotion.

Objective 1: To increase brand awareness of the next Life Alive location through earned media before the grand opening.

Objective 2: To increase flagship café's quarterly sales by 3 percent in fourth quarter 2018.

Objective 3: Donate $2,000 or more to wellness nonprofits through point-of-service sales in fourth quarter 2018.

With the SMART objectives in place, Life Alive and Adam Ritchie could move on to the next stage of the LUPE model: *Plan* to develop a campaign to support the achievement of the goals and objectives identified in the *Understand* phase, which established a benchmark from which to measure progress through the remainder of the campaign.

Plan

Using the social dialogue, attributes, behaviors, and buying patterns of the target audience as learned in the previous stages, tactics, a timeline, and a budget would be derived for the *Plan* stage. Here, the agency took a unique approach to planning and utilized the brand mythology tradition of storytelling, with the aim of inspiring a contagious level of emotion among the influencers by treating them like an elite cohort, moving through an experience together, and mapping the path, which would allow them to be the heroes of their own online stories … around food.

Taking inspiration from Joseph Campbell's hero's journey[16] and modifying it to fit within the confines of influencer, PR. "Mix It Up" would be a quest with four chapters.[17] Chapter 1, The Call to Adventure: a welcome dinner for the entire group, where the owner would brief them on the idea. Chapter 2, Meeting the Mentor: one-on-one prep sessions in the kitchen with the brand's culinary director. Chapter 3, The Transformation: their social handles turning into signature dishes sold for one week. Chapter 4, The Return: their delivery of funds to their chosen nonprofits.

---

[16] Joseph Campbell, *The Hero's Journey: Joseph Campbell on His Life and Work* (N.p.: New World Library, 2014).

[17] Ibid.

Structuring the program this way created four opportunities for each influencer to willingly post about Life Alive as they moved through their journey: a scenario where millions of targeted social impressions could be sustained across several months on a $0 PR expense budget.

Even though the flagship opening was a bust, going forward, this campaign media strategy would include breaking news of Life Alive's next planned location by showcasing the existing flagship café as its template, and highlight the owner's fast-casual dining expertise by positioning Life Alive as the third act in a play which began when he founded Panera and Au Bon Pain.

With the planning stage securely in place, the business owner moved on to the next phase of the LUPE model, *Execute and Evaluate*, where this plan will be implemented and program executed.

Execute and Evaluate

A well-executed campaign has power to engage and inspire action. An intimate welcome dinner brought together the handpicked food, healthy living and college lifestyle influencers at the flagship café. It had the feel of an initiation combined with a family reunion as the influencer cohort sat around a single table with the owner. They all opted in and the first chapter of posts.

@anaalarcon Instagram.

The one-on-one prep sessions in the months that followed brought each collaborator into the kitchen, where the culinary director set out ingredients and guided them through their Mix It Up creation. We asked them to share flavor memories from their personal backgrounds. One made deconstructed tacos to honor her Mexican heritage and said, "They taste like my grandma's frijoles!" Another made Asian peanut noodles to share her memories of home cooking. Another made a Mediterranean-inspired falafel salad to recognize her Greek roots. We helped document their experiences and equipped them with content for their second chapter of posts where they teased their Life Alive collaborations.

(continued)

@eatrunandallinbetween Instagram.

We worked with Life Alive's design team on point-of-sale materials to promote the unveiling of each dish. We introduced one per week over several months, worked with our collaborators to alert their followers and celebrated each launch with them, achieving the third chapter of posts.

@bostonfoodies Instagram.

Finally, the influencers were invited to document the delivery of the funds they helped raise.

For press offsite, a series of food drops to bring the Life Alive experience directly to editors occurred to coincide with the campaign. Each received a small taste of the menu and a press kit with a pitch about the recent opening and the next location, personally delivered by the culinary director and the PR team.

@lifealivecafe Instagram story.

@lifealive Instagram story.

For press onsite, national food media were invited into the café to view the space and interview the owner about his legendary fast casual experience in the context of Life Alive's expansion. Then we fed the influencer program directly into the press program as a fresh angle and presented the whole Life Alive story for a well-balanced meal.

(continued)

The *Evaluation* stage of the LUPE model involves first assessing whether the campaign met its overall goal and SMART objectives, which can demonstrate the overall effectiveness of the program execution against its defined objectives. Traditionally, financial analysis of programs occurs during this phase of the model that identifies any revenue impacts to the client as a result of the campaign efforts.

Objective 1: To increase brand awareness of the next Life Alive location through earned media before the grand opening.

15.4 million target consumers were reached through earned social. The agency tripled the brand's social interactions through influencer posts on the experimental dishes and generated a 4x increase in demand with earned comments and shares like, "I Def have to get this! All my fav things" (tastes2totango), "Omg I wanna try this so bad" (lizzzeats) and "@hannah_meiseles we need to go here" (northyeastern). It drew owned post comments like, "Can we go here @dianabarrie :) :) :)" (leannkosior), "@smgs219 omg go go go! I'm so jealous" (lilmarissaleigh) and "@rachel_nadolny omg definitely need to get this" (hmonbleau).

Thirty-one million target consumers were reached through earned media—31 times the previous period. Life Alive was solidified as a top healthy eating destination in the resulting coverage which included, "The best healthy restaurants in Boston,"[18] "Life Alive is a favorite, and made it their mission to provide you with tons of healthy options"[19] and "Life Alive makes healthy eating delicious, accessible."[20] The owner was positioned as a fast casual authority bringing his extensive fast casual expertise to the brand: "Panera founder has quietly launched a fast-casual empire"[21] and "Panera and Au Bon Pain founder Ron Shaich is driving Life Alive's next era of expansion."[22] The Boston Herald called our Mix It Up dishes "recipes from local tastemakers."[23]

Objective 2: To increase flagship café's quarterly sales by 3 percent in fourth quarter 2018.

This campaign contributed to a 6 percent increase in flagship café quarterly sales. Beyond the objectives, the program produced content for more than 1/3 of the brand's social posts, sold 509 special dishes through PR and PR-driven point-of-sale and raised

[18] Melissa Malamut, "The Best Healthy Restaurants in Boston," *Bon Appetit* (blog), September 11, 2018, accessed November 12, 2019, https://www.bonappetit.com/gallery/the-best-healthy-restaurants-in-boston.

[19] Samantha Lauren Poccia, "Life Alive Is Now Dishing Out Its Healthy, Organic Eats in Brookline," *Fitt* (blog), April 15, 2019, accessed December 12, 2019, https://fitt.co/boston/articles/life-alive-brookline.

[20] "Life Alive Makes Healthy Eating Delicious, Accessible," *BrooklineHub* (blog), October 2, 2018, accessed October 10, 2019, https://www.brooklinehub.com/life-alive-makes-healthy-eating-delicious-accessible/.

[21] Oset Babur, "Panera Founder Has Quietly Launched a Fast-Casual Empire from Boston," *Food & Wine* (blog), October 15, 2018, accessed December 3, 2019, https://www.foodandwine.com/news/panera-founder-ron-shaich-fast-casual-boston.

[22] Rachel Leah Blumenthal, "Life Alive Will Bring Its Vegetable-Packed Grain Bowls to Back Bay Next," *Eater Boston* (blog), September 19, 2018, accessed December 12, 2019, https://boston.eater.com/2018/9/19/17879512/life-alive-back-bay-expansion-boylston-street.

[23] J. Q. Louise, "It's Tasty Tuesday!," *Boston Herald* (blog), November 13, 2018, accessed December 12, 2019, https://www.bostonherald.com/2018/11/13/its-tasty-tuesday/.

$2,250 for wellness nonprofits. Five items created by the campaign even became permanent menu options, where they continue helping the company's bottom line today.

Goal: To increase awareness and generate foot traffic through unique creative experience that go beyond promotion.

Emotion would drive the posts, and everything came down to how well the campaign could inspire our influencers to post willingly. One was moved to tears during her prep session.[24]

@twist_of_lemons Instagram.

Another mentioned having her own dish was a dream come true and made her feel like she'd "arrived."[25]

@anaalarcon Instagram.

---

[24]@twist_of_lemons, Instagram, November 26, 2018, accessed December 1, 2019, https://www.instagram.com/p/BqqeKhOHUcf/.

[25]@annalarcon, Instagram, October 17, 2018, accessed December 1, 2019, https://www.instagram.com/p/BpDJv8IbeV5/.

(continued)

Another brought his parents, who said how proud they were.[26]

@samuel.thompson Instagram.

Another said she'd never had the ability to create beyond her photo feed before.[27]

@bostonfoodgram Instagram.

Data and Influence

This case study showed that public relations and data can drive product development, marshal client internal resources, and carry an idea across multiple platforms. PR owned idea creation and cross-channel storytelling as only PR can,

---

[26] @samuel.thompson, Instagram, November 5, 2018, accessed December 1, 2019, https://www.instagram.com/p/Bp0oaf2AMiP/.

[27] @bostonfoodgram, Instagram, October 20, 2018, accessed December 1, 2019, https://www.instagram.com/p/BpKA9gCgaDo/.

through research and data integration to create solid outcomes, not just outputs. The "Mix It Up" campaign put Life Alive at the center of the city's healthy living, food, and student scenes; elevated the brand to the national level; nourished non-profits; and baked an authentic personal story into every digital dish.[28] Overall, this case demonstrated the value of the micro-influencer with clear evidence of the insight that data analysis partnered with creativity can provide to business owners even when working on a less-than-ideal time frame if executed properly.

---

[28]"Case Film—Mix It Up," YouTube, posted by Adam Ritchie, February 7, 2019, accessed October 18, 2019, https://www.youtube.com/watch?v=qmc7vhpTtRw&feature=youtu.be.

CONCLUSION

Brands, organizations, and even individuals can publish new content using various channels, creating countless opportunities to influence through content creation. Influencers are increasingly open to collaborating with brands to help build their personal profiles or audiences. In the past, organizations would often need to hire a communications and PR firm to engage successfully with their audiences. In today's connected landscape, targeted communications can be completed simply by sending a **direct message (DM)**. This is important when considering that the concepts of brand loyalty and institutional trust are at an all-time low, with short consumer attention spans and less effective traditional advertising outcomes.[18]

A study conducted by the World Federation of Advertisers (WFA) revealed that 65 percent of the multinational brands surveyed plan to make significant investments in influencer marketing programs over the next 12 months, with the goal of improving brand awareness.[19] However, public relations, marketing, and advertising practitioners are also proceeding with caution when identifying and pursuing potential influencers. Of the brands cited in the survey, the majority identified the most important criteria in selecting an influencer as the "quality of followers," with "credibility and reputation" coming in a close second.[20]

As the practice of influence marketing continues to evolve, so do the technology services that monitor the degree to which individuals are considered *influential*. It is important that data-driven public relations and marketing leaders understand how to create, manage, and measure brand influencers in social media marketing.

DISCUSSION QUESTIONS AND EXERCISES

1. Discuss the insights gleaned through social listening tools and how they impact consumer behavior.
2. The chapter discussed how social intelligence influences brand perception. Search for a brand that understand this principle. Discuss how you think they have leveraged influence on impact band positioning and how insights can be leveraged to impact brand positioning.
3. Categories of influencers were explained throughout the chapter. Identify an influencer in each category along with the brand or organization they represent. Break into small groups explain why they are the influencer chosen.

4. Compare and contrast the FTC guidelines and the ASA guidelines surrounding regulations about influencer marketing. Are they adequate? If not, how would you suggest improving them? Do you believe an average consumer gives much thought to regulations on influencer marketing?

5. Discuss the unethical principles associated with influencer marketing. Why is this a topic of utmost importance to brands now?

6. *Small group exercise:* Examine your own sphere of influence. Look at the people you connect with most often. Research people you want to know better. Now build out a network in which you can connect with your identified influencers. In what way could they help you achiever your personal professional goals?

KEY TERMS

advocate	direct message (DM)	influencee
ambassador	Federal Trade	influencer
celebrity	Commission (FTC)	influencer marketing

NOTES

1. "Introduction to Psychology," Lumen Learning, accessed January 2, 2020, https://courses.lumenlearning.com/wmopen-psychology/chapter/what-is-social-psychology/.

2. Neal Beam, Bill Chamberlin, Jane Collins, Susan Emerick, Michael Fein, Amy Laine, Ashley Libby, and Dhara Naik, "Influencer Guidebook, WOMMA, 2013, https://susanemerick.com/wommas-2013-influencer-guidebook/.

3. Mona Hellenkemper, "Influencer Relations—the Way to Go in 2018?," *InfluencerDB* (blog), November 18, 2019, https://influencerdb.com/blog/influencer-relations/.

4. Charles Arthur, "What Is the % Rule?," *Guardian*, July 20, 2006, https://www.theguardian.com/technology/2006/jul/20/guardianweeklytechnologysection2.

5. "7 Tips for Creating a B2B Social Influence Strategy," Sensei Marketing, April 10, 2017, accessed October 30, 2018, https://senseimarketing.com/7-tips-for-creating-a-b2b-social-influence-strategy/.

6. Chris Boudreaux, and Susan F. Emerick, *The Most Powerful Brand on Earth: How to Transform Teams, Empower Employees, Integrate Partners and Mobilize Customers to Beat the Competition in Digital and Social Media* (Upper Saddle River, NJ: Prentice Hall, 2014).

7. Jessica Liu and Arleen Chien, "The Forrester Wave™: Social Listening Platforms, Q3 2018; The 10 Providers that Matter Most and How They Stack Up," August 21, 2018, https://www.forrester.com/report/The+Forrester+Wave+Social+Listening+Platforms+Q3+2018/-/E-RES137843?objectid=RES137843.

8. Ibid. See also Jessica Liu and Arleen Chien, "Social Listening Platforms Forrester Wave Leader," Synthesio, October 4, 2019, https://www.synthesio.com/analyst-reports/social-listening-platforms/.

9. "2018 Social Intelligence Report: Consumer Products," *NetBase*, 2018, www.netbase.com/project/2018-social-intelligence-report-consumer-products/?utm_

medium=Email&utm_source=Gated&utm_campaign=AR-2018-SocInt-Consumer Products.

10. Rand Fishkin, "Can SEOs Stop Worrying about Keywords and Just Focus on Topics?—Whiteboard Friday," *Moz* (blog), February 5, 2016, https://moz.com/blog/can-seos-stop-worrying-keywords-focus-topics-whiteboard-friday.

11. "Definitive Practical Guide to Influencer Relationship Management," *Onalytica* (blog), January 5, 2018, http://www.onalytica.com/blog/posts/white-paper-the-definitive-practical-guide-to-influencer-relationship-management/.

12. Danny Brown and Sam Fiorella, *Influence Marketing: How to Create, Manage, and Measure Brand Influencers in Social Media Marketing* (Indianapolis, IN: Que, 2013).

13. "What You Need to Know About FTC Influencer Marketing Guidelines," *IZEA* (blog), October 8, 2018, https://www.exeter.ac.uk/media/universityofexeter/collegeofsocialsciencesandinternationalstudies/politics/research/crpr/2018_SSIS_028_-_Changing_Food_Cultures_Report.pdf.

14. Ibid.

15. Amelia Tait, "Flat Tummy Tea: Why the ASA Is Cracking Down on Influencers Shilling Detox Drinks," *New Statesman*, September 13, 2017, https://www.newstatesman.com/politics/business/2017/09/flat-tummy-tea-why-asa-cracking-down-influencers-shilling-detox-drinks.

16. Sam Burne James, "Geordie Shore Star Ordered by ASA to Remove Instagram Post on Detox Tea Brand," *PR Daily*, September 13, 2017, https://www.prweek.com/article/1444417/geordie-shore-star-ordered-asa-remove-instagram-post-detox-tea-brand-health-claims.

17. "About Joy," Joy the Baker, April 10, 2018, https://joythebaker.com/2018/04/bourbon-caramel-brownies-a-kentucky-derby-giveaway/.

18. Alicia Russell, "White Paper: Definitive Practical Guide to IRM," *Onalytica* (blog), August 17, 2017, https://www.onalytica.com/blog/posts/white-paper-the-definitive-practical-guide-to-influencer-relationship-management/.

19. "Brands to Invest More on Influencers," World Federation of Advertisers, October 17, 2019, https://wfanet.org/knowledge/item/2018/07/20/Brands-to-invest-more-on-influencers.

20. Ibid. See also Erica Sweeney, "96% of Marketers Put 'Quality of Followers' at the Top of Influencer Checklists, Study Finds," Marketing Dive, July 23, 2018, https://www.marketingdive.com/news/96-of-marketers-put-quality-of-followers-at-the-top-of-influencer-checkl/528334/.

CHAPTER 6

Creating Compelling Content through Visual Storytelling

KEY LEARNING OUTCOMES

Recognize the benefits of visual storytelling.

Anticipate how an image will impact a campaign or brand.

Explain the best uses for visuals in a strategic plan.

Describe the process for incorporating visuals within a strategy.

Apply principles learned to develop a storytelling blueprint.

Understand the link between personal engagement and
visual storytelling.

Differentiate areas of visual storytelling within public relations
and marketing.

VISUALLY ENHANCED WORLD

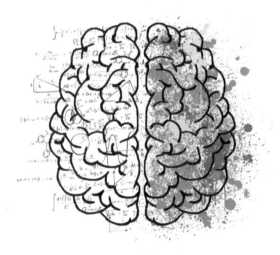

Visual storytelling is becoming an increasingly essential skill for public relations, marketing, and advertising practitioners. From photos on Instagram to videos on YouTube, consumer visual content consumption increases daily and is predicted to continue at rapid pace. In fact, 32 percent of professionals note that images are the most important aspect of their visual storytelling strategy.[1] Approximately 5 billion videos are watched on YouTube each day.[2] A rise in video viewing on almost all social media platforms is being seen across the social sphere. "Views of branded video content have increased by 99 percent on YouTube and by 258 percent on Facebook, while videos on Twitter are six times more likely to be retweeted than one with an image."[3]

This chapter delves into the power of visual storytelling and how practitioners can use this technique to evoke emotion, inspire action, drive **engagement**, grow business, and strengthen **brand recognition** by leveraging photos, videos, **infographics**, presentations, and other rich media together with words.

Seeing is believing. More importantly, though, seeing is remembering. Visual images are impactful and vital in the marketplace of ideas, values, and connections between an organization and their audience. Historically, humans have used images to convey stories for centuries. One of the oldest and earliest recordings of an image found in Indonesia was suggested to be at least 35,400 years old.[4] According to art historian Martin Fox, early cave drawings indicated a symbol of creativity.[5] This rationale is not unlike the reasoning to use visual elements today.

According to authors of *The Power of Visual Storytelling* and *The Laws of Brand Storytelling*, visual storytelling experts Ekaterina Walter and Jessica Gioglio explain the modern-day visual revolution began in the late 1990s, when bloggers emerged and myspace began providing opportunities to personalize profiles.[6] During this time, people began rapidly adopting social networking, and their behaviors on the social web began to change. The Internet saw a rise in photo sharing sites such as Flickr, which made its debut in 2004; the introduction of video sharing with YouTube in 2005; and the founding of Pinterest in 2009, which allows users to create visually attractive inspiration boards.

While Facebook embarked on a platform transformation that became an early footprint of photo engagement, it was not until 2013 when Facebook changed its trajectory to a visual platform that we experience today. Mark Zuckerberg stated publicly that the company was committing to focus on bigger images, access to multiple feeds, and mobile optimization when he radically changed the news feed.[7] A quick look at some of the top global brands will quickly illustrate the change. To market without a digital and social web visually oriented strategy would be detrimental to a brand.

COMPONENTS OF VISUAL STORYTELLING

Campaigns that are successful motivate people to act upon a call to action. This means that the call to action in the storyline is so compelling that people will do what is asked of them. Nonprofits seek donations. Politicians seek votes.

For-profit companies look to consumers to buy their products. No company wants their messages to go unheard. Therefore, the storyline must be powerful enough to inspire action and evoke emotions. Visual storytelling through digital experiences and social media allows for meaningful two-way dialogue exchanges, which build loyalty, **brand awareness**, and trust. Visual storytelling strategies that achieve success employ three main components: authenticity, emotion, and data visualizations.

At 129 million fans, *National Geographic* is the biggest non-celebrity brand on Instagram. What's more, due to the magazine's cross-promotional visual storytelling strategy, they have been the top brand on social media since 2014. According to *The Hustle*, in a time when other brands struggle to find their place in a crowded social sphere, *National Geographic* leveraged a variety of visual formats—from photos to videos—adding their print magazine to their online presence.[1]

---

[1]"Thanks to Its Forward-Thinking Strategy, a 130-year Company Is #1 on Social Media," The Hustle, June 28, 2018, accessed September 22, 2018, https://thehustle.co/ nat-geo-instagram/.

Personalized Engagement through Visual Storytelling

Consumers seek content that speaks to them personally. According to digital strategist Jeff Bullas, "Articles that contain images get 94% more views than articles without."[8] Fabricated, airbrushed, and posed visuals are seen as less likely to resonate with today's consumer.[9] People are looking for sincere moments that speak to human emotions and that capture everyday life. **Authenticity** is connected to the passions of an audience, releasing human emotion that allows the audience to imagine themselves within the images. This elixir turns the audience into eager advocates of the story a brand is attempting to convey.

For brands, authenticity is not only difficult to define, but challenging to project. Brands strive to be genuine and authentic. Visual storytelling helps brands represent brand values, portraying what they stand for transparently to their target audience. In a world based on skepticism, doubt, and uncertainty, brands must connect in new ways, and they are finding visual storytelling in social and digital to be a promising engagement approach. Both **millennials** and **Generation Z**, the first generations of **digital natives**, were raised with continual access to the Internet, which means that practitioners must rethink strategies to reach these enigmas of an audience. Today's consumers turn to Internet search engines as a primary and preferred way to conduct research about organizations, brands, products, services, people, and much more. As they do, these consumers are evaluating a brand's values, purpose, and business practices, in addition to considering what others have shared about their personal experiences with the organization.[10]

Visual storytelling is a central component in conveying authenticity. Two companies that have successfully implemented such strategies utilizing these techniques are GoPro and REI. Both are examples of organizations that dominate the marketplace with original content connecting their target audience with their products through user-generated content.

The Power of UGC in Storytelling

User-generated content (UGC), also known as **user-created content (UCC)**, takes the forms of videos, pictures, blog posts, or social mentions. Such content is commonly created and shared across the social sphere by fans and followers of a brand, without compensation.[1] Consider Coca-Cola's "Share a Coke" campaign or Burberry's the "Art of the Trench Coat" phenomenon: both of these examples motivated loyal fans to share their original content with others. When 86 percent of millennials note that UGC is an indicator of brand quality and can influence purchases, brands and practitioners should incorporate a solid strategy that supports content generated from their users.[2]

---

[1] Megan Marrs, "UGC 101: A Guide to User-Generated Content Marketing," April 12, 2019, https://www.wordstream.com/blog/ws/2014/04/28/user-generated-content.

[2] Jose Angelo Gallegos, "What Is User Generated Content (and Why You Should Be Using It)," *TINT* (blog), September 29, 2018, accessed October 13, 2018, https://www.tintup.com/blog/user-generated-content-definition/.

The Authentic Brands study, conducted by Cohn & Wolfe, a global communications agency, examined the role of authenticity in business, the impact on consumers, and attitudes and behaviors of investors and employees.[11] The study, which surveyed more than 1,400 brands by more than 200 global companies, including more than 15,000 consumers in 15 markets, revealed that these brands had one common thread: they could connect their overall brand messaging to the right media and their core target audience.[12] The report noted that for a brand to stand out and exude authenticity, stock photos needed to be eliminated. When consumers are influenced by visual enhancements within a campaign, a deep connection is created that drives loyalty. Original images will always outshine standard visuals.[13]

One company that made Cohn & Wolfe's Authentic Brands list was Danone. An authentic photo used on the company's Instagram page show a Danone employee taking part in their annual Corporate Challenge to raise money for their local Feeding America organization. A scroll through the company's Instagram account (danonenorthamerica) reveals hundreds of photos that incorporate actual employees donating time and resources. According to Micha Schwing, the director of content strategy for Getty Images, "authenticity, openness and the everyday tap into strong and important ideas. Through the realness of slice-of-life images, brands show that they understand consumers, their life, and their concerns."[14] Authenticity and emotion inextricably intertwined. Stories that are authentic include emotions that connect brands with customers.

Emotion in Visual Storytelling

Evoking emotion has long been a key component of developing an effective public relations and marketing campaign. According to Scott Magdis, Alan Zorfas, and Daniel Leemon, researchers and authors of the article "The New Science of Customer Emotions" published in *Harvard Business Review*, emotional connections between an audience and an organization can outweigh even customer satisfaction. According to the study, the researchers developed what they call "emotional motivators" by applying data analytics to detailed customer data sets, which in turn revealed 300 motivators.[15] The study purports that consumers are emotionally connected to a brand when the brand aligns with a person's private motivations and helps the person fulfill individual desires.[16] Some of the most emotional motivators revealed through this study included the desire to "stand out from the crowd," "have confidence in the future," and "enjoy a sense of well-being."[17]

Armed with this knowledge, brands can develop emotionally charged stories to help identify and leverage a strategy to connect with consumers. For some brands it is easy to make emotional connections.[18] For example, the Make-A-Wish Foundation has to put forth very little effort to develop an emotional connection between their target audiences and their mission. Inherently, most of us want to help sick and dying children live out their last dream. Photos and videos, typography, color, shape, and recognizable icons are all elements of visual storytelling that help tell that story. Therefore, the emotional connection is evident before any story needs to be told.

What happens, though, if your brand does not have such clear, structured, emotional motivators? Consider brands such as Eucerin, Heinz Ketchup, Scotts Lawn Care, or Crocs shoes. Identifying emotional connectors for these consumer product brands may be more challenging than developing an emotionally charged connection for the Make-A-Wish Foundation.

The key to tapping into the emotions of your target audience comes down to understanding what your customers want and need. Emotional motivators vary by brand and industry. For example, car companies may elicit feelings of safety and security, while vacation resorts may elicit rest and relaxation.

By developing real stories that are relatable, it's easy for brands to successfully make emotional connections. In JetBlue's Mother's Day campaign known as FlyBabies, the company used video storytelling to recognize the angst that many mothers feel when flying with children. Both mothers and passengers alike can relate. Feelings of anxiety, annoyance, nervousness, frustration, and fear are just some emotions that come to mind when we think of flying with a baby. The FlyBabies campaign addressed many of the real challenges faced by parents traveling with children.[19] The video's relatability is evident from the first moment through to the end. An emotional connection is developed, and the viewer immediately understands the purpose. This example demonstrates how good stories can come from any number of areas, including customer emotions, company values, the ways that products and services are used, company milestones, or even current events.[20]

Conducting social listening and data analytics to discover insights allows companies to connect with consumers in ways that will most resonate. Data-driven strategies allow a company to understand what makes their customers tick, the values they hold true, and how they can evoke emotions connecting more directly in personalized ways. Emotional connections, backed by data to make better-informed decisions on optimal visuals that motivate or solicit the desired response, create a competitive advantage and ultimate growth for a company.[21]

Data-Driven Insights and Visual Storytelling

Public relations, marketing, and advertising practitioners should view data as a tool of empowerment. As explained in previous chapters, data-driven decision making is foundational: it is a necessary element to allow insights from analysis to effectively aid us in uncovering patterns, spotting trends, connecting with your core audience, and making sound business decisions. Website analytics, social media analytics, email analytics, user experience research, program specific metrics, and company databases are all suitable resources to use when mining and examining data for insights.[22] Social listening platforms—such as Meltwater, Hubspot, Salesforce Social Studio, and Cyfe, just to name a few—data sets that can be used to produce analytical reports so that public relations, marketing, and advertising practitioners have a clearer understanding of brand challenges, message receptivity, and even opportunities to maximize connections to an audience through data visualizations. Data is the vehicle to inform and drive insights. As described in the LUPE model, foundational research and data analysis provide brands with the advantage of data-driven insights to better understand who a target audience is and what motivators are present, and to conduct **A/B testing** of various content forms and layouts to determine performance. Analyzing key trends from a brand's consumer data sets—such as purchase, subscription, or donation history—can reveal triggers or patterns that provide clarity on why consumers behaviors changed. More specifically, an organization may seek to understand why a longtime donor segment has stopped donating to a cause or why sales on a product spiked, or to assess whether a crisis may be brewing. Armed with such knowledge, an effective strategic plan can be developed.

DATA VISUALIZATION: TURNING INSIGHTS INTO VISUAL STORIES

Daniel Waisberg, author of *Tell a Meaningful Story with Data*, reminds us that communicators can tailor a story to the audience by effectively using insights from data analysis to complement a narrative.[23] The combination of decision intelligence from data and a good story can make a connection with the consumer that is unforgettable. As we have already noted, good storytelling includes authenticity and an emotional connection.

In his book *Facts Are Sacred*, Simon Rogers identifies several lessons learned in building the *Guardian*'s Datablog. Three of these principles can be applied to how source data is used in analytics for visual storytelling:[24]

1. Choosing the most appropriate data sources is a form of curation—companies are overloaded with data; therefore, it's important to find the right data to analyze to ensure relevant insights are delivered to aid in decision making. Public relations, marketing, and advertising practitioners should work with their statisticians, data scientists, or business analysts to understand which pieces of information are most important, and why and how they can be used within data-driven decision making for a campaign.

2. Analysis does not have to be complicated—sometimes public relations, marketing, and advertising practitioners are given data sets and immediately feel overwhelmed. While data collection and analysis are rigorous and even time-consuming, there are times when a simple data point is all that is necessary.

3. Focus on the story, not the data—practitioners should focus on the story that they want to convey. In doing so, the visual element—whether it is an infographic, chart, video, or photo—will manifest. Insights revealed from the analysis of key data sets help guide and reinforce strategic decision making.

Public relations, marketing, and advertising practitioners should remember that humans are visual beings and that actions and decisions are based on emotions, which means that visual elements are among the most effective forms of successful communication. That's not to say that the narrative is less important, only that the two complement one another.

FOCUS ON STRATEGY: INCORPORATING VISUALS TO COMPLEMENT THE NARRATIVE

Communicators are responsible for developing effective messaging that resonates with their audiences, which means they often become the conduit between the story and the interpretation of the data delivered from analysis and determining the most relevant insights to take action on. A solid strategy should be in place for stories that influence and engage an audience both emotionally and logically. By aligning content practices—visual and written—public relations, marketing, and advertising practitioners can shape a brand's visual story.

A/B Testing

A central component to developing content that resonates is testing both copy and images. A/B testing is a process in which brands compare audience reactions to two versions of something—such as a website, social media ad, or even an app—to see which one performs better. Online tools, such as Optimizely, have made conducting A/B tests affordable. Practitioners can test on owned platforms such as websites, within emails, or on social channels. Even with small budgets, a company can run several ads concurrently on Facebook to see which visuals and accompanying content generate the most interactions. Almost all social media platforms allow for A/B testing. On YouTube, brands can test still images from video reels, while Pinterest allows for brands to analyze likes and repins. Nearly every platform provides capabilities to measure and evaluate content effectiveness, so take advantage of these tools to help your brand tell its best story.

Harmony between Messages and Visual Elements

Text and images reinforce messaging. Cognitive scientists call this **dual coding theory**.[25] When humans take in visual information together with verbal or written information, their ability to encode the information into long-term memory is enhanced. A study from the University of Cambridge revealed that combining visuals with text increased learning by 89 percent over text-only information.[26] If text sends one message and a visual element sends another, there will be a disconnect with your audience. The last thing any public relations, marketing, and advertising practitioner wants is for visuals to compete with content. Regardless of the intended message, the visual wins. Joseph Cappella, professor of communication at the Annenberg School for Communication, found that when people are shown smoking in an anti-smoking campaign, the image has the opposite of the desired effect. Rather than deter people from smoking, they are driven in the exact opposite direction. The Truth Campaign, sponsored by Truth Initiative, America's largest nonprofit public health organization dedicated to eliminating tobacco use, is an anti-tobacco campaign that has been in place since 1998.[27] The long-standing effectiveness of the campaign can be attributed to the impactful use of strong visuals, accompanied by pointed text across paid, earned, shared, and owned media channels. The campaign uses several guiding principles when creating images with text, quotes, or stats that are helpful for public relations, marketing, and advertising practitioners to keep in mind:[28]

- communicate clearly and succinctly—write in short, definitive phrases;
- numbers make an impact—use statistics and data visualizations to reinforce key messages; and
- inject humor, which resonates with people, and when appropriate include funny copy or images.

Public relations, marketing, and advertising practitioners are the digital curators for a brand. As such, they must keep in mind not only the brand persona, but also the various platforms for which content and visual elements are created. There are key elements deployed when maximizing visual elements.

Photos and Video

Traditional photos, a staple within public relations and marketing departments, have been used on brochures, fliers, websites, advertisements, and more. Today's practitioners must also view these images through a social media lens. To create best-in-class

Bridget, the person behind darkfaerietales_ on Instagram, has a knack for creating images that resonate with her audience.

images, ensure that you start with the highest resolution possible. Regardless of the camera, to create dynamic photos, you will want crisp, clear photos. Applying the rule of thirds, by dividing your image into thirds horizontally or vertically and then aligning the image just off center, creates a more engaging and visually appealing photo.[29] Have fun by framing the shot, working with odd angles, and cropping images. Color, emotion, and creativity all play a fundamental role in curating stunning photos.

Typography

Factors such as **typography** can enhance a visual experience or break it all together. Public relations, marketing, and advertising practitioners should never overlook or discount the importance of font choices.[30] Work with a skilled art director or graphic designer to choose the correct font for the visual messaging. If you are using an off-the-shelf tool such as Adobe Spark Posts, the tool itself will help identify the correct font choice depending on the template.

Color

Color is part of the visual element of language and can create a mood or inspire engagement.[31] People feel blue, see red, or become green with envy. Colors pairings work in concert to generate various moods for the audience. One can hardly think of world-famous jeweler Tiffany's without immediately picturing their quintessential little blue box. Color is powerful; don't underestimate its impact.

Shape

Shapes should be simple. Overly complex layouts and designs can confound the audience. Anna Guerrero from Canva, a digital asset management software platform, suggests using shapes to frame content or for emphasis.[32] To add professional design effects to text, boxes and shapes such as circles, squares, or triangles can be incorporated with any visual elements.

Icons and Emojis

Icons, visual representations of objects, people, or abstract forms,[33] create a sense of familiarity; **emojis**, images used to express emotions or ideas, have become a universal language.[34] Because icons and emojis are so simple, they can send a strong, universally understood visual message.

DEVELOPING A CONTENT STRATEGY

As discussed in earlier chapters, the backbone of successful campaigns, programs, and initiatives center around consistently delivering useful content that resonates with the intended audience. As readers, we know how we feel when experiencing content that is authentic and engaging. When we read or see such content, our sense of curiosity increases. Consumers may be inspired, moved, or feel an emotional response. Content that elicits these responses is more likely to be noticed, liked, and shared across the social web. Public relations, marketing, and advertising practitioners must capitalize on opportunities to develop snackable content that inspires engagement and motivates action.

Storytelling Blueprints: Checklists for Visual Components

The Visual Storytelling Lab offers free resources for practitioners to utilize and customize. The following checklist outlines the basic steps for developing a strategic approach when it comes to visual elements within a campaign:[1]

- Plan the visual elements that evoke emotions and tell your brand's story.

  - Set the stage—be explicit regarding when and where the story unravels.
  - Develop the characters—decide who is part of the story, and why these characters matter to the audience.

- Test images to ensure they resonate with your target audience.

- Decide whether or not to use original images or stock photos, original video or stock video. As noted within the chapter, original images are far more powerful, but when a company has a small budget, stock images will suffice. Resources such as Pixaby.com or Unsplash.com provide high-quality, Creative Commons images.

---

[1]Liz Banse, *Visual Storytelling Guide*, Resource Media, April 2013, http://www.resource-media.org/wp-content/uploads/2013/04/Visual-storytelling-guide.pdf.

- Choose your lead photo with great care. First impressions matter. Your lead photo will set the tone for the campaign ign.
- Create captions and copy that enhances images. The copy should be aligned with the overarching strategy of the campaign.
- Pay attention to consistency of quality, size, color, and brand identity across all platforms and channels.

M.O.M. Squad Storytelling Saves the Day
Adam Ritchie, APR, a Ritch Brand

Introduction

The development of Web 2.0 (websites that emphasize user-generated content, ease of use, participatory culture, and interoperability for end users)[1] and now Web 3.0 (technologies that emphasize machine-facilitated understanding of information in order to provide a more productive and intuitive user experience)[2] have the ability to provide the concepts of information contribution, diffusion, and exchange moderated uniquely and succinctly, through stories.[3] Storytelling can have great business impact when the stories communicate a clear theme that enhances imagination, motivates, elicits emotions, and encourages action.[4] Digital storytelling isn't a new concept in communications,[5] and as digital tools have become more usable so, too, have the insights that we as communicators can glean from their data; however, communicating that data is sometimes easier said than done.

To make sense from data, especially to a public, communicators will often use it to create a story in an effort to convey the importance of the data but in an easier to digest format.[6] Additionally, there is an important reduction of information, or limiting impact in scenario building, when passing research and analysis to the storytelling phase to process and increase the impact of that data that would not exist if not for the concentration of the information to create

---

[1]Tim O'Reilly, "What Is Web 2.0 Design Patterns and Business Models for the Next Generation of Software," O'Reilly, last modified September 30, 2005, accessed October 10, 2019, https://www.oreilly.com/pub/a/web2/archive/what-is-web-20.html.

[2]John Markoff, "A Web Guided by Common Sense?," *New York Times*, November 11, 2006, accessed November 10, 2019, https://www.nytimes.com/2006/11/12/technology/12iht-web.1112web.3496525.html?.

[3]Zheng Xu et al., "Building the Multi-modal Storytelling of Urban Emergency Events Based on Crowdsensing of Social Media Analytics," *Mobile Networks and Applications* 22, no. 2 (2017): 218–27.

[4]Esther K. Choy, *Let the Story Do the Work: The Art of Storytelling for Business Success* (New York: Amacom, 2017).

[5]Klaus Fog, Christian Budtz, Baris Yakaboylu, and SpringerLink, *Storytelling: Branding in Practice* (Berlin, Heidelberg: Springer Berlin Heidelberg, 2005).

[6]Cole Nussbaumer Knaflic, *Storytelling with Data: A Data Visualization Guide for Business Professionals* (Hoboken, NJ: Wiley, 2015).

that story.[7] More recently, brands have used storytelling through social media channels to reach larger and/or more targeted audiences to advance the brand promise or convey brand value to shareholders of all kinds, both internal and external.[8]

So, who can a brand turn to when its biggest retailer closes its doors, sales are down, and social engagement is flat? Public relations can help it reconnect with consumers and find the hero in each of them. In this case study, a diverse group of pregnant influencers from across the country were transformed into the world's first team of pregnant comic book superheroes, equipped with products from the line and brought together for Mother's Day. The M.O.M. Squad carried the brand's message of support across six media categories, doubled the brand's social interactions, and drove sales while celebrating the hero in every mom.

Using the LUPE model, this case study details the use of influencers in an integrated campaign conducted by Adam Ritchie Brand Promotion for client Summer Infant. The aim is to showcase how effective storytelling can create sound return on investment for integrated campaigns when the client is flexible and the practitioner uses research and creativity to solve complicated ecommerce issues.

Listen and Learn

The case study applies the first stage of the LUPE model, *Listen and Learn*; to develop the opportunity or problem involved, ranking the most significant aspects of the issue; determine priorities for effective research; and conduct social listening and monitoring as a means for primary research—in addition to using secondary research methods in order to determine market trends and attitudes, consider consumer sentiment, and address attitudes present in the environment.

In this case, baby gear company Summer Infant was in a bind. Its biggest retail partner, Babies"R"Us, had just gone out of business. Sales were down. Social engagement was flat. The corporate outlook was uneasy. The brand needed a jump-start. It wanted to reach expectant parents and parents of newborns to three-year-olds through positive national coverage in parenting media and beyond, reinforce the brand's message of support (*"Baby has you. You have us"*), spark positive social media conversations around the brand, and drive sales—all in time for Mother's Day. Summer Infant's VP of marketing was a true believer in the ability of public relations to transform brands, and, as such, she partnered with Adam Ritchie to create a content-driven converged media campaign incorporating rich storytelling, from scratch.

---

[7]Javier Carbonell, Antonio Sánchez-Esguevillas, and Belén Carro, "From Data Analysis to Storytelling in Scenario Building: A Semiotic Approach to Purpose-Dependent Writing of Stories," *Futures* 88 (2017): 15–29.

[8]Gabrielle Dolan, Yamini Naidu, and Ebooks Corporation, *Hooked: How Leaders Connect, Engage and Inspire with Storytelling* (Milton, Queensland, Australia: Wiley, 2013).

(continued)

A trip to the movie theater resulted in a flash of inspiration that was cross-checked to determine viability. Marquees were filled with superhero films. Families from all backgrounds were spotted lining up at ticket windows. The agency dug into the national superhero obsession and the role these movies play in family entertainment. Secondary research showed women and men were equally excited about these films.[9] *Wonder Woman* had recently become the top-grossing superhero origin movie of all time (Forbes),[10] *Black Panther* had crossed the $1 billion mark,[11] and audiences were asking for greater diversity[12]—specifically, more women in these films.[13] Taking these insights into account, Summer Infant agreed that parents want to be superheroes to their children and always save the day, and their products gave them extra abilities. The agency then shaped these insights into a concept that would tap into the superhero trend, tie in the empowering message of the women's movement, and break through with an unforgettable visual. It would create a pregnant superhero. A woman with top-notch gadgetry to heighten her powers. She'd be Batman with a baby bump, and nothing would stand in her way. Completing this research stage allows for data-driven analysis, which is essential for the agency to understand

- powerful social trends,
- economic factors at play across an industry sector, and
- the type of community tactics that would inspire the target audience to act.

Without the insights gathered in the *Listen and Learn* stage, the agency could not have tapped into a strong sentiment among the target audience, nor would they have understood the alignment with pop culture elements at play and how those two would or could potentially intersect, creating a campaign like no other. This research allowed for influencer discovery—or, in this case, creation: the ability to plan media planning or programmatic media buying to optimize conversion and continue social listening and media monitoring to improve the campaign as it continued. Without the impact of this knowledge, the agency could not have moved into the next stage of the LUPE model: *Understand.*

---

[9]Gemma Joyce, "The Most Hotly Anticipated Superhero Movies 2018," *Brandwatch* (blog), January 12, 2018, accessed November 8, 2019, https://www.brandwatch.com/blog/react-superhero-movies-2018/.

[10]Mark Hughes, "'Wonder Woman' Is Officially the Highest-Grossing Superhero Origin Film, " *Forbes*, November 2, 2017, accessed November 8, 2019, https://www.forbes.com/sites/markhughes/2017/11/02/wonder-woman-is-officially-the-highest-grossing-superhero-origin-film/#666c5b4aebd9.

[11]Andrew Liptak, "Black Panther Has Crossed the $1 Billion Mark Worldwide," *The Verge* (blog), March 11, 2018, accessed November 8, 2019, https://www.cnbc.com/2018/03/11/black-panther-has-crossed-the-1-billion-mark-worldwide.html.

[12]Nicol Turner Lee, "Black Panther: Lessons in Hollywood Diversity and Black Pride," Brookings, last modified February 26, 2018, accessed November 8, 2019, https://www.brookings.edu/blog/up-front/2018/02/26/black-panther-lessons-in-hollywood-diversity-and-black-pride/.

[13]Joanna Piacenza, "Superhero Movies Possess Staying Power with Viewers." *Morning Consult* (blog), April 26, 2018, accessed November 8, 2019, https://morningconsult.com/2018/04/26/superhero-movies-possess-staying-power-with-viewers/.

Understand

In the *Understand* stage, insights gathered from the previous stage are used to develop strategies and articulate their necessary components such as goals and SMART objectives. Drawing from the audience demographic data from Facebook Insights, the business owner developed the following goals and objectives.

Goal: To increase awareness and generate enthusiasm for the Summer Infant brand.

Objective 1: To increase brand awareness in parents of newborns to three-year-olds through positive national coverage in parenting media and beyond by Mother's Day.

Objective 2: To increase sales in the online store by 10 percent by Mother's Day.

With these strategic components in place, the business owner could move on to the next stage of the LUPE model: *Plan* to develop a campaign to support the achievement of the goals and objectives identified in the *Understand* phase.

Plan

Using the social dialogue, attributes, behaviors, and buying patterns of the target audience as learned in the previous stages, tactics would be derived for the *Plan* stage. Here the agency created the Target Audience, Tactics, and Timeline and Budget. Since the client loved the idea and wanted more than one character, the agency suggested banding them together as a unit: the world's first team of pregnant superheroes. They'd come together from all walks of life and all stages of pregnancy to kick butt and celebrate all moms as heroes to their little ones. (*"Baby has you."*) Each would be equipped with a Summer Infant product as her tool of choice: a monitor, a potty, a stroller and a bath seat. (*"You have us."*) They'd be the living embodiment of the brand message.

The agency went further and suggested the characters be based on real-life pregnant micro-influencers from across the country, in the target audience, to bring a concept based in fantasy into reality. It outlined the criteria for the four women who would make up the group and emphasized diversity.

It was important for the characters to break old comic book stereotypes of women drawn by men, so the agency asked Summer Infant to hire a female comic book artist. Illustrator Viera Boudreau was chosen to bring the characters to life with powerful art that would turn heads and drive the narrative.

The M.O.M. Squad was born. Its members were Agent Momitor, Professor Potty, The MotherLoad, and AquaMom—each based on a real pregnant woman with her own story to tell. To connect with moms, a light would be shone on the superhero in each of them.

With a major juvenile products industry trade show to support before this could start, it had to be content creation at the speed of pop culture. Most campaigns are brand- or product-focused. This campaign was designed to be both. As many campaigns focus on a single holiday, this campaign used a pair of one-day holidays as goalposts to land results between. It would kick off just before National Superhero Day (April 28) and culminate on Mother's Day (May 13). The team had just 2.5 weeks to conduct the outreach with a production and paid media budget of $30,000.

(continued)

Agent Momitor

Aqua Mom

Professor Potty

The MotherLoad

With the *Planning* stage in place, the business owner moved on to the next phase of the LUPE model, *Execute*.

Execute and Evaluate

Marvel Entertainment was invited to amplify Summer Infant's positive announcement on their social platforms. They declined but appreciated the idea, and we moved forward solo, undaunted. Next a video trailer was scripted[14] introducing

[14]"The World's First Team of Pregnant Superheroes," posted by Summer, April 25, 2018, accessed November 8, 2019, https://www.youtube.com/watch?v=9JVhpiHiOoU&feature=youtu.be.

the female comic book illustrator, showing the real women morphing into superheroes and inviting consumers to share and tag the supermoms in their own lives.

Moments after the trailer was finalized, it was pitched to the most influential online parenting outlet in the country: The Bump. Once we broke the news, we used The Bump placement as proof-of-concept to broaden our outreach horizons and propel the story out of parenting media and into noncompeting outlets in lifestyle, women's, pop culture, news and business segments, with angles tailored to each.

Summer Infant launched a microsite[15] and promoted Facebook posts where consumers were asked to tag their personal supermoms. Three consumers would receive the full line of products used by the heroes, and Summer Infant gift cards. An email blast was sent, and the video trailer was promoted with TrueView.

To pitch to media outlets, a different take on the news release was conceived,[16] as an open letter to Marvel Entertainment, extolling the virtues of pregnant superheroes and inviting them to write future M.O.M. Squad adventures together with Summer Infant. It was a lighthearted note to boost media interest and the brand's search engine optimization (SEO).

Finally, the inspirational women behind the M.O.M. Squad characters were available for interviews—along with the female comic book illustrator and the client—and suggested editors might ask readers what their own superpowers would be. This showed the story's potential for engaging readers and helped sell the pitch.

The *Evaluation* stage of the LUPE model involved first assessing whether the Mother's Day campaign met its overall goal and SMART objectives, and then evaluating other metrics to assess the campaign's performance in relation to the Christmas campaign when the digital agency had control.

Objective 1: To increase brand awareness in parents of newborns to three-year-olds through positive national coverage in parenting media and beyond by Mother's Day.

Stories were secured across six different media segments and reached 93.3 million target consumers. The messaging we placed carried Summer Infant's message of support and changed the tone of previously skeptical company coverage: "Summer Infant supports you";[17] "Summer Infant's mission to sing moms' praises is an overdue and important one";[18] "This badass team of comic

---

[15] "Meet the M.O.M Squad," Summer Infant, accessed December 8, 2019, https://summerinfant.com/meet-the-mom-squad.

[16] Adam Ritchie, "The World's First Team of Pregnant Superheroes Is Born," April 26, 2018, accessed October 9, 2019, https://www.prweb.com/releases/2018/04/prweb15443216.htm.

[17] Anisa Arsenault, "4 Real-Life Moms Get a Superhero Alter Ego—Because Moms Can Multitask Way Better than Batman," The Bump, last modified April 26, 2018, accessed November 9, 2019, https://www.thebump.com/news/summer-infant-superhero-moms.

[18] Maressa Brown, "There's a New Squad of Pregnant Superheroes in Town & It's About Time," *What to Expect* (blog), May 9, 2018, accessed November 25, 2019, https://www.whattoexpect.com/news/pregnancy/pregnant-superheroes-summer-infant/.

(continued)

book characters gives heroism a whole new perspective . . . it [could] challenge the way our society thinks about mothers";[19] "This innovative brand is all about family";[20] "Summer Infant has taken the superhero concept to the next level";[21] "What I love about this campaign are the stories being told and the conversations being started";[22] "Illustrative and empowering";[23] "Who can't get behind a little mom-as-superhero action this Mother's Day?"[24] The compelling artwork we commissioned was used up front in every story.

Objective 2: To increase social media interaction and sales in the online store by 10% by Mother's Day.

The brand's social media interactions more than doubled (likes/comments/ shares) from the previous period and reached 5.4 million target consumers. The M.O.M. Squad resonated with users who tagged their own supermoms and

[19]"World's First Team of Pregnant Superheroes Celebrating Motherhood This Mother's Day," *GirlTalkHQ* (blog), May 10, 2018, accessed November 8, 2019, https://www.girltalkhq.com/ worlds-first-team-of-pregnant-superheroes-celebrating-motherhood-this-mothers-day/.

[20]Gloria Mellinger, "We're Celebrating #NationalSuperheroDay with the M.O.M. Squad of Pregnant Superheroes!," *Celebrity Baby Trends* (blog), April 27, 2018, accessed November 8, 2019, https://celebritybabytrends.com/this-saturday-is-national-superhero-day-celebrate-your-supermom.

[21]Kelly Guidry, "Meet the First Team of Pregnant Superheroes, Inspired by Real Life Moms," *New York Family* (blog), May 11, 2018, accessed November 8, 2019, https://www.newyork-family.com/meet-the-first-team-of-pregnant-superheroes-inspired-by-real-life-moms/.

[22]Kali Moulton, "Moms Are Super: Meet the M.O.M Squad," *Geek Mom* (blog), May 13, 2018, accessed November 8, 2019, https://geekmom.com/2018/05/ moms-are-super-meet-the-m-o-m-squad/.

[23]Ellen Smith, "Summer Infant's M.O.M Squad Depicts Moms as Heroes," *Trend Hunter* (blog), May 22, 2018, accessed November 8, 2019, https://www.trendhunter.com/trends/ mom-squad.

[24]Amy Joyce, "These Moms Were Given Their Own Superhero Personas. What's Your Superpower?," *Washington Post*, May 13, 2018, accessed November 8, 2019, https:// www.washingtonpost.com/news/parenting/wp/2018/05/13/these-moms-were-given-their-own-superhero-personas-whats-your-superpower/.

said, "Hannelore Moore literally is a super hero already! Love you Hanni! xoxo." "Stephanie Stevens you are a superhero Mom to those charming boys!!" "Alex Umstead! We are totes M.O.M. squad superheroes!!!" M.O.M. Squad members (Image 2)[25] posted their characters and said, "I am in tears seeing this actually come to life!"

In a week, the combined earned and paid campaign drove 29,934 YouTube views (70x the brand's previous video performance), a 56.4 percent view rate blowing away the YouTube retail benchmark of 15.7 percent,[26] a 10 percent email open rate and a 6 percent clickthrough rate. The story spread and generated 3,974 landing page sessions. Coverage backlinked to each product's purchase page and contributed to a 13.3 percent increase in quarterly sales.

Goal: To increase awareness and generate enthusiasm for the Summer Infant brand. In addition to satisfying both SMART objectives, months after the campaign, its assets continued to be shared by consumers around the world. PR sparked the creative process, marshaled the client's internal resources, and drove an interagency team to carry an idea across disciplines and channels. It owned idea creation and multimedia storytelling as only PR can. The client called it "inspiring . . . an excellent return on investment . . . generated excitement within the organization" and added, "The brand had not received this level of coverage [in all of its 33 years]."

The M.O.M. Squad carried the brand's message of support across six media categories, doubled the brand's social interactions, and drove sales while celebrating the hero in every mom. There were no celebrity spokespeople. No big spends. Just an original idea to celebrate the heroics of everyday women and elevate them to superhero status, while helping a brand recover its superpowers.

The case study demonstrated how the use of creative problem-solving through storytelling propelled a brand through a sales slump and rejuvenated brand recognition and enthusiasm through earned media as a result. This campaign employed the LUPE model and used research and insight to construct and inform its structure and implementation, and it met its goal and SMART objectives. During the *Evaluate* step, data provided the sales information and engagement required to analyze the campaign in its entirety and provided "next steps" in moving the story forward. Lastly, this case study provided clear evidence of the insight that data can have on content creation and curation to invigorate a brand that seemed to be otherwise "stalled" and provide a new lexicon through which to tell the brand story, through the M.O.M Squad.

---

[25]@_livingforjasmin, Instagram, April 26, 2018, accessed November 8, 2019, https://www.instagram.com/p/BiCdoSpjY3L/.

[26]YouTube, "The Big Picture: 2017 YouTube Benchmark Report," accessed November 8, 2019, https://downloads.ctfassets.net/82kv66k4hmlh/6xsAwDYwbCYgEycgGq6o4e/bb47786681deccc965c0ba494c9a6dea/2017_YouTube_Data_Report.pdf?id=main-cta&mkt_tok=eyJpIjoiTURFeU1qaGtaRFkxWkdNMiIsInQiOiJaVzdVZGGx3N0tnSDQ0SitUTDZMbmJzNGNZeFlsNTM1MGoweExTTm5qVmhOe.

How to Create Narrative Images in 5 Easy Steps

By Shlomi Ron, CEO, Visual Storytelling Institute LLC

Images are today's lingua franca of visual communications. So, knowing how to create images with compelling narratives is crucial to stand out from the crowd.

We naturally look at static photos in the present time and see them as time capsules of an event that took place in the past. According to Sarah Elise Väre, author of *Storytelling Advertising: A Visual Marketing Analysis*, "the past group shows the ending of a story, the present group the middle, and the future group the beginning. The all-tenses group shows both the beginning, the middle, and the end of a story."[1]

However, not all photos are so clear cut. Since we are constant seekers of meanings, we're all players in our own movies where we play the hero, the director, the cameraman and most importantly the editor—then we edit what we see in order to create meanings that fit our internal narratives and beliefs. Such editing work could play with the narrative timeline back and forth until landing on a story we find personally meaningful.

Follow these five easy steps to create compelling narrative images. Just to caveat, the narrative images we're talking about are ideally those you plan in advance vs. the ones you spontaneously take as they allow you more control:

1. **Plan your story:** Come up with the story (setting, conflict, and resolution) your audience truly cares about.

2. **Select your storytelling picture type:** As outlined above there are four types of narrative pictures, select the one you want to focus on and emphasize 1–2 narrative clues (e.g., time of day, salient accessories, the interaction between characters shown etc.) that will help your viewers conjure the right story.

3. **Add captions and hashtags:** There are two types of captions: (a) Descriptive: Where the caption describes what happens in the image and (b) Inferential: Where the caption uses the image as a springboard to convey a larger single idea. On VSIs Instagram, we typically use the latter as it allows us to vividly amplify the power of the visual to support a larger visual storytelling principle we're looking to relay. Lastly, research what hashtags resonate the most with your audience along with what top influencers in your space are using—and integrate them into the caption second half. Leave your opening caption without hashtags so it's easy to read.

4. **Select your target emotion:** According to Fractl's study, The Role of Emotions in Viral Content, the most impactful recipes include: "positive emotions along with surprise were found to result in massive shares Pair 'low-arousal' emotions (sadness, relaxation, and depression) with admiration or surprise

[1]Sarah Elise Väre, "Storytelling Advertising—a Visual Marketing Analysis," Harken School of Economics, May 2014, https://pdfs.semanticscholar.org/3f39/551004dc5cde471dfa136fddb 257664a4261.pdf.

Play up high-arousal emotions (anxiety, anger and excitement) in unsurprising, negative content."[2]

5. Test your picture: Create several executions of your picture and test them with your colleagues. You'll often discover that the story you had in mind may be processed differently by your audience, which means you need to further amplify your narrative clues.

[2]"Why Certain Emotional Combinations Make People Share," Fractl, accessed January 12, 2020, https://www.frac.tl/work/marketing-research/viral-content-emotions-study/. Reprinted with permission of Shlomi Ron.

CONCLUSION

It has never been easier for public relations, marketing, and advertising practitioners to develop emotionally compelling stories using strong visual component. Today's technology enables practitioners to make images and video essential elements within a communications plan. To move people to act, public relations and marketing strategies must connect brand emotions with human emotion, supported by data. With the right visual component and a strong message, campaigns can unite people with the brands they trust.

DISCUSSION QUESTIONS AND EXERCISES

1. Assemble a list of the benefits of visual storytelling for public relations, marketing, and advertising practitioners.
2. Based on what you have read in the chapter, formulate a strategy for how images and video will impact a campaign, brand, or organization.
3. We often hear that consumers are overloaded with information. One way to break through the noise is by using photos and videos to tell compelling stories. Do you agree that it is harder to break through to consumers? Are poignant images and video the answer?
4. Find a brand on Pinterest, Instagram, YouTube, and Facebook. Compare how the brand utilizes each platform. Are the same images or videos used throughout? Do you think they have reached their intended audience? Should they adjust content in any way? Is there harmony across each platform and through the images and videos?
5. The M.O.M. Squad campaign used emotional imagery to move people to action. Discuss why this campaign was so powerful.
6. *Small group exercise:* Assumptions about individual customers must encompass more than an "audience persona" outlining likes, dislikes, demographics, or even characteristics.[35] Decisions about customers should be made based on

their online behaviors. Take a moment to search for a product on Amazon or a streaming video on Hulu or Netflix—and then identify and discuss the keywords chosen and the options revealed. Do you see phrases such as "Because you watched" or "Customers who bought this item also bought"? What does this tell you about your online search habits and who you are as a customer?

KEY TERMS

A/B testing	emoji	user-created content
authenticity	engagement	(UCC)
brand awareness	Generation Z	user-generated content
brand recognition	infographics	(UGC)
digital natives	millennials	visual storytelling
dual coding theory	typography	

NOTES

1. Jesse Mawhinney, "45 Visual Content Marketing Statistics You Should Know in 2018," HubSpot Blog, May 2018, accessed October 13, 2018, https://blog.hubspot.com/marketing/visual-content-marketing-strategy.
2. "37 Mind Blowing YouTube Facts, Figures and Statistics—2019," MerchDope, November 2, 2019, https://merchdope.com/youtube-stats/.
3. "Why Video Is Exploding on Social Media in 2018," Wyzowl, 2018, https://www.wyzowl.com/video-social-media-2018/. See also Young Entrepreneur Council, "How to Refocus Your Personal Brand with Video," Inc., August 31, 2018, https://www.inc.com/young-entrepreneur-council/how-to-refocus-your-personal-brand-with-video.html.
4. John Noble Wilford, "Cave Paintings in Indonesia May Be among the Oldest Known," New York Times, December 21, 2017, accessed August 27, 2018, https://www.nytimes.com/2014/10/09/science/ancient-indonesian-find-may-rival-oldest-known-cave-art.html.
5. Martin Fox, "Why Are Cave Paintings Important?," March 24, 2017, https://www.quora.com/Why-are-cave-paintings-important.
6. Ekaterina Walter and Jessica Gioglio, The Power of Visual Storytelling: How to Use Visuals, Videos, and Social Media to Market Your Brand (New York: McGraw-Hill, 2014).
7. Christina Warren, "Facebook Unveils a Radically Redesigned News Feed," Mashable, March 7, 2013, accessed August 27, 2018, https://mashable.com/2013/03/07/new-facebook-news-feed/#cMkKRZBrwPqE.
8. Jeff Bullas, "6 Types of Visual Content You Need to Use in Your Marketing Campaigns," Neil Patel (blog), December 20, 2019, https://neilpatel.com/blog/visual-content-you-need-to-use-in-your-marketing-campaign/.
9. Bulldog Reporter, "Consumers Say Visuals Are Most Important Factor in Online Shopping," Agility PR Solutions, August 25, 2017, https://www.agilitypr.com/pr-news/public-relations/consumers-say-visuals-important-factor-online-shopping/.
10. Adam Fridman, "Brand Authenticity: Powered by the Science of Purpose," Inc., May 31, 2017, https://www.inc.com/adam-fridman/brand-authenticity-powered-by-the-science-of-purpose.html.

11. Cohn & Wolfe, "Global Study from Cohn & Wolfe Defines Authenticity in the Eyes of Consumers and Reveals the 100 Most Authentic Brands," PR Newswire, June 29, 2018, https://www.prnewswire.com/news-releases/global-study-from-cohn--wolfe-defines-authenticity-in-the-eyes-of-consumers-and-reveals-the-100-most-authentic-brands-300253451.html.

12. Cohn & Wolfe, "Authentic 100," Authentic Brands, June 2017, http://www.authentic100.com/.

13. Tyler Walch, "How to Build Brand Authenticity Like the Top 100 Brands," DIYMarketers, April 26, 2018, https://diymarketers.com/most-authentic-brands-brand-authenticity/.

14. Newscred Insights, "Whitepaper: The Power of Visual Storytelling; The Power of Visual Storytelling—4 Principles from Newscred & Getty Images," August 3, 2016, http://visualstorytelling.newscred.com/p/2.

15. Louisa S, "How to Build Emotional Customer Connections," Research by Design, August 21, 2018, https://researchbydesign.com.au/how-to-build-emotional-customer-connections/.

16. Ibid.

17. Scott Magids, Alan Zorfas, and Daniel Leemon, "The New Science of Customer Emotions: A Better Way to Drive Growth and Profitability," *Harvard Business Review* 93 (November 2015): 66–74, 76.

18. Philipp Wolf, "6 Ways to Make Emotional Connections with Potential Customers," Custify, June 7, 2019, https://www.custify.com/6-ways-to-make-emotional-connections-with-potential-customers.

19. Shawna Kaszer, "JetBlue's 'FlyBabies' Misses the Mark," Huffington Post, December 7, 2017, https://www.huffingtonpost.com/shawna-kaszer/jetblues-flybabies-misses_b_9843648.html.

20. Ivy Cohen, "5 Ways to Get to the Heart of Emotional Marketing," *Entrepreneur*, July 25, 2017, https://www.entrepreneur.com/article/297367.

21. Magids, Zorfas, and Leemon, "New Science of Customer Emotions."

22. Kristen Twiford, "3 Tips for Impactful Data-Driven Visual Storytelling," AMA, https://www.ama.org/publications/MarketingNews/Pages/3-tips-for-impactful-data-driven-visual-storytelling.aspx.

23. Daniel Waisberg, "Tell a Meaningful Story with Data," Think with Google, March 2014, https://www.thinkwithgoogle.com/intl/en-145/marketing-strategies/data-and-measurement/tell-meaningful-story-data/.

24. Simon Rogers, *Facts Are Sacred* (London: Faber and Faber, 2013).

25. Mark Sadoski and Allan Paivio, *Imagery and Text: A Dual Coding Theory of Reading and Writing* (New York: Routledge, 2013). See also Donna L. Murdaugh, Jose O. Maximo, Claire E. Cordes, Sarah E. O'Kelley, and Rajesh K. Kana, "From Word Reading to Multisentence Comprehension: Improvements in Brain Activity in Children with Autism after Reading Intervention," *NeuroImage: Clinical* 16 (2017): 303–12.

26. Richard E. Mayer, *Multimedia Learning* (Cambridge: Cambridge University Press, 2001).

27. "Who We Are," Truth Initiative, accessed January 12, 2020, https://truthinitiative.org/who-we-are.

28. rdelder1, "Being Clear and Concise," University of Bradford, Academic Voice.docx, accessed December 31, 2019, https://www.bradford.ac.uk/t4-ssis/ruski-files/academic-voice/page_06.htm.

29. Sean, "Rule of Thirds," PhotographyTalk, April 19, 2019, https://www.photographytalk.com/rule-of-thirds.

30. Steven Bleicher, *Contemporary Color: Theory and Use* (Clifton Park, NY: Delmar Cengage Learning, 2012), 48–52.

31. Nick Babich, "How to Build and Maintain a Visual Language," Shopify, November 13, 2019, https://www.shopify.com/partners/blog/visual-language.

32. Anna Guerrero, "5 Ways to Use Shapes Creatively in Your Designs," Canva, May 18, 2018, https://www.canva.com/learn/use-shapes-creatively-design/.

33. "Ikon," Vocabulary.com, accessed January 12, 2020, https://www.vocabulary.com/dictionary/ikon.

34. Oxford English Dictionary, "Emoji," Lexico.com, accessed January 12, 2020, https://www.lexico.com/en/definition/emoji.

35. Gary DeAsi, "How to Use Customer Behavior Data to Drive Revenue (Like Amazon, Netflix & Google)," Pointillist, August 14, 2018, accessed January 20, 2019, https://www.pointillist.com/blog/customer-behavior-data/.

CHAPTER 7

Corporate Social Responsibility and Corporate Activism

KEY LEARNING OUTCOMES

Understand and differentiate between corporate social responsibility (CSR), corporate activism, and cause-related marketing (CR-M).

Grasp the evolution of corporate social responsibility, corporate activism, and cause-based marketing.

Explain the role that corporate activism plays in today's social media–driven marketplace.

Assess the role that millennials and Generation Z play in organization's achieving goals of giving back.

Critique organizational motivations that inspire brands to utilize CSR strategies that incorporate ethics and transparency in their mission of giving back.

Identify the main considerations for implementing a strategy that incorporates CSR, CR-M, and corporate activism.

THE STATE OF GIVING BACK

Research in today's marketplace reveals that giving back matters to consumers. In fact, corporate debacles over the past few years have fueled the fire for companies understanding and adopting more genuine ways in which to connect with consumers. Some notable examples include Kendall Jenner's misrepresentation of the Black Lives Matter campaign,[1] H&M's "Coolest Monkey in the Jungle,"[2] Shea Moisturizer's campaign that outraged its key demographic,[3] and Dove's mishap that showed an image of an African American woman removing a dark brown shirt to reveal a white woman.[4] All were the result of brands not fully researching before executing their strategies. Debacles such as these have negative implications on consumers' attitudes and brand perceptions.

In the past, companies could win over consumers with a simple apology. Today, however, consumers expect more from their favorite brands. Given the plethora of data available to brands, mistakes like these should not happen. Corporate social responsibility, corporate activism, and caused-based marketing are significant for public relations, marketing, and advertising practitioners. This chapter explores the foundations of corporate social responsibility through the exploration of corporate activism and cause-based marketing campaigns prompted a new generation of consumers and the subsequent partnerships between nonprofits and corporations.

Today's consumer is engaged and is holding organizations accountable for their actions. They pay attention to how a company is giving back through corporate social responsibility and corporate activism.

Corporate Social Responsibility

The concept of a brand, organization, or corporation giving back has been a staple since the early 1950s.[5] In fact, Henry Ford, who championed himself as the common man, is quoted as saying, "Business is a service, not a bonanza."[6] The premise behind what Ford was alluding to is what researchers Anjan Thakor and Robert Quinn call the **economics of higher purpose**. The idea is that organizations must shift from a bottom-line, transaction-oriented focus to a purpose-driven mindset. The economics of higher purpose is the foundation of **corporate social responsibility (CSR)**: the principle of developing stronger bonds with employees, the community, stakeholders, and consumers. There are many interpretations of CSR. Researchers Brent Beal and Cristina Neesham defined CSR as "the moral and practical obligation of market participants to consider the effect of their actions on collective or system-level outcomes and to then regulate their behavior in order to contribute to bringing those outcomes into congruence with societal expectations."[7] CSR comes down to creating a direct connection back to the global marketplace by acting ethically and morally.

In the early days of CSR, public relations, marketing, and advertising practitioners were tasked with improving the reputation and citizenship of their organizations by volunteering to participate in company-sponsored initiatives such as donating their time, giving financial support through sponsorships, or partnering with a nonprofit for a cause that tied back to their organization's mission.

Today, CSR strategies are more than reputation building activities: they've evolved to align values, build trust, and genuinely connect with consumers. There is increasing evidence, as outlined below, that proves consumers are socially conscious and are tuned in to what a company stands for and the causes it may or may not support.[8]

Corporate Activism

Corporate activism uses the underpinning of an organization's values to actively fight obstructions in the market and issues in society that in turn push the boundaries of CSR.[9] According to the U.S. Bureau of Labor Statistics, 90 million Americans identify themselves as conscious consumers and over 72 percent of consumers report that they actively seek out brands that align with their values.[10] The CEO of Spend Consciously, Matt Colbert, says that "consumers want to know more than whether a corporation is socially responsible. They want to make purchasing decisions based on their values and understand which companies are not aligned with their values."[11] When employing a corporate activism strategy, corporations must become completely transparent or consumers will spend their money elsewhere.[12]

Target, Apple, Wal-Mart, Starbucks, and Nike are just a few of the companies taking positions on politically polarizing social justice issues such as gay rights, reproductive rights, and modern-day civil rights. There was a time, however, not too long ago, when companies went along with the status quo. Take, for example, the 1960 Greensboro, North Carolina, Woolworth sit-in protest led by students at the segregated lunch counter. According to University of Michigan professor and researcher Jerry Davis, "Woolworth's corporate policy had been to 'abide by local custom' and keep black and white patrons separated. By supporting the status quo, Woolworth and others like it stood in the way of progress."[13] In 1996, when Walt Disney enacted "gay day" in support of the LGBTQ+ community, the Southern Baptists initiated an eight-year boycott against the company.[14] The boycott was ineffective. American families still wanted to see that smiling mouse. Brands today are taking stronger stances for causes they believe in.

The rise in social media has fueled such movements with the ability to easily mobilize like-minded supporters. Social media provides an accessible platform that allows consumers to have a voice, organize, rally, activate, and advocate. "Clicktivism," or "hashtag activism," draws attention to an issue to demonstrate support for change.[15] Some form of activism is likely to be a constant presence for corporations in the future.[16] Many believe this change is largely correlated with social consciousness expectations of millennials and Generation Z and their collective impact on brands prioritizing corporate activism.[17]

Cause-Related Marketing

According to research by Rajan Varadarajan and Anil Menon, **cause-related marketing (C-RM)** is an increasingly popular strategy among corporate social responsibility (CSR) initiatives because this approach offers consumers the opportunity to engage in altruistic acts that benefit a social cause they wish to support, satisfying individual and organizational objectives.[18] C-RM has risen to become a popular strategy to increase business value through profit-motivated giving.[19]

Companies like Tom's Shoes and Bombas fashion their business model on the 1-1 giving principle. Essentially, you buy a pair, and they give a pair to those in need—whether it's shoes, socks, or some other product. This strategy resonates with younger consumers. According to Cone Communications, 94 percent of Generation Z believe that companies should assist in addressing social as well as environmental issues; while 87 percent of millennials and 85 percent of the general population do as well.[20] Chipotle takes pride in supporting sustainability efforts; Starbucks promotes fair trade, marriage equality, and racial justice. These brands understand what their customers want and will support causes that resonate.

A NEW GENERATION OF CONSUMERS

Changing times require a change in strategy. Brands must respond to evolving consumer expectations. And many are doing so through authentic action. Customers speak through buying power that is fueled by personal convictions. Data shows that millennial and Generation Z customers expect more from brands than previous generations. Millennials appreciate brands that practice CSR. According to a 2015 Cone Communications study on millennials and CSR, "more than 9-in-10 Millennials would switch brands to one associated with a cause," because millennials noted that they are "prepared to make personal sacrifices to make an impact on issues they care about, whether that's paying more for a product, sharing products rather than buying, or taking a pay cut to work for a responsible company."[21] In 2017 Cone Communications once again conducted a generational study, this time examining Generation Z and their viewpoints. They found that 89 percent of Generation Z purchase from brands that support social and environmental issues. In fact, 65 percent pay close attention to the efforts put forth by companies regarding CSR. This should not come as a surprise to public relations, marketing, and advertising practitioners. This generation was raised on understanding the impact of climate change, took part in recycling programs, and learned about diversity within education, and as a result they are highly empathetic and socially conscious. This means that the pressure to effectively communicate an organization's corporate activism goals and philanthropic contributions to society falls to public relations and marketing teams.

Research shows that this generation has access to $44 billion in buying power—and significant influence (93 percent) on family buying decisions. And they are using their power for good. Nearly 9 in 10 (89 percent) say they would rather buy from a company addressing social or environmental issues over one that is not, and 92 percent would switch brands to one associated with a good cause, given similar price and quality, skewing just slightly higher than the national average (89 percent).[22]

CSR activities play an important role in building loyalty, soliciting feedback, and meeting the needs of consumers. Savvy brands understand this and have CSR built into the core of their business DNA. Utilizing the LUPE model, let's examine how Patagonia embraces corporate social responsibility.

Patagonia: Can a Self-Imposed 1 Percent Tax Really Change the World?

Today's successful companies actively "give back," supporting select causes aligned with their mission and values. It's no longer acceptable to simply exist as a company, but rather, companies must attempt to "do better." This case study will demonstrate how a company can achieve the economics of higher purpose to "do good," remain authentic, and still succeed in the marketplace.

Patagonia, Inc. (Patagonia) is a Ventura, California–based outdoor clothing company, founded in 1973 by Yvon Chouinard. It has annual sales exceeding $500 million. Long before the establishment of Certified B Corporations (B Corps) and the B Economy[1]—which is a special designation for business that meet the highest standards of verified social and environmental performance, public transparency, and legal accountability to balance profit and purpose—Patagonia has sought to solve some of the stickiest global issues plaguing the planet. For more than 40 years, its mission statement, what they call their "reason for being," had been to build the best product, cause no unnecessary harm, use business to inspire and implement solutions to the environmental crisis. Patagonia since the beginning has used a rather radical idea, the notion of a self-imposed 1 percent tax on sales, which it donates to the preservation and restoration of natural environments.

Since 1985, Patagonia has supported grassroots groups working hard to find viable solutions to the crisis plaguing the environment, delivering over $100 million to grantees to fund systematic change. Going one step further, they have promised to support these grantees on issues regarding land, water, climate, communities, and biodiversity by connecting people to their grantees to take on the most controversial and urgent issues facing our world.

In line with Patagonia's self-imposed business responsibility model, the company goes so far as to offer up tools in the form of checklists right from their website in the area of conservation, borrowing from B Corporation and nongovernmental organizations worldwide to aid in the spread of these ideas.

Using the LUPE model, the aim of this case study is to show how authentic corporate social responsibility can please stakeholders and achieve economic prosperity for a brand at the same time. While unconventional, this case study looks to inform the nature of Patagonia's CSR philosophy through a strategic model using the LUPE model.

Listen and Learn

In the first stage of the LUPE model, *Listen and Learn*, framing and using initial research helps determine what significant, beneficial, or even dangerous aspects to an issue are at hand. This is a chance for practitioners to establish the scope of an issue or opportunity, align other competing company determinants, and listen to what consumers think, feel, as well as understanding how they will act. The use of social listening research techniques aids in determining the market conditions, changing dynamics, societal conditions, political views, environmental trends, and more that might impact an action. All of this data is used for a proper risk analysis to address time, money, and other resource-saving measures in order to decrease financial and reputational risk to the brand. In this case, Patagonia played a role of trendsetter in what would later become corporate environmental activism.

---

[1] "About B Corps," B Corporation, accessed November 11, 2019, https://bcorporation.net/about-b-corps.

(continued)

In this stage, Patagonia made a few decisions based on both internal and external factors. First, it sought knowledge from research on what it means for a company to be responsible, seeking out views from shareholders and stakeholders. While it might not surprise you to know that companies are continuously revising corporate strategy, you may not have spent a great deal of time thinking about the responsibilities of a corporation established in 1970 versus the CSR responsibilities of a company today. Evolution, modification, and refinement of company ideals was required for Patagonia founder Yvon Chouinard, whose original humble focus was 'building the best outdoor equipment' but has evolved to his current mission of being 'in business to save the planet.'[2] Finally, none of this was done without research, being open to listening to shareholders and stakeholders, learning about consumers' changing needs and the dynamic political environment, and observing dramatic environmental factors like loss of biodiversity, deforestation, ocean pollution, and desertification.[3]

Completing this stage of research, it is essential to

- learn about powerful trends of consumer wants/needs;
- examine economic factors at play across an industry sector;
- use data-driven insights to inform and define or refine a clear purpose;
- understand the role of Patagonia in the greater corporate environment; and
- redefine purpose over time with economic and environmental changes.

If Patagonia had not invested time and resources to listening and learning from stakeholders and shareholders, or was tone deaf to the political and economic forces at play within a global context, the brand leadership could not have corroborated audience research, nor would they have tapped into a strong sentiment expressed by its target audience to arrive at this value proposition. Without this knowledge, they could not have moved into the next stage of the LUPE model: *Understand*.

Understand

The *Understand* stage from the LUPE model focuses on analysis to determine key insights from the research stage. Data-driven insights are applied to construct strategies and write SMART objectives to guide brand strategy. Drawing from these insights, the company developed the following goals and objectives,

Goal: To save the home planet through progressive business practices, environmental, and social responsibility.

Objective 1: To fund grassroots solutions to the environmental crisis by donating 1 percent of sales to the preservation and restoration of natural environments.

Objective 2: To change business practices and share information learned through doing less harm and more good.

Gone are the days of a company staying neutral on political and other "hot-button" issues. As revealed in the Edelman Earned Brand Report,[4] consumers

---

[2]Ben Court, "Yvon Chouinard, the Founder of Patagonia, Is on a Mission to Save the Planet," *Men's Health*, last modified October 25, 2018, accessed November 17, 2019, https://www. menshealth.com/trending-news/a23878672/yvon-chouinard-patagonia/.
[3]Yvon Chouinard and Vincent Stanley, *The Responsible Company: What We've Learned from Patagonia's First 40 Years*, 2nd ed. (Ventura, CA: Patagonia Books, 2016), Kindle.
[4]"Edelman Earned Brand Report," Edelman, last modified 2018, accessed January 11, 2020, https://www.edelman.com/research/brand-trust-2020

demand an authentic stand and are willing to vote their support with their dollars. A company with a true CSR will be inseparable from the idea of their social responsibility and will find a way to embolden consumers with mission-related promises and not fabrications of sales projections or promises of shareholder returns. This bold authenticity is not always embraced. With company goals and objectives in place, the brand then moved on to the next stage of the LUPE model: *Plan* to develop a robust action plan to support the achievement of the goals and objectives identified in the *Understand* stage, aided by research.

Plan

Creating the *Plan* as articulated in the LUPE model, Patagonia would have to shelve the idea of safety and embrace risk in an effort to protect and restore the stability, integrity, and beauty of the web of life. Part of this plan has been to limit ecological impacts, creating "goods that last for generations or can be recycled so the materials in them remain in use. Making the best product matters for saving the planet."[5]

Patagonia would embrace contrarian behaviors and buying patterns of the target audience ascertained from the *Learn* and *Understand* stages, and apply specific messaging, strategies, channel, and communication preferences while developing tactics to create action through tactics and timeline creation—plus formulate a budget based on these elements. Outside of their ongoing 1 percent tax revenue discussed in the introduction, Patagonia has routinely gone the extra mile to provide a healthier environment and a smaller retail footprint through creative campaigns targeting consumerism.

With the *Plan* stage established, the brand continued to the next stage of the LUPE model, *Execute*.

Execute and Evaluate

No stranger to high-impact campaigns, Patagonia has been eschewing the American capitalist "holiday" Black Friday with contrarian efforts in support of their goal for decades. Two of the most popular campaign actions based on their CSR efforts came in the early 2000s in a holiday catalog. The brand featured a "Don't Buy This Shirt" campaign, which supported the company's "Common Thread" initiative to reduce, renew, reuse, or repair fashion consumables.

Then in 2011, via a full-page ad in the *New York Times*, they launched an anti-consumption campaign on Black Friday, perhaps the highest consumption-based day of the year, with the "Don't Buy This Jacket"[6] campaign, which urged consumers not to purchase the popular winter jacket unless it was absolutely necessary.[7] The campaign improved the the company's sustainability image, yet at the same time was dubbed an "attention grab" to increase sales during a busy gift-giving time.

In 2016, following the U.S. presidential election of Donald Trump—who previously questioned global warming, suggesting it was a myth created by China—Patagonia took yet another Black Friday stand and donated 100 percent of its sales to grassroots environmental groups on one of the largest netting retail days of the

---

[5]"Patagonia's Mission Statement," Patagonia, accessed December 11, 2019, https://www.patagonia.com/company-info.html.

[6]"Don't Buy This Jacket, Black Friday and the New York Times," Patagonia, last modified November 25, 2011, accessed December 9, 2020, https://www.patagonia.com/blog/2011/11/dont-buy-this-jacket-black-friday-and-the-new-york-times/.

[7]Chanmi Hwang, Youngji Lee, Sonali Diddi, and Elena Karpova, "Don't Buy This Jacket," *Journal of Fashion Marketing and Management* 20, no. 4 (2016): 435–52, http://dx.doi.org/10.1108/JFMM-12-2014-0087.

(*continued*)

year. Marketing director Alex Weller explained that the idea behind this strategy was not to be deliberately disruptive, but rather to find a way to effectively communicate and demonstrate brand values to the public:

> "The idea of Black Friday is that you reduce your price aggressively and you make it possible for lots of people to buy lots more stuff in a truly short space of time. The idea of encouraging purchase purely based on a reduced price point goes completely against the philosophy and values of a company like Patagonia," Weller tells Marketing Week.

> "We will never engage in something like Black Friday for what it is, but of course there is an opportunity for us to creatively bring our own mission and values, our own purpose, to the fore during that moment." ...

> "You can't reverse into a mission and values through marketing. The organisations that are struggling with this are probably the ones that are thinking about marketing first. The role of marketing is to authentically elevate that mission and purpose and engage people in it, but the purpose needs to be the business."[8]

In 2018, as the United States Environmental Protection Agency (EPA) began to roll back environmental protections and the federal government began to retract its position on issues of land preservation and climate change, Patagonia created "Action Works," a digital tool that facilitates human connection while doing the critical work of grassroots interaction.[9] In doing so, Patagonia set out to create a response that matches the urgency of the matters they, as a company, value and wish to convey. Patagonia funds only environmental work, and their reported reason for existence is that they are "in business to save our home planet."

How can I get involved?

We built patagonia action works to connect committed individuals to organizations working on environmental issues in the same community. It's now possible for anyone to discover and connect with environmental action groups and get involved with the work they do.

| Find out about **events** happening in your area | Sign **petitions** supporting issues you care about | Have a skill that an organization is looking for? Find out how to **volunteer** your time | **Donate** money to local causes. |

In 2019, Patagonia took their efforts one step further toward their brand promise and closed its doors for the day during the Global Climate Strike, part of Climate Week, so that employees could march in an effort to remind the U.S. Congress and

---

[8]Charlotte Rogers, "Patagonia on Why Brands 'Can't Reverse into Purpose' through Marketing," *Marketing Week*, last modified July 18, 2018, accessed January 2, 2020, https://www.marketingweek.com/patagonia-you-cant-reverse-into-values-through-marketing/.
[9]Patagonia, "Patagonia Action Works," YouTube, February 6, 2018, accessed January 11, 2020, https://youtu.be/NXWGudS8DV4.

other world leaders that there is simply no room in government for climate change deniers. In an article on LinkedIn, Patagonia's CEO Rose Marcario explained that the closure of the retail stores is "in solidarity with the young people who are striking for climate action."[10] This action ran alongside a digital advertising campaign enlisting teen activists for the cause, which described the extinction of the human species in a powerful video and print campaign.[11]

Also in 2019, Patagonia announced that its community raised over $10 million in donations in just 17 days. On Black Friday, again Patagonia launched a commitment to match individual donations to Action Works, their online grassroots connection tool, between Black Friday and year end, resulting in a $10 million match for environmental nonprofits. This improved their reach for environmental causes to five new countries and drew attention to the fact that in the United States at least, environmental nonprofits receive only roughly 3 percent of philanthropic giving.[12]

Featured here is an anti-consumption ad from Patagonia.

The *Evaluate* stage of the LUPE model involved first assessing whether the effort met its overall goal and SMART objectives.

While scrutiny arrived soon after the anti-consumption ad in the early 2000s as the company sales jumped to $543 million (a 30 percent increase), which resulted in many more questions regarding the authentic of the brand promise.[13] The transparency and authenticity of the brand allowed those to remain loyal and served as sort of a public trust bank for allegations from media regarding their success.

[10]Rose Marcario, "Enough Is Enough: Join the Climate Strikes and Demand Action," LinkedIn, last modified September 12, 2019, accessed December 11, 2019, https://www.linkedin.com/pulse/enough-join-climate-strikes-demand-action-rose-marcario/.
[11]Jeff Beer, "Patagonia Enlists Teen Activists to Speak Out for Global Climate Strike Campaign," Fast Company, last modified September 19, 2019, accessed January 11, 2020, https://www.fastcompany.com/90406565/patagonia-enlists-teen-activists-to-speak-out-for-global-climate-strike-campaign.
[12]Corey Simpson, "Patagonia Community Raises $10 Million for the Planet in 17 Days, Company Will Match," Patagonia Works, last modified December 16, 2019, accessed January 1, 2020, http://www.patagoniaworks.com/press/2019/12/16/patagonia-community-raises-10-million-for-the-planet-in-17-days-company-will-match.
[13]Hugo Martin, "Outdoor Retailer Patagonia Puts Environment Ahead of Sales Growth," *Los Angeles Times*, last modified May 24, 2012, accessed December 5, 2019, https://www.latimes.com/business/la-xpm-2012-may-24-la-fi-patagonia-20120525-story.html.

(*continued*)

Objective 1: To fund grassroots solutions to the environmental crisis by donating 1 percent of sales to the preservation and restoration of natural environments.

To date, Patagonia has pledged 1 percent of sales to various grassroots restorative and natural environment organizations, which equals a cool $89 million of cash and in-kind donations to nonprofits globally. Grounded in a core belief that the environmental crisis has reached the tipping point, Patagonia has used 1 percent as a benchmark for a self-induced tax to combat climate change. Sam Murch, activism marketing coordinator for Action Works, explains why Patagonia focuses on grassroots activism:

> If we take action by supporting the grassroots environmental organizations that protect the places and communities we care about, we turn the tide on the idea that environmental harm is a necessary part of doing business.
>
> … [W]e can measure the value we provide to our grantees via this nonmonetary support mechanism. We might give an organization a grant worth a few thousand dollars, but with Patagonia Action Works, we can augment our grant dollars with valuable capacity-building support and message amplification. We estimate that we have saved participating grantees over half a million dollars in costs since we launched the platform to our grantees in December.[14]

Objective 2: To change business practices and share information learned though doing less harm and more good.

Berkeley native David R. Brower, the first executive director of the Sierra Club, is considered by most to be the father of the modern environmental movement, once said, "There is no business to be done on a dead planet"[15]—and it seems Patagonia has taken this message to heart, from its founding leaders to present-day CEO Rose Marcario. The outdoor retailer booked over $1 billion in revenue last year and somehow managed to persuade more than 400 companies to walk the walk as well—from environmental causes to policy-driven change making to endorsement of political candidates who stand with them on issues relating to the planet.[16] While this objective is ongoing, it seems that the "activist company" is galvanizing the members of the outdoor industry and others to donate money gleaned from the 2016 Trump tax cuts for corporations, on top of the 1 percent they already donate, back into nurturing environmental grassroots groups. In an interview with *Inc.* after earning Company of the Year honors, CEO Marcario admits that because Patagonia is a privately held company, it has more freedom to be

---

[14]Mary Mazzoni and Rachel Zurer, "Engage Your Customers for Impact: Lessons from Patagonia's Activism Experts," Conscious Company, last modified May 31, 2018, accessed December 11, 2019, https://consciouscompanymedia.com/sustainable-business/engage-your-customers-for-impact-lessons-from-patagonias-activism-experts/.

[15]"Who Was David Brower," David Brower Center, accessed January 11, 2020, https://browercenter.org/about/who-was-david-brower/.

[16]Yvon Chouinard and Vincent Stanley, *The Responsible Company: What We've Learned from Patagonia's First 40 Years*, 2nd ed. (Ventura, CA: Patagonia Books, 2016), Kindle.

"bold in its actions," but even so, when Patagonia succeeds with this home planet mission, they will "make it hard and uncomfortable for other businesses not to follow our lead."[17]

Authenticity in CSR

Patagonia represents authentic corporate social responsibility, including a wild idea that an activist company can actually "save the planet." Using the stages of the LUPE model we examined through the *Listen and Learn* stage, Patagonia would have

- learned about powerful trends of consumer wants/needs;
- examined economic factors at play across an industry sector;
- defined a clear purpose;
- understood the role of Patagonia in the greater corporate environment; and
- redefined purpose over time with economic and environmental changes.

To truly *Understand* the target audience and to ensure that campaigns and other CSR efforts were authentic and appropriate, Patagonia could have applied powerful market intelligence from secondary research sources like the Edelman Brand Report to validate the changes to their business goals in 2017, realigned to "save the home planet" through progressive business practices that demonstrate their commitments to environmental and social responsibility. This would have mitigated some of the risk involved with changing a business mission statement to "go all in" on projects like Patagonia Action Works and progressive campaigns like "Don't Buy This Jacket" and backing political candidates whose values most closely aligned with their mission. In *Plan*, Patagonia aligned outputs with outcomes in order to lead change in the vast business environment. They did not just act alone, but created incentive for other large companies to evolve as well in order to *Execute* high-impact campaigns that align their CSR with their sales. In *Evaluate*, founder Chouinard wrote in his award-winning book *Let My People Go Surfing* about maintaining "a controlled growth rate of about five percent."[18] Since 2009, annual growth climbed to 14 percent, according to *Fortune*.[19] Patagonia now controls 9 percent of the outdoor industry's apparel market, a figure that doesn't include the company's massive direct-to-consumer business.[20]

---

[17]Lindsay Blakley, "Patagonia's Unapologetically Political Strategy and the Massive Business It Has Built," *Inc.*, last modified 2018, accessed December 11, 2019, https://www.inc.com/lindsay-blakely/patagonia-2018-company-of-the-year-nominee.html.

[18]Yvon Chouinard, *Let My People Go Surfing: The Education of a Reluctant Businessman*, 2nd ed. (New York: Portfolio/Penguin, 2016), Kindle.

[19]Ryan Bradley, "The Woman Driving Patagonia to Be (Even More) Radical," *Fortune*, last modified September 14, 2015, accessed November 15, 2019, https://fortune.com/2015/09/14/rose-marcario-patagonia/.

[20]Alana Semuels, "Rampant Consumerism Is Not Attractive. Patagonia Is Climbing to the Top — and Reimagining Capitalism Along the Way," *Time*, last modified September 23, 2019, accessed December 15, 2019, https://time.com/5684011/patagonia/.

(continued)

CONCLUSION

Consumers believe that corporate activism—giving back and standing for causes—matters, according to the 2018 Edelman Earned Brand report, conducted to study how brands can earn, strengthen, and protect consumer-brand relationships.

The number of belief-driven buyers, who choose a brand based on its position on social issues, is growing worldwide, representing 59 percent of all shoppers in the United States, based on the 40,000 consumers surveyed by in the Edelman study.[23] Here are some interesting statistics from this study:[24]

- Sixty-four percent of those surveyed say that CEOs should take the lead on change rather than waiting for government to impose it.
- Sixty-seven percent of belief-driven buyers bought products from a brand for the first time because of its stance on a controversial issue.
- Sixty-five percent will not purchase from a brand because it stayed silent on an issue it had an obligation to address.
- One in two people are belief-driven buyers and choose, switch, avoid, or boycott a brand based on its stand on societal issues.

The numbers speak for themselves. It's clear that when companies support worthy causes, they often find they have loyal customers.

DISCUSSION QUESTIONS AND EXERCISES

1. Identify and explain the differences between of corporate social responsibility, corporate activism, and cause-based marketing.
2. This chapter covered many aspects of organizations giving back. Which resonated with you most, and why?
3. How are millennials and Gen Z impacting how marketing and public relations professional create campaigns? Do you think these generations truly have an impact on corporations? Substantiate your responses.
4. Provide examples of companies utilizing CSR, corporate activism, and CR-M. What is the impact for the brand? What is the impact for the consumer?
5. One could argue that Patagonia exemplifies many of the characteristics of modern-day CSR initiatives. Do you agree? Do you support companies that use corporate political advocacy? Or do you think companies should be uninvolved in politics? Why?
6. *Small group exercise:* Look up your favorite brand, company, or store. Identify their CSR activities. What organizations do they give back to? Are your personal beliefs aligned with what you are finding? If not, will you continue to buy their products or engage with their company, or will you find a company that provides a similar product or service? Compare your response with those of your classmates.

KEY TERMS

cause-related marketing (C-RM)

corporate activism

corporate social responsibility (CSR)

economics of higher purpose

NOTES

1. E. J. Schultz and A. C. Diaz, "Pepsi Is Pulling Its Widely Mocked Kendall Jenner Ad," *Advertising Age*, April 5, 2017, http://adage.com/article/cmo-strategy/pepsi-pulling-widely-mocked-kendall-jenner-ad/308575/.
2. S. West, "H&M Faced Backlash Over Its 'Monkey' Sweatshirt Ad, but It Isn't the Company's Only Controversy," *Chicago Tribune*, January 20, 2018, http://www.chicagotribune.com/lifestyles/style/ct-h-m-race-backlash-20180119-story.html.
3. Regina Luttrell, *Social Media: How to Engage, Share, and Connect* (Lanham, MD: Rowman & Littlefield, 2019).
4. Ibid.
5. Andrew Crane, *The Oxford Handbook of Corporate Social Responsibility* (Oxford, UK: Oxford University Press, 2012).
6. Anjan V. Thakor and Robert E. Quinn, "The Economics of Higher Purpose" (ECGI—Finance Working Paper No. 395/2013, 2013), https://ssrn.com/abstract=2362454.
7. B. D. Beal and C. Neesham, "Systemic Corporate Social Responsibility: Micro-to-Macro Transitions, Collective Outcomes and Self-Regulation," *Social Responsibility Journal* 12, no. 2 (2016): 209–27, doi:10.1108/srj-01-2015-0011; B. D. Beal and C. Neesham, *Systemic CSR: Insourcing the Invisible Hand* (Tyler, TX: The University of Tyler at Texas, 2013).
8. B. Monaghan, "PR for a Purpose: Bringing Corporate Social Responsibility Back to Basics," *Forbes*, February 13, 2018, https://www.forbes.com/sites/forbesagencycouncil/2018/02/13/pr-for-a-purpose-bringing-corporate-social-responsibility-back-to-basics/#2b975d2c54e9.
9. Real Leaders, "Corporate Activism Is on the Rise," RealLeaders, October 27, 2018, https://real-leaders.com/corporate-activism-rise/.
10. Dante A. Disparte and Timothy Gentry, "Corporate Activism Is on the Rise," *International Policy Digest*, July 6, 2015, https://intpolicydigest.org/2015/07/06/corporate-activism-is-on-the-rise/.
11. Real Leaders, "Corporate Activism."
12. Ibid.
13. Jerry Davis, "When Did Che Guevara Become CEO? The Roots of the New Corporate Activism," *The Conversation*, September 27, 2016, https://theconversation.com/when-did-che-guevara-become-ceo-the-roots-of-the-new-corporate-activism-64203.
14. Ibid.
15. Jerry Davis, "What's Driving Corporate Activism?," *New Republic*, September 27, 2016, https://newrepublic.com/article/137252/whats-driving-corporate-activism.
16. Ibid.

17. "Getting Gen Z Primed to Save the World," *Atlantic*, accessed January 8, 2020, https://www. theatlantic.com/sponsored/allstate/getting-gen-z-primed-to-save-the-world/747/.

18. P. Rajan Varadarajan and Anil Menon, "Cause-Related Marketing: A Coalignment of Marketing Strategy and Corporate Philanthropy," *Journal of Marketing* 52, no. 3 (1988): 58–74.

19. João Guerreiro, Paulo Rita, and Duarte Trigueiros, "A Text Mining-Based Review of Cause-Related Marketing Literature," *Journal of Business Ethics* 139, no. 1 (2015): 111–28, https://doi.org/10.1007/s10551-015-2622-4.

20. Sophie Komornicki, "2017 Cone Communications CSR Study," Cone Communications, May 17, 2017, https://www.conecomm.com/research-blog/2017-csr-study.

21. "2015 Cone Communications Millennials CSR Study," Cone Communications, http://www.conecomm.com/research-blog/2015-cone-communications-millennial-csr-study.

22. Sophie Komornicki, "Gen Z Sees Social Media Activity as More Effective than Community Involvement According to New Research by Cone Communications," Cone Communications, September 13, 2017, https://www.conecomm.com/news-blog/2017/9/12/gen-z-sees-social-media-activity-as-more-effective-than-community-involvement-according-to-new-research-by-cone-communications. See also Richard Carufel, "How to Speak Z: Examining Teens' CSR Voice of Choice," Agility PR Solutions, March 24, 2019, https://www.agilitypr.com/pr-news/public-relations/speak-z-examining-teens-csr-voice-choice/.

23. Alana Semuels, "Patagonia CEO Rose Marcario Has a Plan to Fix Capitalism," *Time*, September 23, 2019, https://time.com/5684011/patagonia/; Edelman, "Edelman Earned Brand Report."

24. Ibid.

CHAPTER 8

Engagement through Crowdsourcing and User-Generated Content

KEY LEARNING OUTCOMES

Recognize the essential components of crowdsourcing and user-generated content.

Recognize how the evolution of technologies has made original user-generated content possible to be crowdsourced.

Understand how crowdsourcing and user-generated content work together.

Explain the role of user-generated content and how it enables individuals, organizations, and brands to mobilize content.

Assess the role that crowdsourced content plays within the strategy of a campaign.

Identify the main considerations and benefits of using crowdsourcing to inspire consumer engagement and brand advocacy.

INFORMATION OVERLOAD

We're experiencing unprecedented volumes of digital and social content that competes for our attention as information originating from friends and family, organizations, brands, politicians, and countless other news sources becomes the norm in today's news-hungry society. *New York Times* writer Dennis Overbye says that most of the population is in a state of constant information overload. He explains that our devices possess more data than the Apollo mission control, which contributes to information overload.[1] Our world now contains 300 exabytes—300,000,000,000,000,000,000 pieces—of human-made digital information. What does this mean for public relations, marketing, and advertising practitioners aiming to break through the noise and clutter? Let's explore how practitioners can tap into the power of crowdsourcing and user-generated content (UGC).

CROWDSOURCING DRIVES EFFICIENCY
AND CUSTOMER ENGAGEMENT

The onset of the information age and subsequent adoption of social networks and social media have brought about new means for individuals and collective groups to tap into the power of digital to mobilize and capture our attention. From photo sharing to querying consumer opinions, and even co-creating content, brands are beginning to rely on customers to help drive messaging. An era of collective consumer action has arrived. This is called **crowdsourcing**,[2] a practice that empowers businesses to expand reach and connect on deeper levels with their target audiences.

In other words, businesses and individuals alike can tap into the benefits of a crowd of people rather than completing tasks independently. This phenomenon began to gather traction in large part due to technological advancements within product design software and digital video cameras, further connecting a brand with its audience. Crowdsourcing allows for everyday people with interest in each topic to be supported by the power of a group of other like-minded individuals. The process of crowdsourcing may be a preferential option to outsourcing.

The concept of crowdsourcing is not new; rather, it is a modern-day extension of what Aristotle first described as the *wisdom of the crowd*. This concept leverages and values the collective opinion of a group over that of a single individual and continues to evolve in response to the ever-changing online environment.[3]

CROWDSOURCING DEBUTS
IN THE ENGLISH LEXICON

In 2013, the term crowdsourcing was added to the world-renowned *Oxford English Dictionary* (*OED*), breaking its own rule that a word must be "current for ten years" before it can be included into the dictionary.[4] Oxford defines crowdsourcing as "obtaining information or input into a particular task or project by enlisting the services of a number of people, either paid or unpaid, typically via the Internet."[5]

A couple of years later, in 2015, authors Mimi Onuoha, Jeanne Pinder, and Jan Schaffer published their "Guide to Crowdsourcing" report through the Tow Center for Digital Journalism at Columbia's Graduate School of Journalism. In this summary, the concept of journalism crowdsourcing was researched and explained as being an act of inviting specific groups of individuals through a targeted, open approach, who will then support a particular reporting task, including data collection, the gathering of news, or some degree of data analysis and interpretation.[6] With these definitions in mind, the two predominant forms that crowdsourcing generally take are the following:[7]

- *Unstructured call-out*: an open call to contact a journalist to provide input on the requested information.
- *Structured call-out*: targeted outreach to solicit responses for a particular request. Responses can be received through a variety of channels such as email, text, a micro-site, or a Google form.

Crowdsourcing Drives Behavioral Change

The process of crowdsourcing through social networks is shaping the way companies interact with consumers and changing the business landscape.[8] Crowdsourcing is also changing consumer buying consideration, evaluation, and the decision-making processes. Trust is sliding in corporate advertising as well in social media giants such as Facebook.[9] However, trusting opinions of others who are willing to share their product or service experience through ratings, reviews, or other commentary about a purchase experience on social networks or otherwise through social media has become a source of information with increasing trust and reliance. When considering a purchase, in addition to receiving messages via paid media, consumers can also rely on input or referrals from people they know and trust such as family, friends, or colleagues. This is the heart of crowdsourcing.[10]

Nielsen, a global media and market research firm, identified a measurable shift in consumers' trust in advertising. Their Trust in Advertising study revealed that credible and trusted advertising generally results from the influences of personal acquaintances. In fact, this study highlighted that nearly 83 percent of participants highly trusted recommendations coming from either friends or family.[11] Additionally, of those same participants, nearly two-thirds indicated that they highly trusted consumer opinions that are posted online, with owned channels or brand managed websites also contributing to a 70 percent rate of consumer confidence.

UGC AND CROWDSOURCING WORKING TOGETHER

More and more, individuals, organizations, and brands are using crowdsourcing to mobilize movements, inspire action, create news, and even boost campaigns. Crowdsourcing and **user-generated content (UGC)** are linked.[12] One cannot exist without the other. UGC is content created by users of a brand. According to Lili Török, a content creator at Veem, consumers are 50 percent more likely to trust content generated by their peers than that coming from a company.[13] She goes on to explain that UGC includes comments on a blog, testimonials on a website, social media posts, blog articles, videos, Instagram stories, pictures, and essentially any content that is generated by a customer or a user.[14]

Users who develop original content are encouraged to share and promote their content within their social sphere, which drives further engagement and fosters their conversion to brand advocates in the process. As a result, UGC and crowdsourcing allow organizations to gain quality content in various forms—such as images, videos, and text-based content like commentary, quotes, or endorsements—at a fraction of the cost. This reduces or negates the need to hire expensive resources such as agencies and production crews to capture, edit, and produce brand content artifacts. Additionally, UGC and crowdsourced content provides brands with the ability to secure content from locations around the world that otherwise would have been cost prohibitive. Lastly, allowing consumers to have their say through sharing opinions, product feedback, and preferences provides brands the opportunity to build brand loyalty while consumers reap the benefit of being heard and respected for their feedback.

Bringing people together to share their opinions, provide feedback, and engage in discussions allows brands to utilize social listening research methods to mine public discourse, derive insights, and apply findings to strategic planning using the LUPE model.

PIONEERING BRANDS TAPPING
INTO CROWDSOURCING AND UGC

Many organizations are using extrinsic rewards or incentives to drive interest in creating UGC and participation in crowdsourcing to support their public relations and marketing goals. Leading brands are implementing programs with explicit parameters and specific calls to action that encourage crowdsourcing through structured campaigns. Companies are inspiring action to create original content in easy steps such as click, save, share, and reap rewards. Crowdsourcing encourages boundless UGC contributions from a multitude of constituencies, fans, customers, and even employees. Some of the top brands utilizing this method to connect with consumers include GoPro, Starbucks, and M·A·C Cosmetics.

GoPro

One of the early innovators in crowdsourcing, with over 7.7 million subscribers to their YouTube channel, is the camera company GoPro.[15] Recognized as a top YouTube brand, GoPro has earned this honor by crowdsourcing and releasing video footage from customers multiple times per day. GoPro fans and customers alike share vivid imagery and video from around the world documenting their adventurous lifestyles and breathtaking natural surroundings with photo snapshots, raw clips, and video footage. GoPro is leading the way with their crowdsourcing program "GoPro Awards," which gives cash rewards to people submitting UGC in various categories. For example, the brand calls for those traveling off the beaten path to share what they discover on Twitter tagging @GoPro and using the hashtag #TRIPON and encourages consumers to share their love of their camera model by posting to GoPro's official Twitter account with the hashtag #GoPro. Customers can even share their thoughts on the latest product release or adventures their camera has taken them on. In this way, consumers highlight the versatility of the product, allowing others to live vicariously through them with video, emotion, and storytelling—all from the consumer's point of view.

The official GoPro Twitter handle allows customers to communicate directly with the company.

Starbucks' White Cup Contest

When Starbucks tapped into their consumers by launching a cup design competition, they received nearly 4,000 entries. Customers in North America were encouraged to decorate a Starbucks reusable cup with their original customized art and submit a photo through social media using the hashtag #WhiteCupContest. This UGC crowdsourced campaign resulted in a boost in traffic to Starbucks stores, the company website, and social media brand channels.[16]

Starbucks' White Cup Contest winning design, by Brita Lynn Thompson.

Brita Lynn Thompson, an art student at the time, won the inaugural crowdsourced campaign. Here she describes how it changed her life:

> Ever since the day Starbucks announced that I was the winner, my life changed. It has never been this great. I get choked up thinking about it sometimes because it is truly an amazing feeling to have thousands and thousands of strangers say that I, Brita Lynn Thompson, inspire them to create. I never thought in a million years I would be such an inspiration to that many people or to anyone at all. Being able to connect with people all around the world through what I love to do makes me happy. I'm lucky and grateful.[17]

In addition to having her design printed on a limited-edition Starbucks cup, she received a $300 gift card, which she then used to start her own business.

Utilizing crowdsourcing to supplement product development processes, gather feedback, and test products before launching can render important changes as well as lead to product extensions or new product uses.[18]

M·A·C Cosmetics

The highly acclaimed crowdsourced campaign from M.A.C. Cosmetics, conceived by senior makeup artist John Stapleton and Regan Rabanal, was originally developed to encourage and engage a global community of beauty and makeup artists to share their craft using M.A.C.'s vivid cosmetics line. They launched the first campaign in 2015 on Instagram during the Halloween season using the hashtag #SeniorArtistSlayHalloween.[19] Annually, makeup artists showcase their own skills by turning themselves into mythical beasts, famous characters, and other

Halloween-inspired creations, while in turn, customers create their own spooky inspirations using M.A.C. cosmetics.

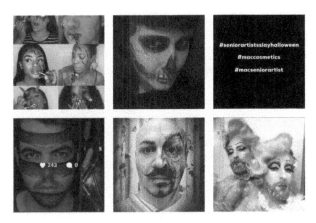

To engage their audience, MAC Cosmetics regularly holds makeup contests on their Instagram account.

Let's take a closer look at a full-blown campaign. Using the LUPE model, Kyle Heim breaks down how Lay's masterfully utilizes data-driven strategies to run a successful crowdsourcing campaign.

Crunching the Data: Crowdsourcing and the Lay's Potato Chip "Do Us a Flavor" Contest

By Kyle Heim, Ph.D., Shippensburg University

Southern Biscuits and Gravy. Chicken & Waffles. Cheddar Bacon Mac & Cheese.

They sound like comfort foods you might see on the menu at a local diner, not flavors you would expect to encounter in the grocery store snack aisle. Yet these were just a few of the winning entries and runners-up in Frito-Lay's "Do Us a Flavor" contest, a nationwide search for the next new Lay's potato chip flavor that began in 2012 and was repeated three more times through 2017. The millions of flavor combinations vying for the $1 million grand prize and a place on store shelves did not originate in the offices or test kitchens of Frito-Lay but in the imaginations of potato chip lovers across the United States. The campaign was an award-winning example of crowdsourcing, which harnesses the talent and creativity of large groups of people to generate ideas, solve problems, or develop new products.

Although "Do Us a Flavor" underwent numerous revisions between its launch and its final run, the basic contest rules and procedures remained unchanged. Contestants submitted their Lay's potato chip flavor ideas, consisting of up to three ingredients, via a website and social media. A judging panel narrowed the submissions to three or four finalist flavors, which made their way into production and onto store shelves. The public then had several months to sample the new potato chip varieties and vote for their favorites. Each year's winner received $1 million or 1 percent of the flavor's net sales in that year (whichever was greater) while the finalists each received $50,000. The contest was heavily promoted online, accompanied by personalized videos, photo galleries, and maps showcasing the entries and the most popular ingredients.

By employing multiple social media platforms and applications, Lay's created an interactive, immersive experience for snack food fans to enjoy. The contest generated millions of submissions while attracting favorable press and word-of-mouth. But "Do Us a Flavor" was much more than fun and games and unusual flavors. Every time fans submitted an idea, cast a vote, or discussed the contest on social media, they were creating or sharing data. The data were then used by Frito-Lay to evaluate and improve the contest, as well as to conduct market research and tailor the company's products to consumers' tastes. Ram Krishnan, a Frito-Lay executive who helped spearhead the contest, observed that "the marketers who will be successful—and the brands that will be successful—will make the leap from marketing as a creative function to be a technology discipline using data."[1]

The Company and the Contest

Frito-Lay, a leader in the consumer-packaged goods industry, is responsible for some of the most popular snack brands on the market, including not only Lay's but also Ruffles potato chips, Fritos corn chips, Doritos and Tostitos tortilla chips, and Cheetos cheese-flavored snacks. *The New York Times* noted that "Frito-Lay has long dominated the snack-food business by relentlessly focusing on the middle swath of America that eats chips and pretzels and party mix without regard to the effect on the waistline."[2]

FRITO-LAY'S HISTORY AND CULTURE Frito-Lay North America, headquartered in Plano, Texas, employs nearly 55,000 people and reported more than $15 billion in revenue in 2016.[3] The company operates as a wholly owned subsidiary of PepsiCo.

"Do Us a Flavor" was not the first time that Frito-Lay had looked to consumers for ideas and inspiration. From 2006 to 2016, it hosted "Crash the Super Bowl," which invited members of the public to create their own Doritos commercials, one or more of which would air each year during the televised football game.[4] In addition, Frito-Lay's international divisions had run contests similar to "Do Us a Flavor" in 15 other countries dating back to 2008, producing such potato chip flavors as Cajun Squirrel in the United Kingdom and Spicy Crab in Thailand.[5] But Lay's had never before run a create-a-chip campaign in the United States.

"Do Us a Flavor" came to America in July 2012, timed to commemorate the 75th anniversary of the Lay's brand. The campaign grew out of parent company PepsiCo's desire to improve its sales and image among two key age demographics: the technology pioneers or millennials, who were born between 1981 and 1996,

---

[1]Susan Kuchinskas, "Frito-Lay CMO Krishnan Uses Data to Cash in on His Chips," CMO.com, December 28, 2018, accessed February 17, 2016, https://www.cmo.com/interviews/articles/2015/12/28/the-cmocom-interview-ram-krishnan-cmo-fritolay-north-america.html.

[2]Stephanie Strom, "Frito-Lay Takes New Tack on Snacks," *New York Times*, June 12, 2012, https://www.nytimes.com/2012/06/13/business/frito-lay-strategy-aims-for-top-and-bottom-of-market.html.

[3]"Frito-Lay North America Fact Sheet," Frito-Lay North America Inc., January 2018, https://www.fritolay.com/docs/default-source/media-assets/flna-fact-sheet--final-1-25-18.pdf.

[4]E. J. Schultz, "How 'Crash the Super Bowl' Changed Advertising," *AdAge*, January 4, 2016, https://adage.com/article/special-report-super-bowl/crash-super-bowl-changed-advertising/301966.

[5]David D. Burstein, "How Lay's Is Tapping Its Audience for Its Next Big Chip Idea," *Fast Company*, August 1, 2012, https://www.fastcompany.com/1681333/how-lays-is-tapping-its-audience-for-its-next-big-chip-idea.

(continued)

and the digital natives of Generation Z, born between 1997 and 2015.[6] Millennials and Gen Z'ers often tune out traditional advertising and marketing campaigns, but social media can be a highly effective means of engaging them. In a survey by Yes Lifecycle Marketing, more than 80 percent of Gen Z'ers and 74 percent of millennials said their shopping habits were influenced by social media.[7]

Social media campaigns are a popular way for brands to promote their products, but social platforms can be incorporated into product development strategies as well. For companies such as Frito-Lay, social media can supplement or even replace traditional forms of research and development. Conversations on Facebook or Twitter can be mined for consumer feedback at a fraction of the cost needed to conduct surveys or focus group sessions. Social media users can be tapped to participate in the process of creating a new product, enabling customer preferences and behavior to be measured even before the product reaches the market. In the case of Lay's "Do Us a Flavor," by the time the judging panel in the inaugural year of the competition sifted through 3.8 million submissions to select three finalists, the contest already had generated online buzz and yielded valuable data. As Dave Kerpen, the author of *Likeable Social Media*, put it, "Who wouldn't want to launch a new product that 3.8 million people already felt they had connected to before it even hit the shelves?"[8]

Of course, running the "Do Us a Flavor" contest was not as simple as issuing a call via social media and then watching the submissions and votes roll in. Crowdsourcing ventures must be nurtured by a corporate culture that values open innovation, the creative deployment of new technology, and the use of data-driven insights to inform decision making. In a 2012 study, more than 100 management consultants and industry practitioners were asked to rate the importance of a series of **key performance indicators (KPIs)**—forms of measurement used to quantify the success of a key business objective—related to the initiation and implementation of various types of business innovation projects. For innovation contests designed to generate ideas, the survey respondents rated the degree of management commitment to the initiative highest among the KPIs,[9] indicating that buy-in from senior executives is essential to the success of such contests.

"Do Us a Flavor" enjoyed strong support from top management. The campaign was embraced by Frito-Lay executives because it fit well with the company's culture of innovation, which emphasizes experimentation, technology, and Big Data. Ram Krishnan, who has held a variety of leadership roles within the company, including chief marketing officer, was the driving force behind the promotion. Krishnan's Twitter handle (@Ramalytics) and website (www.ramalytics .com) reveal his love of all things data-related. In an interview with CMO.com, Krishnan explained that the marketing function at Frito-Lay has changed dramatically in recent years, which he attributed to three trends: consumers' growing

[6]Linda Tucci, "Frito-Lay: 'Omniculturals' at the Intersection of IT and Marketing," *TotalCIO* (blog), October 16, 2015, https://searchcio.techtarget.com/blog/TotalCIO/ Frito-Lay-Omniculturals-at-the-intersection-of-IT-and-marketing.

[7]David Kirkpatrick and Peter Adams, "Study: More than 80% of Gen Zers Report Social Media Influences Shopping Habits," *Marketing Dive*, July 18, 2017, https://www.marketingdive.com/news/ study-more-than-80-of-gen-zers-report-social-media-influences-shopping-ha/447303/.

[8]Dave Kerpen, *Likeable Social Media*, 2nd ed. (New York: McGraw Hill, 2015), 131.

[9]Marc Erkens, Susanne Wosch, Frank Piller, and Dirk Lüttgens, "Measuring Open Innovation," *Performance* 6, no. 2 (2014): 20.

expectation of two-way communication with brands, their increasing willingness to share data about themselves as long as they receive something of value in return, and the exponential growth in ways for companies to connect with their customers due to advances in technology. "I keep telling our marketers, 'Your job description has changed. You are no longer a marketer; you're a marketing technologist,'" Krishnan said.[10]

THE HISTORY OF "DO US A FLAVOR" Frito-Lay worked with several partners to develop, promote, and execute the "Do Us a Flavor" contest during its four-year run, and the campaign earned many accolades. For example, the campaign won a 2014 FAB (Food And Beverage) Award for advertising effectiveness[11] and was a finalist in the best consumer brand category of the 2015 Shorty Awards,[12] which recognize outstanding social media usage by brands, organizations, and influencers.

Frito-Lay announced the first contest in July 2012. The launch coincided with the opening of a Lay's pop-up store in New York City's Times Square, where consumers could sample existing Lay's flavors and learn about potato chips from around the world. Actress and restaurateur Eva Longoria and TV chef Michael Symon were enlisted as celebrity spokespeople and appeared in ads for the campaign.[13] To enter the contest, consumers needed to select up to three ingredients for their potato chip flavor, give it a name, and include a 140-character description. Submissions were accepted via Facebook, a website, or text messaging. A judging panel made up of Longoria, Symon, and other food experts chose three finalist flavors, which were then developed by Frito-Lay chefs and food scientists and introduced to store shelves. Fans voted for their favorite via Facebook, Twitter, or text message.

In 2015, the Lay's "Do Us a Flavor" contest celebrated "Tastes of America," asking participants to include the location that inspired their flavor creations.
SOURCE: Frito-Lay "Do Us a Flavor" homepage (2015).

---

[10]Kuchinskas, "Frito-Lay CMO Krishnan."

[11]"Lay's Do Us a Flavor," FAB Awards, https://fabawards.com/fab-entry/lays-do-us-a-flavor/.

[12]"From the 7th Annual Shorty Awards: Lay's Do Us a Flavor," Shorty Awards, https://shorty-awards.com/7th/lays-do-us-a-flavor#menu.

[13]Frito-Lay, "Lay's Potato Chips Teams Up with Eva Longoria and Iron Chef Michael Symon to Invite Consumers to Create the Next Great Potato Chip Flavor," PR Newswire, July 20, 2012, https://www.prnewswire.com/news-releases/lays-potato-chips-teams-up-with-eva-longoria-and-iron-chef-michael-symon-to-invite-consumers-to-create-the-next-great-potato-chip-flavor-163156706.html.

(continued)

The contest returned in 2014 with several new twists: Fans could now choose from three types of potato chips—original, kettle cooked, and wavy—for their flavor ideas. Frito-Lay increased the number of finalists to four and expanded the social media options for submitting entries and voting.[14] Lay's also partnered with Uber for a two-day urban picnic in Manhattan, delivering 200 free picnic baskets filled with the finalist flavors, plus sandwiches, fruit, and water.[15] Comedian Wayne Brady added some star power to the campaign. Brady selected a small number of submissions on launch day and recorded comedic videos for YouTube and Twitter riffing on their flavor ideas.[16] A contest-inspired tune, "The Yummy Song," developed by the Deep Focus digital creative agency, became a YouTube sensation, earning more than 12 million views.[17] Deep Focus also monitored Twitter conversations about the contest to create "instajingles" tailored to individual tweets.[18]

The third competition in 2015 celebrated regional cuisines by asking contributors to include the location that inspired their flavor creations. Recording artist and restaurateur Nick Lachey teamed with Lay's to travel the country, paying surprise visits to the four finalists.[19] The Deep Focus agency beefed up its creative efforts by shooting and uploading impromptu one-minute video clips, featuring two potato-themed puppets known as the Taste Spuds, in response to Twitter conversations about the contest.[20]

After a one-year absence, "Do Us a Flavor" returned in 2017 for its final run. This time, participants were asked to include a pitch for their flavor in the form of a photo, video, or written description.[21] An extra level of competition was added, with the selection of 10 semifinalists. The winners of each year's contest and their million-dollar flavors appear in Table 1, along with the finalist flavors.

[14]Liz Webber, "Winner: Frito-Lay," *Supermarket News* 62, no. 18 (October 20, 2014): 32.

[15]E. J. Schultz, "Lay's Is Launching an Urban Picnic, Brought to You by Uber," *AdAge*, August 15, 2014, https://adage.com/article/digital/lay-s-launching-urban-picnic-brought-uber/294591.

[16]Frito-Lay North America, "Lay's 'Do Us A Flavor' Contest Is Back: Fans Invited to Submit Next Great Potato Chip Flavor Idea for the Chance to Win $1 Million," *PR Newswire*, January 14, 2014, https://www.prnewswire.com/news-releases/lays-do-us-a-flavor-contest-is-back-fans-invited-to-submit-next-great-potato-chip-flavor-idea-for-the-chance-to-win-1-million-240093481.html.

[17]"Lay's DUAF," Moment Studio, http://www.momentstudio.com/index.php/project/lays-duaf/.

[18]Ibid.

[19]Frito-Lay North America, "Lay's 'Do Us a Flavor' Contest Returns to the U.S. with $1 Million Grand Prize for Best Potato Chip Flavor Idea," *PR Newswire*, January 20, 2015, https://www.prnewswire.com/news-releases/lays-do-us-a-flavor-contest-returns-to-the-us-with-1-million-grand-prize-for-best-potato-chip-flavor-idea-300021897.html

[20]Lauren Johnson, "How Lay's Is Adding More Social Zest to Its Popular Flavor-Creation Campaign," *Adweek*, February 27, 2015, https://www.adweek.com/digital/how-lays-adding-more-social-zest-its-popular-flavor-creation-campaign-163173/.

[21]Frito-Lay North America, "Get Your Pitch On! Lay's 'Do Us a Flavor' Seeks America's Next Great Potato Chip Flavor and Celebrates the Stories Behind the Flavors with $1 Million Award," *PR Newswire*, January 10, 2017, https://www.prnewswire.com/news-releases/get-your-pitch-on-lays-do-us-a-flavor-seeks-americas-next-great-potato-chip-flavor-and-celebrates-the-stories-behind-the-flavors-with-1-million-award-300388806.html.

Table 1 "Do Us a Flavor" Winners and Finalists

	2012-13	2014	2015	2017
Winner	Karen Weber-Mendham; Land O' Lakes, WI	Meneko Spigner McBeth; Deptford, NJ	Hailey Green; Noblesville, IN	Ellen Sarem; San Antonio, TX
Winning Flavor	Cheesy Garlic Bread	Kettle Cooked Wasabi Ginger	Southern Biscuits and Gravy	Crispy Taco
Finalist Flavors	Chicken & Waffles	Cheddar Bacon Mac & Cheese	Wavy West Coast Truffle Fries	Kettle Cooked Everything Bagel with Cream Cheese
	Sriracha	Wavy Mango Salsa	New York Reuben	Wavy Fried Green Tomato
		Cappuccino	Kettle Cooked Greektown Gyro	

Sources: Frito-Lay, PR Newswire

The Characteristics of Crowdsourcing

"If you want something done right, do it yourself" is a quote that has been attributed to both 19th-century playwright Charles-Guillaume Étienne and the French emperor Napoleon Bonaparte.[22] It also sums up the approach that guided business innovation throughout most of history—one in which all of a company's functions were handled in-house. Today, however, many companies are looking beyond the walls of their workplaces for ideas. Crowdsourcing is one strategy that turns tasks into solutions by turning consumers into developers, designers, and problem-solvers.

OPEN INNOVATION, COLLECTIVE INTELLIGENCE, AND CROWDSOURCING In the classic model of **closed innovation**, a company maintains control of the innovation process from start to finish—creating new products, then marketing, distributing, servicing, and supporting them.[23] All tasks are performed internally by employees who possess the necessary knowledge and skills. This model of innovation began to break down, however, as workers became more highly educated and more mobile. Soon, companies were looking to their suppliers, their customers, and even their competitors for ideas. Closed innovation gave way to **open innovation**, defined by Henry W. Chesbrough as "a paradigm that assumes that firms can and should use external ideas as well as internal ideas, and internal and external paths to markets, as the firms look to advance their technology."[24]

The concept of **collective intelligence** takes open innovation a step further. The term "collective" in this context refers to large groups of individuals who do not necessarily share the same attitudes or viewpoints.[25] Such groups, when solicited

---

[22]Jurgen Appelo, "If You Want Something Done, Delegate It Yourself," *Forbes*, November 27, 2015, https://www.forbes.com/sites/jurgenappelo/2015/11/27/if-you-want-something-done-delegate-it-yourself.

[23]Henry W. Chesbrough, *Open Innovation: The New Imperative for Creating and Profiting from Technology* (Boston: Harvard Business School Press, 2003), xx.

[24]Ibid., xxiv.

[25]Jan Marco Leimeister, "Collective Intelligence," *Business & Information Systems Engineering* 2, no. 4 (2010): 245.

(continued)

for their input, often produce better results than would be obtained by relying on experts or professionals.[26] James Surowiecki's 2005 best-selling book, *The Wisdom of Crowds*, cites several instances in which the collective intelligence of a crowd outperformed experts or professionals. For example, contestants who were stumped by trivia questions on the TV game show "Who Wants to Be a Millionaire?" were better off polling the studio audience, which supplied the correct answer 91 percent of the time, than turning to a trusted friend or expert as a lifeline, which yielded a much lower accuracy rate of 65 percent.[27]

The power of collective intelligence has implications far beyond game shows. Corporate America has tapped the wisdom of crowds by seeking the public's contributions in industries as diverse as fashion and pharmaceuticals. Jeff Howe coined the term **crowdsourcing** in a 2006 *Wired* magazine article to describe this phenomenon:[28] He defines it as "the act of taking a job traditionally performed by a designated agent (usually an employee) and outsourcing it to an undefined, generally large group of people in the form of an open call."[29]

Crowdsourcing can take at least four forms, depending on the nature of the crowdsourced work:[30]

- **Crowdprocessing** relies on the crowd to perform mundane tasks in large quantities. An example is Amazon's Mechanical Turk (MTurk), in which clients post tasks online that independent workers can choose to complete for a small sum of money.

- **Crowdsolving** harnesses the diversity and creativity of the crowd to identify multiple solutions to a challenge. This form of crowdsourcing may be used to solve complex problems or to generate novel ideas. For example, Starbucks' White Cup Contest [discussed earlier in this chapter] in 2014 invited customers to treat the coffeehouse chain's reusable plastic cups as a blank canvas and submit their design suggestions.

- **Crowdrating** asks the crowd to provide collective assessments or predictions. Online sites such as Yelp or TripAdvisor that aggregate customer reviews rely on this form of crowdsourcing.

- **Crowdcreating** seeks contributions from individual crowd members to create a physical or digital product, such as the online encyclopedia Wikipedia.

Frito-Lay's "Do Us a Flavor" contest blended elements of both crowdsolving (by asking consumers to solve the challenge of creating a new potato chip flavor) and crowdrating (by asking them to vote for their favorite submissions).

CHALLENGES AND BENEFITS OF CROWDSOURCING Inviting a large number of people to participate in a crowdsourcing contest is no guarantee that any of them will accept the call. One danger is that members of the crowd will feel exploited. They may resent being asked to perform tasks, usually for little or no pay, that would normally be handled by employees or professionals. The opportunities for exploitation are especially great in an online environment where there are few standards

---

[26]Ibid.

[27]James Surowiecki, *The Wisdom of Crowds* (New York: Anchor Books, 2005), 3–4.

[28]Howe, "The Rise of Crowdsourcing."

[29]Jeff Howe, "Crowdsourcing: A Definition," *Crowdsourcing* (blog), June 2, 2006, https://crowdsourcing.typepad.com/cs/2006/06/crowdsourcing_a.html.

[30]Benedikt Morschheuser, Juho Hamari, Jonna Koivisto, and Alexander Maedche, "Gamified Crowdsourcing: Conceptualization, Literature Review, and Future Agenda," *International Journal of Human-Computer Studies* 106 (2017): 27.

governing crowdsourced labor and no face-to-face contact between the crowd and the contest sponsors.[31] Crowd members might see little incentive to produce high-quality work or to participate at all.

One way to overcome this resistance is to offer a cash prize or other economic incentives. For would-be potato chip chefs, what could be more enticing than the prospect that your contest entry could make you $1 million richer? Yet cash prizes may not be as strong a motivator as one would assume, especially when the odds of being a prize winner are minuscule. Moreover, those individuals who do contribute but come away empty-handed might not bother to participate the next time the contest is offered. Research shows that nearly two-thirds of contributors to companies' online crowdsourcing contests do not come back more than twice, and that most of the rest quit after a few attempts.[32] The problem of user churn is especially acute when a contest has only one prize winner. Not only are participants in winner-takes-all contests unlikely to return for more, but those who do contribute again show significantly less effort the second time around.[33]

Companies can try to boost participation by awarding multiple prizes. Offering feedback during the contest also has been shown to generate more submissions.[34] Ultimately, however, a reliance on monetary rewards and other forms of **extrinsic motivation**—motivation that is external to the work itself[35]—may not be enough. **Intrinsic motivation**—"the motivation to engage in work for its own sake because the work itself is interesting or satisfying"[36]—tends to be a much greater impetus for participation in crowdsourcing contests.[37]

In the case of "Do Us a Flavor," Frito-Lay officials understood the need for intrinsic motivation. They realized that the contest had to connect with consumers on a personal level while building enthusiasm for the Lay's brand. As Bart LaCount, a marketing director for Frito-Lay North America, told delegates at a 2015 Brand Activation Association (BAA) event: "We needed to create an immersive consumer experience. This wasn't just about submitting a flavor for people. This was an idea that they wanted to get excited [about] and really rally behind."[38]

How does a company generate that level of excitement and make contest participants feel empowered, not exploited? There is no single answer, but one way to build intrinsic motivation is through **gamification**, defined as the use of game

[31]Michelle Chen, "Is Crowdsourcing Bad for Workers?," *The Nation* (blog), January 5, 2015, https://www.thenation.com/article/crowdsourcing-bad-workers/.

[32]Reto Hofstetter, Z. John Zhang, and Andreas Herrmann, "The Hidden Pitfall of Innovation Prizes," *Harvard Business Review*, November 27, 2017, 2.

[33]Ibid., 3.

[34]Lian Jian, Sha Yang, Sulin Ba, Li Lu, and Li Crystal Jiang, "Managing the Crowds: The Effect of Prize Guarantees and In-Process Feedback on Participation in Crowdsourcing Contests," *Management Information Systems Quarterly* 43, no. 1 (March 2019): 109.

[35]Haichao Zheng, Dahui Li, and Wenhua Hou, "Task Design, Motivation, and Participation in Crowdsourcing Contests," *International Journal of Electronic Commerce* 15, no. 4 (Summer 2011): 60.

[36]Ibid.

[37]Ibid., 76.

[38]"How a Lay's Marketing Campaign Rebranded the Chip" (archived version), *Immersive Youth Marketing* (blog), 2016, https://web.archive.org/web/20161113001414/http://www.immersiveyouthmarketing.com/blog/how-a-lays-marketing-campaign-rebranded-the-chip.

(continued)

design elements in a non-game environment.³⁹ Replicating some of the fun features of video games can make even ordinary tasks more enjoyable. Foursquare, which launched in 2009, was one of the earliest examples of gamification. The location-based app gamified the activity of visiting places by awarding "badges" and "mayorships" to users who frequently checked in to particular venues.⁴⁰ Avatars, leaderboards, stickers, and "level-ups" are some of the other features associated with gamified crowdsourcing.

"Do Us a Flavor" gamified the task of inventing new potato chip flavors by using technology to give the contest interactive and personal touches. Facebook users could join their friends and other contestants in head-to-head "flavor showdowns," where Facebook's iconic "Like" button was replaced by an "I'd Eat That" button. In the contest's third year, Frito-Lay partnered with Google and the Frank Collective creative agency to create the "Daily Flavorcast," a regularly updated U.S. map showing the most-searched-for ingredients in each state, and a "movie trailer" feature allowing fans to create characters based on their flavor ingredients and then insert them into the plot of their favorite film genres.

A voting tracker showed the popularity of the four finalist flavors in each state during the 2015 Lay's "Do Us a Flavor" contest.
SOURCE: Frito-Lay "Do Us a Flavor" homepage (2015).

These efforts clearly paid off, if Twitter posts using the #DoUsAFlavor hashtag are any indication. One Twitter user wrote, "Is it silly how much fun I'm having

³⁹Sebastian Deterding, Dan Dixon, Rilla Khaled, and Lennart Nacke, "From Game Design Elements to Gamefulness: Defining Gamification," in *Proceedings of the 15th International Academic MindTrek Conference: Envisioning Future Media Environments, Tampere, Finland, September 28–30, 2011* (New York: ACM, 2011): 9–15; Kai Huotari and Juho Hamari, "A Definition for Gamification: Anchoring Gamification in the Service Marketing Literature," *Electronic Markets* 27 (2017): 21–31.

⁴⁰In 2014, the Foursquare app was split in two, and most of the check-in functions migrated to the Swarm app.

creating weird flavors for the Lay's Do Us a Flavor contest?"[41] Another fan commented, "We love the annual #DoUsAFlavor Lay's Campaign—We even had a voting party!"[42] Participants in the crowdsourcing campaign transferred their positive feelings for the contest to the Lay's brand, building brand loyalty. When they shared their enthusiasm in conversations on social media, the crowd became a community of brand ambassadors, potentially bolstering the brand's image.

While crowdsourcing can have many positive outcomes for brands and their customers, it is not without its pitfalls. Any time a brand relinquishes control over the innovation process to the crowd, there is the risk that the crowd will use that power to embarrass or damage the brand. Mountain Dew learned this lesson when it invited Internet users to name its new green apple-flavored soft drink. The suggestions that topped the online leaderboard included "Diabeetus" and "Hitler did nothing wrong."[43]

In the "Do Us a Flavor" contest, a small number of individuals suggested some truly bizarre flavors, including Kitten, Despair, and Blood of My Enemies,[44] but the presence of a few rogue entries did not seem to spoil the fun. By having a judging panel of experts, rather than the crowd, select the finalists, Lay's was able to weed out any mischief-makers and ensure that the winning flavors would be tasty, not tasteless.

"Do Us a Flavor," Data, and Measurement

It is impossible to measure and evaluate the success of "Do Us a Flavor" without an appreciation of Frito-Lay's reasons for holding the crowdsourcing contest. To the public, the competition was all about creating new potato chip flavors to satisfy snack lovers, but to Frito-Lay, the competition took on a different meaning. Southern Biscuits and Gravy or Wasabi Ginger never were intended to outsell classic flavors such as Sour Cream and Onion or Barbecue; the winning flavors were novelty products that would remain in stores for a limited time. For Frito-Lay, the main goals of the contest were to engage the millennial and Generation Z audiences and build brand awareness and loyalty, which in turn could boost sales of the full range of Lay's products.

Why stage such an elaborate contest? The answer lies in the information collected each time someone cast a vote, posted a comment, or submitted an entry. When a Facebook user installed the "Do Us a Flavor" app, the user gave the app permission to access information such as his or her location, gender, birthdate, photos, list of friends and status updates, and products he or she had "liked."[45] For each contest entry, Lay's harvested the participant's contact information in addition to the flavor name, ingredients, and description.[46] Social media behavior, including clicks, comments, likes, and shares, also could be tracked for the duration

---

[41] Alison Reeger Cook, Twitter post, March 18, 2014, https://twitter.com/ARCookAuthor/status/446058629985488896.

[42] DonnaHup, Twitter post, May 29, 2017, https://twitter.com/donnahup/status/869438253673451522.

[43] Everett Rosenfeld, "Mountain Dew's 'Dub the Dew' Online Poll Goes Horribly Wrong," *Time*, August 14, 2012, http://newsfeed.time.com/2012/08/14/mountain-dews-dub-the-dew-online-poll-goes-horribly-wrong/.

[44] Sean Kelley, "Lay's Do Us a Flavor Campaign Is Out of Control and It's Awesome," *lonelybrand* (blog), February 12, 2014, https://lonelybrand.com/blog/lays-us-flavor-campaign-control-awesome/.

[45] Stephanie Clifford, "Social Media Act as a Guide for Marketers," *New York Times*, July 31, 2012, A3.

[46] Andy Jolls, "What's Sustaining the Popularity of Lay's 'Do Us a Flavor' Market Research Initiative?," LinkedIn, October 14, 2015, https://www.linkedin.com/pulse/whats-sustaining-popularity-lays-do-us-flavor-market-research-jolls.

(continued)

of the contest. The value of this information extended beyond "Do Us a Flavor" to aid in Frito-Lay's market research and future product development.

Analyzing the data collected during a crowdsourcing project can be overwhelming. Brands must identify key **metrics** that will elicit the most meaningful insights. A metric is defined as "a set of figures or statistics that measure results."[47] It is beyond the scope of this chapter to consider all of the metrics related to the "Do Us a Flavor" campaign. Much of the data was never made public. But the LUPE (Listen and Learn, Understand, Plan, Execute and Evaluate) model provides a framework for examining some of the key ways in which Frito-Lay used data-driven insights during various stages of the campaign.

LISTEN AND LEARN Successful brands are always listening to their stakeholders to uncover consumer trends and identify new brand opportunities. At Frito-Lay, listening and research are top priorities of the marketing team. Jennifer Saenz, who became chief marketing officer in 2016, described the company's approach in an interview with the web publication *MarTech Today* "I think, to be successful, you have to have a listen-first mentality with consumers. You need to consistently listen and give them what they're looking for, give them what excites them. . . . A listen-first mindset and approach are critical, especially in a modern landscape where there's an abundance of choice and an abundance of options."[48]

In the past, much of this listening took place during focus group sessions. Today, social media channels can be monitored for conversations relevant to the brand. Social listening enables companies to see in real time what people are saying about their brands, as well as the competition. It provides a broader cross-section of consumer feedback because social media platforms tend to attract members of the younger demographics—highly coveted by marketers and advertisers—who may be reluctant to participate in focus group sessions.[49] The social media approach also produces a much larger volume of data at lower cost.[50]

Through social listening, Frito-Lay parent company PepsiCo identified a problem with the Lay's brand: It was not connecting with young consumers. The message young people were sending was clear: "Lay's is what my parents ate. Lay's isn't really relevant to my lifestyle."[51] But research also identified three values that suggested a way forward: self-expression, authenticity, and recognition.[52] If the Lay's brand could create experiences that encouraged teens and young adults to express their individuality, that seemed real and credible to them, and that respected them and gave them a voice, it might be able to turn them into loyal customers.

UNDERSTAND The second step of the LUPE model challenges marketers to build upon the findings of the social listening process in order to understand their target audiences and set goals and strategies.

Frito-Lay targeted the millennial and Generation Z age demographics as it sought to reinvigorate the Lay's brand. When researching the behavior of these

---

[47]Eoin Cullina, Kieran Conboy, and Lorraine Morgan, "Measuring the Crowd—a Preliminary Taxonomy of Crowdsourcing Metrics," in *Proceedings of the International Symposium on Open Collaboration (OpenSym 2015), San Francisco, August 19–21, 2015* (New York: ACM, 2015): 2.

[48]Amy Gesenhues, "Frito-Lay CMO Says Marketers Need a Listen-First Mentality to Be Successful," *MarTech Today*, January 4, 2018, https://martechtoday.com/frito-lay-cmo-says-marketers-need-listen-first-mentality-successful-208595.

[49]Clifford, "Social Media Act as a Guide."

[50]Ibid.

[51]"How a Lay's Marketing Campaign."

[52]Ibid.

generations, technology was a recurring theme. "Technology has been omnipresent throughout their lives and is a universal language for these two cohorts," observed Ram Krishnan, the former Frito-Lay CMO.[53] Krishnan identified three attributes of millennials and Gen Z'ers that are of particular interest to marketers: First, they use a variety of electronic devices, so marketing campaigns must be designed for multiple screens. Second, they put more care into cultivating their digital presence than they do their physical living spaces. Third, they feel self-imposed pressure to lead interesting lives and to share memorable moments on social media. Hashtags, in particular, are a way for them to organize their experiences and connect with peers.[54]

When it comes to designing marketing strategies for target audiences, Frito-Lay has shifted the primary focus away from snack segments such as potato chips or pretzels to "moments" such as the Super Bowl that bring people and snacks together.[55] Taking its cue from this approach, Frito-Lay wanted to create memorable moments that would bring people together around the Lay's potato chip brand, which is exactly what it did with the "Do Us a Flavor" contest. "We created tools that allowed people to celebrate their passion for food. Lay's became a communication device for people to share about their daily lives," Ann Mukherjee, president of the company's global snacks group and global insights division, told a retailers conference in 2015.[56]

PLAN Crowdsourcing campaigns take tangible form in the planning stage of the LUPE model as broad strategies are translated into specific, concrete tactics. In addition, timelines and budgets are established, and communication channels are selected. Based on the insights gleaned from the first two stages of LUPE, "Do Us a Flavor" was born. Frito-Lay used a variety of tactics for the crowdsourcing contest, many of which were discussed earlier in the chapter. Using an **iterative** approach, the contest was repeated several times. Lessons learned were applied improving overall effectiveness. Originally, "Do Us a Flavor" was intended to be a one-time event, but its continued success kept it alive for three more iterations.[57]

In its first year, the contest was mostly an exercise in one-way communication. With the exception of the finalists, participants received little feedback or recognition from Lay's or its partners. In future iterations, Frito-Lay turned to the creative minds of comedian Wayne Brady and the Deep Focus agency. They created personalized videos and jingles on the fly, responding directly to specific submissions and contest-related Twitter conversations. Now, fans could see that Lay's was listening to them and even talking back.

Other changes over time centered on the choice of communication channels. Facebook was the star platform when "Do Us a Flavor" began in 2012. A contest website, Twitter, and text messaging played supporting roles. Visitors to the dousaflavor.com website were directed to a Facebook app that served as the contest's home base. Flavor ideas could be submitted via Facebook or text message. For those who

---

[53]Tucci, "Frito-Lay: 'Omniculturals.'"

[54]Ibid.

[55]David M. Grome, "Human Emotion Inspires Marketers' Data-Driven Decisions," *AMA (American Marketing Association) Rochester* (blog), October 27, 2014, http://www.ama-rochester.org/2014/10/27/human-emotion-inspires-marketers-data-driven-decisions/.

[56]"How PepsiCo Convinced You That Lays Were Cool Again," Knowledge@Wharton, Wharton School of the University of Pennsylvania, April 30, 2015, https://knowledge.wharton.upenn.edu/article/how-pepsico-convinced-you-that-lays-were-cool-again/.

[57]"How a Lay's Marketing Campaign."

(continued)

needed some extra inspiration, the Facebook app provided a "flavorizer" tool. This feature searched their Facebook timelines and suggested flavors and cuisine styles based on restaurants where they had recently checked in. Once all submissions were reviewed and the three finalists were selected, voting for the winner was conducted via Facebook, the contest website, text messaging, and Twitter.

LaCount explained that Facebook was a logical hub for the contest because it was the best channel to reach the intended audience: "We really decided to focus on Facebook [to give] us the scale we needed with our millennial target. That was where they were and spent the majority of their time. That was the relevant place for us to be."[58] Soon, other platforms would challenge Facebook's dominance. As social media habits changed, Frito-Lay responded accordingly. In the competition's second year, Twitter and YouTube were added to the list of platforms for contest entries, and photo and video sharing apps Instagram and Vine were new options for voting. By 2017, the contest's final year, fans also could vote via the Snapchat messaging app.

EXECUTE AND EVALUATE The final step in the LUPE model involves measuring and evaluating the effectiveness of a crowdsourcing campaign in meeting its stated objectives. Here, several layers of metrics must be considered, each providing a different set of insights.

One layer of metrics for the "Do Us a Flavor" contest would measure contest participation by totaling the number of submissions entered and votes cast, then comparing the totals against predefined targets to determine whether objectives were met. Table 2 shows submission and vote totals for the first year of "Do Us a Flavor." The 3.8 million contest submissions[59] and 4 million votes[60] far exceeded the targets set by Frito-Lay. These totals then became benchmarks for subsequent years. In the contest's second year, submissions and votes more than tripled. Frito-Lay reported about 14.4 million[61] submissions and 14 million votes.[62] (Totals were not available for the third and fourth years.)

Table 2 First-Year Submission and Vote Totals

	PERIOD	TARGET	ACTUAL
Contest submissions	July 20 – Oct. 6, 2012	1.2 million	3.8 million
Votes	Feb. 12 – May 12, 2013	1 million	4 million

Sources: Frito-Lay, PR Newswire

Note: Numbers are approximations.

---

[58]Ibid.

[59]Frito-Lay North America, "Lay's Brand Names Cheesy Garlic Bread Flavored Potato Chips as 'Do Us A Flavor' Contest Winner; Creator Receives $1 Million or More in Grand Prize Winnings," *PR Newswire*, May 7, 2013, https://www.prnewswire.com/news-releases/lays-brand-names-cheesy-garlic-bread-flavored-potato-chips-as-do-us-a-flavor-contest-winner-creator-receives-1-million-or-more-in-grand-prize-winnings-206392591.html.

[60]"How PepsiCo Convinced You."

[61]Frito-Lay, "Lay's Brand Issues Last Call for Votes in Its 'Do Us A Flavor' Contest; $1 Million Grand Prize on the Line for Finalist Who Submits Winning Flavor Idea," *PR Newswire*, October 2, 2014, https://www.prnewswire.com/news-releases/lays-brand-issues-last-call-for-votes-in-its-do-us-a-flavor-contest-1-million-grand-prize-on-the-line-for-finalist-who-submits-winning-flavor-idea-277863501.html.

[62]"How PepsiCo Convinced You."

Although these numbers clearly show that the contest was a hit with fans, they do not indicate whether it produced the desired effects on engagement and sales. Therefore, we need to dig deeper.

The next layer of metrics would focus on trends in social media activity during or after the contest. These metrics might include measurements of audience reach or size (such as number of friends or followers and numbers of mentions), engagement or interaction (number of likes or favorites, comments, shares or retweets, etc.), and the sentiment (positive, negative, or neutral tone) of social media conversations related to the brand.

Many of these statistics were not readily available, but Frito-Lay did release some figures about Facebook activity for the initial 2012–13 contest. During the 10-month campaign, the Lay's Facebook page averaged 22.5 million visits per week,[63] and generated 1.2 billion impressions[64] (meaning the total number of times a post from the Lay's Facebook page was displayed in users' News Feeds). These numbers are impressive, but it is not clear how they compared with the number of visits or impressions in the months before the contest. Nor is it clear from these metrics alone whether any of the chatter on Facebook had an effect on brand loyalty or the Lay's bottom line.

Consumer attitudes and behavior represent the next layer of metrics. YouGov BrandIndex, which conducts interviews to measure public perception of thousands of brands, tracked Lay's consumer ratings during the voting period of the second "Do Us a Flavor" contest in 2014. The results suggest that the contest had a powerful impact on attitudes toward the brand among the contest's target audience.[65] Among 18- to 34-year-olds, the Lay's "buzz score" (calculated by asking people if they had heard anything positive or negative about the brand in the past two weeks and subtracting negative feedback from positive) rose by 6 points over the voting period (on a scale from -100 to +100). In addition, intent to purchase Lay's products increased by 4 percent during the period.[66]

Sales statistics for the Lay's brand during the first year's contest showed an 8 percent increase in the three months following the "Do Us a Flavor" launch,[67] and overall year-to-year sales growth of 12 percent during the duration of the initial contest, far surpassing the target of a 3 percent increase.[68] Still, Lay's could not be certain that the increased sales were entirely due to the crowdsourcing campaign. Other factors may have contributed to the sales growth, making it possible that the increase would have occurred even without a contest.

Cause-and-effect relationships among consumers' exposure to marketing campaigns, their social media activity, their attitudes toward brands, and their purchases are difficult to establish, given the multifaceted and often unpredictable

---

[63]"Frito-Lay Lay's Do Us a Flavor—Gold," Chief Marketer, https://www.chiefmarketer.com/pro-awards-winners/best-idea-or-concept-gold.

[64]"How a Lay's Marketing Campaign."

[65]YouGov BrandIndex, "Crowdsourcing Campaign Appears to Boost Brand Perception for Lay's," Forbes, October 11, 2014, https://www.forbes.com/sites/brandindex/2014/10/11/crowdsourcing-campaign-appears-to-boost-brand-perception-for-lays.

[66]Ibid.

[67]Ibid.

[68]Joe Weller, "The Definitive Guide to Marketing Campaign Management," Smartsheet, May 23, 2017, https://www.smartsheet.com/marketing-campaign-management-guide.

(continued)

nature of human behavior. Even consumers themselves may not know what motivated them to buy a particular product or to choose one brand over another. But when datasets from the various layers of metrics are compared through statistical analysis, correlations among variables can be uncovered that make some predictions possible, even if true cause and effect cannot be proved. Thus, the final layer of metrics seeks to connect data from the previous layers for **"closed-loop" measurement**, in which media exposure and consumption are directly linked to purchase decisions.[69]

Officials with Engagement Labs, a data analytics firm, engaged in closed-loop measurement when they analyzed several datasets to develop a comprehensive picture of what leads consumers to purchase the products of several brands, including Lay's.[70] They measured the amount of online conversation about the brands on social media, blogs, and forums, as well as the amount of direct face-to-face conversation about the brands. In addition, they examined weekly advertising expenditures and sales data.

The research, conducted in 2017 during the voting period of the final "Do Us a Flavor" contest, showed that the voting process led to "a surge in both offline word-of-mouth and online social media."[71] Online conversations about Lay's faded quickly, but offline conversations persisted,[72] indicating the campaign's success in generating and sustaining word-of-mouth. As for the impact on sales, for all brands overall, about 19 percent of consumers' purchase decisions could be traced to online and offline conversations.[73] But Lay's fared much better than average. Approximately one-third of all Lays' sales were linked to online and offline conversations, showing that discussion about the Lay's brand during the contest did, in fact, drive sales.[74]

Lessons Learned

By nearly any measure, the Lay's "Do Us a Flavor" contest, held four times between 2012 and 2017, was a crowdsourcing success story. The contest drew millions of submissions, brought favorable publicity to the potato chip brand, and made four people instant millionaires. Consumers appreciated the fun, personal, and interactive nature of the contest. They welcomed the opportunity to brainstorm novel ideas for new potato chip flavors. For Frito-Lay, the main products of the crowdsourcing campaign were not bags of potato chips but gigabytes of data about consumers' online behavior and taste preferences. Other brands can learn from Frito-Lay's eagerness to let customers participate in innovation process and from the company's commitment to data-driven marketing. The insights gleaned from the data collected in the "Do Us a Flavor" contest will enjoy a much longer shelf life than any of the new varieties of potato chips that were introduced.

[69]Kuchinskas, "Frito-Lay CMO Krishnan."

[70]Brad Fay, Ed Keller, Rick Larkin, and Koen Pauwels, "Deriving Value from Conversations about Your Brand," *MIT Sloan Management Review* 60, no. 2 (Winter 2019): 72–77.

[71]Engagement Labs, "Social Engagement Secrets: Lessons for Marketers from Landmark Consumer Conversations Analytics Study," 2018, https://cdn2.hubspot.net/hubfs/2689843/Social%20Engagement%20Secrets/Social%20Engagement%20Secrets_ELABS.pdf.

[72]Ibid.

[73]Fay et al., "Deriving Value," 73–74.

[74]Engagement Labs, "Social Engagement Secrets."

CONCLUSION

The Internet, social networking, and other web-based technologies make crowd-sourcing possible. The ways individuals, organizations, and brands collaborate to create UGC and crowdsource content holds endless possibilities for. The frontrunners of the practice are integrating crowdsourcing into operational processes to achieve improvements in functional efficiency as well as consumer engagement. Social media listening and monitoring provide advanced data mining and analytics capabilities to understand non-solicited publicly shared opinion that can be crowdsourced from citizens around the world as they express viewpoints on social media. There will be continued growth in new technology platforms that are engineered to provide more crowdsourcing solutions. Creators producing engaging marketing content, news, and communities of interest will increasingly rely upon crowdsourcing, bringing a whole new meaning to Aristotle's "wisdom of the crowd" for years to come.

KEY TERMS

"closed-loop" measurement
collective intelligence
crowdcreating
crowdprocessing
crowdrating

crowdsolving
crowdsourcing
extrinsic motivation
gamification
intrinsic motivation
iterative

key performance indicator (KPI)
metrics
open innovation
user-generated content (UGC)

DISCUSSION QUESTIONS AND EXERCISES

1. Identify and explain the benefits of crowdsourcing and UGC.
2. This chapter covered many aspects of how organizations are inspiring action and participation through crowdsourcing. What aspects of crowdsourcing resonated with you most, and why?
3. Using the brand examples provided in this chapter, explain how crowdsourcing provided alternatives to traditional content development approaches at a fraction of the cost. How do you think the role of public relations, marketing, and advertising practitioners has changed as they adopt crowdsourcing to create campaigns?
4. Provide examples of other individuals, organizations, companies, or brands that are utilizing crowdsourcing in an exemplar fashion. What are the benefits? What is the impact for the consumer?
5. What were the most relevant aspects of the Lay's Do Us a Flavor campaign? How did data and crowdsourcing impact decisions and the overall campaign?
6. *Small group exercise:* Debate: divide the class into two groups, with one supporting crowdsourcing content and one being opposed to it and keen on using traditional content creation methods. Students should evaluate the other side's arguments and be prepared to explain and defend their position to the class.

NOTES

1. Daniel J. Levetin, "Why It's So Hard to Pay Attention, Explained by Science," *Fast Company* (blog), September 23, 2015, https://www.fastcompany.com/3051417/why-its-so-hard-to-pay-attention-explained-by-science.

2. Gustavo S. Betini, Tal Avgar, and John M. Fryxell, "Why Are We Not Evaluating Multiple Competing Hypotheses in Ecology and Evolution?," *Royal Society Open Science* 4, no. 1 (2017): 160756.

3. Sara Baase, *A Gift of Fire: Social, Legal, and Ethical Issues for Computing and the Internet*, 3rd ed. (Prentice Hall, 2007), 351–57.

4. Oxford English Dictionary, "Crowdsource," Lexico.com, accessed August 21, 2019, https://www.lexico.com/en/definition/crowdsource.

5. Ibid.

6. Mimi Onuoha, Jeanne Pinder, and Jan Schaffer, "Guide to Crowdsourcing," *Columbia Journalism Review*, Tow Center for Digital Journalism, November 20, 2015, https://www.cjr.org/tow_center_reports/guide_to_crowdsourcing.php.

7. Ibid.

8. Jordi Paniagua and Pawel Korzynski, "Social Media Crowdsourcing," 2017, https://doi.org/10.1007/978-1-4614-6616-1_200009-1.

9. Jesse Moeinifer, "Trust in Facebook Is at an All-Time Low: Here's How Media Companies Can Use That to Their Advantage," *Digital Content Next* (blog), August 5, 2019, http://digitalcontentnext.org/blog/2019/08/05/trust-in-facebook-is-at-an-all-time-low-heres-how-media-companies-can-use-that-to-their-advantage/.

10. Claudia Pelzer, "Why Crowdsource?," Crowdsourcing Week, January 23, 2016, https://crowdsourcingweek.com/blog/why-crowdsource.

11. "Global Trust in Advertising," Nielsen, September 2015, https://www.nielsen.com/wp-content/uploads/sites/3/2019/04/global-trust-in-advertising-report-sept-2015-1.pdf.

12. Mark D. Hall and Dave Chaffey, "5 Ideas for Crowdsourcing and User Generated Content," Smart Insights, November 20, 2011, https://www.smartinsights.com/customer-engagement/crowdsourcing/crowd-sourcing-and-user-generated-content/.

13. Lili Török, "A Complete Guide to Leveraging User Generated Content in 2019," *Mention* (blog), 2019, https://mention.com/blog/user-generated-content-guide/.

14. Ibid.

15. "GoPro," *TrackAnalytics* (blog), 2019, https://www.trackalytics.com/youtube/user/goprocamera/.

16. "One Year Later, Starbucks White Cup Contest Winner Grateful to Inspire Others," Starbucks, August 7, 2015, accessed August 21, 2019, https://stories.starbucks.com/stories/2015/starbucks-white-cup-contest-winner-grateful-to-inspire-others/.

17. UGC University, "Starbucks: White Cup Contest," *StoryBox* (blog), July 28, 2017, https://storybox.io/blog/2017/7/25/tourism-queensland-best-job-in-the-world-z3csp.

18. Debra Zahay, Nick Hajli, and Debika Sihi, "Managerial Perspectives on Crowdsourcing in the New Product Development Process," *Industrial Marketing Management*, November 14, 2017, accessed August 21, 2019, https://www.sciencedirect.com/science/article/abs/pii/S0019850117308350.

19. Devon Ableman, "M.A.C. Makeup Artists Are Slaying Halloween with These Incredible Looks," *Allure*, October 18, 2017, accessed September 14, 2019, https://www.allure.com/story/mac-makeup-artists-halloween-makeup-hashtag.

CHAPTER 9

Social Customer Experience (CX)

KEY LEARNING OUTCOMES

Understand what customer experience is and why brands should focus energy on developing a strategy.

Define customer experience (CX).

Highlight the benefits of using social media to deliver personalized customer support.

Illustrate functional responsibilities of managing customer experience and social media shared across multiple departments.

Explain common mistakes that brands make when social customer care is managed as a siloed initiative.

Identify common consumer expectations for direct customer-to-brand interactions through social media.

THE ROLE SOCIAL MEDIA HAS IN CUSTOMER EXPERIENCES

Social media has transformed the way consumers can directly reach and interact with companies, bringing with it changes in customer expectations. Gone are the days when customers were willing to call a toll-free customer service number, and then wait on hold until (crossing fingers) an actual person answered to help rectify the issue. Today's consumers expect to reach companies directly through the social media channel of their choosing and receive an immediate response to their concerns and inquiries. Such direct access presents new opportunities and challenges for brands in the realm of customer support, **customer service**, and overall **customer experience (CX)**. CX is defined as personalized moments specific for customers focusing on desires, actions, awareness, intentions, and actions.[1] Delivering superior customer service has long been a differentiator. Social media allows organizations across industries to harness the power of the social sphere to delight customers through customer service by efficiently leveraging their social channels. These outlets also provide a higher level of engagement and personalization than other channels. Companies that excel at delivering superior customer service through social media are set apart from those using traditional channels to resolve issues.

In his book *Winning at Social Customer Care: How Top Brands Create Engaging Experiences on Social Media*, author Dan Gingiss simplifies the idea of a customer experience as understanding feelings and relating them to organizational interactions. He suggests that to appropriately leverage the reach and power that social media adds to the customer experience, brands should focus on relating to the needs of the customer by understanding what is important as seen through the consumer lens.[2] Approaching the customer experience from this point of view is important in understanding any challenges or roadblocks that could influence what it truly means to be a patron of a brand. Aligning the organizational mindset with that of the customer helps to extend the larger reach of the brand. A successful customer experience results from fluidity—regardless of where the interactions happen. Each touchpoint should be smooth and complementary ensuring a seamless experience for the customer.[3]

Brands today must address the "consumer of one," meaning that nearly all shoppers feel their relationship with a brand should be unique and special between the brand and themselves. Organizations now focus on many of the following consumer-driven needs as a result of these expectations:

- recognition of the communication preferences of individual customers and multiple social media channels to accommodate several target audiences;
- active management of social media channels to address customer needs;
- personalized engagement that is tailored to customers' individual needs;
- authentic engagement in social conversations, not scripted copy-and-paste responses;
- access to product experts;
- concierge-type services;
- simple, easy-to-use applications and intuitive interfaces requiring little effort; and
- truth, honesty, and integrity—including an expectation that customer data is kept secure and that companies are abiding by ethical business practices that protect personal information.

Eptica, a leading European technology company specializing in intelligent platforms for digital customer experience, notes that consumers have high expectations for organizational response times.[4] A recent poll of a thousand consumers highlighted the anticipated organizational response time when using various social channels to communicate with a brand. Sixty-four percent of consumers using Twitter as a customer service tool assume that they will receive a response within 60 minutes, while 85 percent of consumers using Facebook believe that they will hear back from a company within the first six hours.[5] Although this is a tall order for most companies, **social customer care** has become a necessary investment, typically addressed through digital customer experience transformation initiatives.

Additionally, social media provides an unparalleled opportunity to provide personalized customer care, benefiting the customer and organization alike. Social-based advantages promote **rapid response** intervention and issue remediation, improved relationship building, increased customer retention and loyalty, and reduced costs. When consumers are happy, customer satisfaction improves, and, in turn the organization typically experiences increased sales and revenue.

SOCIAL CUSTOMER CARE TRAINING

According to a report by Acquia, "two out of three consumers can't recall the last time a brand exceeded expectations."[6] Delivering customer care effectively through social media channels brings about new training requirements, and brands cannot simply assume that digital teams have the appropriate skills or practice to advance customer experience strategies. Overwhelming amounts of data produced from online experiences and disparate non-integrated systems, often hinder marketers efforts to improve consumer engagement or service. Traditional customer service training must be adapted for the context and expectations unique to delivering customer support through social media channels. Two entertainment brands that demonstrate excellence in social customer care include Spotify and Netflix.[7]

Spotify, a popular mobile streaming app, established a dedicated social support account that provides specific instructions to customers looking for help on their Twitter page through @SpotifyCares. The company carefully selects customer service agents to manage customer support through the account. They are so well known for this assistance that they even won a Webby Award for their epic social media customer support.

Spotify Cares customer service interaction on Twitter.

Spotify staff is trained on email matters surrounding payment and account-related queries with a longer response turnaround time expectation.[8] This training ground is a prerequisite to providing customer service on social media. where requests are more urgent. Sam Thomas, Spotify's global manager of social media support, mentions on the *Focus on Customer Service* podcast that potential agents must go through multiple writing tests before being considered for a job in social media customer service and, once there, have their Spotify e-mails continuously inspected before advancing to the social support team, as he is really protective over the tone of voice—something "they monitor very, very closely."[9]

Netflix is another brand that demonstrates a focus on **personalized customer engagement**. The accompanying Twitter response shows how the customer care team at Netflix engages using charisma, wit, and humor. From posting regular updates on entertainment-related content to answering and engaging the audience with wit and humor, they stray far from corporate speak.[10] Netflix has the highest engagement rates compared to Hulu, Hotstar, and Amazon Prime Video.[11] They give consumers what they want, listen and follow through with requests, post consistently, and engage in what appears to be a true customer relationship, merging online and offline successful behaviors together to keep the brand on top of the social media heap.[12]

Netflix connects with enthusiastic customers.

A Harvard Business Review Analytic Services Survey correlated positive organizational market growth and influence with superior customer experiences using integrated social media initiatives.[13] The survey indicated that leading-edge businesses do not simply recognize social media integration as just another technology platform or a separate inexpensive marketing channel; rather, they recognize that social media needs to be customer facing, enabling broad contribution to the overall customer experience. In the accompanying image, you can see the functional responsibilities of managing customer experience and social media shared across multiple units.

Customer experience is managed across multiple function
Percentage indicating functions involved in managing
customer experience and social media.

● Customer experience   ● Social media

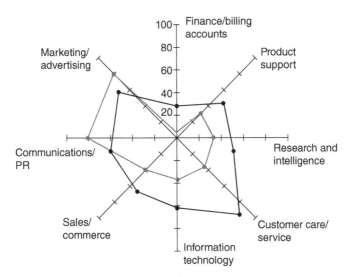

The customer experience illustrated across multiple functions showing that social media and customer service overlap.

The American Marketing Association (AMA) suggests that organizations focus on their online reputation, **social media monitoring**, and responding to customer reviews found on social channels as well as sites such as Yelp. By homing in on these three areas, brands can listen and respond to build relationships with their audience. For a brand to strengthen their relationship with customers, the AMA suggests the following:

- Support online reviews from customers. A simple shout-out or public notification will go a long way in building customer relationships.
- Respond when customers post reviews. This helps support brand loyalty and retention.
- Continuously monitor social media channels because the data provides intelligent insights. Preventative measures can be taken, should an issue arise, before it becomes a full-blown crisis.

Aberdeen Group predicts that 90 percent of customer service interaction will be conducted via corporate social media channels.[14] Today, more than 50 percent of organizations utilize social media as part of their customer care efforts, with an additional 15 percent focusing on outreach tactics.[15] The accompanying figure illustrates the impact that social customer service is having as it continues to expand.[16]

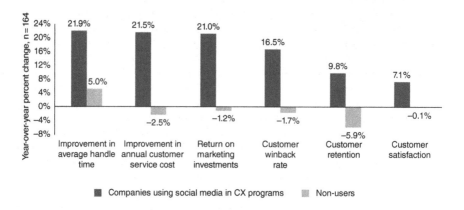

Year-over-year percent change, n = 164

| | Companies using social media in CX programs | Non-users |

- Improvement in average handle time: **21.9%** / 5.0%
- Improvement in annual customer service cost: **21.5%** / −2.5%
- Return on marketing investments: **21.0%** / −1.2%
- Customer winback rate: **16.5%** / −1.7%
- Customer retention: **9.8%** / −5.9%
- Customer satisfaction: **7.1%** / −0.1%

---

5 Key Components of a Social Customer Care Training Program

By Dan Gingiss

Once you've hired the right people to be the face of your social care program, it's time to train them. This may overlap with existing customer service training in your organization, but there will need to be some added elements that are specific to social care.

[Below, Dan expounds on five key components of a social customer care training program and his guide to hiring the right social customer care agents, which he covers in his award-winning book *Winning at Social Customer Care: How Top Brands Create Engaging Experiences on Social Media*.]

Here are 5 key components of an effective social customer care training program:

1. Your Core Business

Social customer service agents need to be a "jack of all trades." Unlike many other customer service agents who may be able to specialize in one area of the business, social care agents will need to act as "super-agents"—knowing at least a little bit about every part of the business and knowing whom to call when the questions get especially complex.

You'll want to quickly expose them to the company's products and services, preferably with leaders from different business units presenting live and answering questions afterward. You'll also want to give them an overview of your industry and direct competitors, as many customer service inquiries will compare your company's product or service to that of a competitor. While it's generally not a best practice to talk about your competitors in social media, it is critical that your social care agents understand how your offerings are superior (or in some cases inferior) to competitors' offerings.

2. Most Frequent Inquiry Types

In most companies, the same questions emerge over and over again in customer service. Teaching your social care employees about the most frequently asked questions will save you (and them) time later when they start to see these repetitive questions from prospects and customers. Many of these will be basic questions that require basic answers, such as:

What are your store hours? What is the price of this product or service? How do I enroll in your program? How does your product or service work? Can I check on the status of my order?

Agents should be able to quickly answer each of these questions and/or direct a customer to the right place on your website to find the answer (this latter method can be helpful to others who scroll through your social feed because they may find the answer to the same question without even having to ask it).

3. Internal Systems and Policies

It's very important that all new employees understand the systems and software that will guide their day-to-day work, so take the time to thoroughly train them. It's a good idea to bring in a representative from your social care technology provider to run the training. Agents should thoroughly understand how to claim a post, tag it appropriately (usually with business or inquiry type classifications), answer the customer's questions, and close the inquiry.

New agents will also need to learn about complementary systems and software, which may include your CRM or account management system, Microsoft Office products, e-mail, and instant messaging software, your company's intranet and Knowledge Base resources (containing FAQs, terms and conditions, etc.) and more. Don't forget to also train your agents on the digital properties that your customers use, like your website, Account Center, and mobile app.

4. Social Media Platforms

Take the time to walk through each social media platform that your company is using, explaining both the general mechanics of each one and the customer service-specific tools and processes. The difference between the platforms, including their nomenclature (posts vs. tweets vs. pins, friends vs. followers, etc.), is critical to understanding consumers' expectations of your brand in each platform. Your social care agents need to be fluent in each channel's functionality, audience type, etiquette and eccentricities (the most obvious one being Twitter's 280-character limit) that will affect how customer service is performed.

This training doesn't end at a new employee's orientation. Social media is notorious for changing on almost a daily basis, and your front-line agents need to be up-to-speed on new features and functionality. There is so much change at the major platforms that it's a good idea to hold monthly sessions with your agents to ensure they know about the latest technology and functionality.

5. Public Customer Service

Performing customer service in public is much different than performing it on the phone. Traditional customer service agents are used to a one-to-one relationship with the customer; that is, the conversation is private between only two people. In social media, that is clearly not the case because there is always an audience. So, while it is important that the agent still tries to establish a one-to-one relationship with the customer—personalizing the conversation with the customer's first name and leveraging available customer information from social media profiles or the company's CRM— the agent must also think about what others will perceive about the conversation.

Agents must thoroughly understand that everything they post is public, on behalf of the brand, and can be shared to a wider audience. A good rule of thumb is to ask of every post whether the company would be OK with it appearing on its own website. If yes, then the post is fine. If there are concerns, then you should look to re-write the post.

(continued)

Social customer care can be fun and rewarding, especially when the company is customer-obsessed, and it already has a lot of fans. Customers love hearing from brands on social media—it makes them feel important and loved, and they will often share those good feelings with their friends and followers. But public customer service can also cause reputational risk to a company if it's not done correctly—if agents aren't properly trained or if posts aren't properly monitored. If you've trained your agents well, you can enter the world's most public customer service channel with confidence that you are helping to improve customer experience and brand reputation.

How to Hire the Right Social Customer Care Agents

No social care program can be successful without the right people interacting with your customers and prospects. The hiring of the front-line social care staff should be thoughtful, strategic, and intentional, as it will set up the rest of the program to be able to scale in the future.

What complicates the hiring process is that the social care agents will likely report up through an Operations or Customer Service division, whereas you as a social media leader may be part of the Marketing or Communications team. Customer Service will likely already have a robust hiring process in place; it is important for you to respect that process but also to introduce some additional stages that will ensure the right kind of agent behind the proverbial wheel.

The first question people usually ask when thinking about hiring for a Social Customer Care team is whether they should prioritize Customer Service experience or social media prowess. Of course, it is preferable that candidates have both, but if you must choose then the choice is clear: It is much easier to teach social media skills than it is to teach someone how to care for a customer.

The patience, empathy, compassion and friendliness that a Customer Service agent must possess to be successful are extremely difficult to teach. Have you ever experienced a cashier who seemed to consider you an interruption to her otherwise pleasant day? What are the chances that you'd be able to train that person to genuinely care about each and every customer as if they were family?

Customer Service Consultant John R. DiJulius III calls this skill "Service Aptitude," which is critical to have in every single employee of your company. In his book, What's The Secret?: To Providing a World-Class Customer Experience, DiJulius defines "Service Aptitude" as: "A person's ability to recognize opportunities to exceed Customers' expectations, regardless of the circumstances."[1]

Just because someone is good at social media doesn't mean they know the first thing about how to treat your customers. Sure, it helps if the candidate is active on Facebook and Twitter and understands the nuances of hashtags and DMs, but the mechanics of the various social media platforms can be taught; empathy cannot.

The first stage is writing a solid job description. Again, you may have to start from an existing Customer Service job description, but that's OK. Generally the types of skills that are found in a telephone, e-mail, or chat agents are transferrable to Social Customer Care. But you'll need to tweak it a bit and add a few more requirements. Specifically:

> *Writing Skills*: These are a must. Social Customer Care agents must be able to communicate effectively with the written word, more so because much of the communication will be public. These public responses are a reflection of your brand, so you don't want them littered with spelling and grammar errors or sentences that don't make sense. Make sure you require at least one writing sample as part of the candidate application.

Writing in 140 Characters: Twitter writing skills are even better. Writing on Twitter is a slightly different skill than writing in other forums. Remember when your high school English teacher told you to "write tight"? She probably explained that it was important to eliminate really superfluous words that needlessly extended your already lengthy sentences even more than they had to be just so you sounded more intelligent to those reading your paper and filled up the entire page with words and . . . well you get the point! This is a critical skill on Twitter given its limitation of 140 characters per tweet. Even in Facebook, it is important for Customer Service agents to get to the point quickly, not waste the customer's time, and not say more than what needs to be said. If the candidate is not active on Twitter, look for related skills like journalism (especially headline writing), copy editing, advertising copy writing, or SMS marketing.

Social Media Experience: While being active on social media is not required, it definitely helps. People who frequently use social media platforms have an inherent sense for how each of them work. They know what a hashtag is, and that one or two is ideal on Twitter but many more are acceptable on Instagram and despite Facebook's efforts, not many people use them there. Perhaps most importantly, people active on social media understand the importance of the "social" in social media—that it's about the conversation and engagement with people, not the brand shouting its message with a megaphone.

Ideally, you or someone on the Social Media team can also be one of the interviewers for each candidate. If left to the Customer Service team to interview alone, the key components listed above likely won't get prioritized. For example, they may not be used to reading and reacting to writing samples or asking about social media experience. Another benefit of the social media team participating in the hiring process is that it forces collaboration with Customer Service. Now both groups will have an incentive to hire the right people for these critical roles.

---

[1] John R. DiJulius III, *What's the Secret?: To Providing a World-Class Customer Experience*, May 2008, https://www.wiley.com/en-us/What%27s+the+Secret%3F%3A+To+Providing+a+World+Class+Customer+Experience-p-9780470196120.

SOURCE: Dan Gingiss, *Winning at Social Customer Care: How Top Brands Design Engaging Experiences on Social Media* (self-pub., CreateSpace, 2017).

MEASURING SOCIAL MEDIA IN THE CONTACT CENTER

Customer care centers are a central component for many large organizations. TELUS International, a global contact center outsourcing company that handles 200 million customer care interactions per year for many global brands, noted that organizations approach customer care through a variety of ways. Some brands rely on metrics, others measure response time, while still others examine direct impact on service. Key performance indicators (KPIs) are used to measure and evaluate service levels within customer care.[17]

Customer care programs that are well thought out can connect directly back to organizational goals such as cost savings, bottom-line revenue impact, or an increase in market share. Strong customer care initiatives move toward the customer of one and move away from serving the masses. Focusing time and individualized attention on customers will only increase in importance. Every customer wants to feel as though the brand cares about them and their needs.

UNIFIED CUSTOMER EXPERIENCE

Organizations that adopt and incorporate a cross-channel content strategy experience improved outcomes related to customer interactions. A common mistake that organizations make results from treating each platform within the cross-channel strategy as a stand-alone entity. Brands should strive to deliver consistent experiences to customers in an integrated fashion and at every touchpoint:

- Digital/web
- Social media
- Mobile
- Call center
- In store
- Point of sale
- Direct mail
- Email

Stacy Martinet, VP of marketing strategy and communications at Adobe, explains that

> a data-driven approach to creativity helps marketers work more productively, create the right content faster, and deliver that content to the right customer, across the right channels, at the right time. One common denominator among today's most innovative companies is a unified view of the customer, pulling data from across multiple sources. Creative teams need to work more closely with their data and analytics teams to better understand the changing behaviors of consumers both online and off. Even further, we'll see enterprises focused on building a seamless flow of connected customer data—behavioral, transactional, financial, operational, and more—to get a true end-to-end view of their customers for immediate actionability.[18]

ACTIONABLE STAGES

Customers no longer accept a "please hold" approach when it comes to customer service. In our 24/7 social media driven society, customers want responses now.[19] Here are five ways to approach customer care with a customer first mindset.

Deliver a Cohesive Customer Experience

Continuity across social channels reinforces brand image. Consistent implementation positively impacts customer experience and builds trust. These efforts also demonstrate a persistent brand identity, reassuring customers of brand values and what degree of service they can expect. This means brands must strive to deliver consistent experiences to customers at every touchpoint.

Deliver Personalized Customer Experiences

Customers expect personalized engagement that is tailored to their individual needs. Accenture, a multinational professional services company that provides services in strategy, consulting, digital, technology and operations, recently found that 81 percent of consumers are interested in brands taking time to better understand their needs. Customers expect that organizations appreciate their communications preferences and will deliver authentic engagement in social conversations using their preferred channels. Brands must understand these partialities and strive to engage effectively with customers where they want to be.

Delight Customers by Anticipating Needs

Customers are savvy and realize that leading companies invest in predicting their needs. Brands need to advance their capabilities to understand and direct future actions to proactively deliver positive customer experiences. Social media enables brands to monitor customer conversation and activity, allowing increased appreciation for customer pain points, desires, and aspirations to deliver appropriate customer value.

Flatten Organizational Silos

Delivering a positive customer experience is the responsibility of all business functions. Social media is an essential channel that every part of the organization needs to prioritize. Information obtained during every customer touchpoint is critical for improving upon the overall customer experience. Mapping the customer interaction points and determining the process for uncovering insights from customer feedback will help guide process improvement priorities that enhance customer experiences.

Invest in Measuring and Monitoring

There are various methods for measuring customer satisfaction. Evaluate which approach provides you with the most straightforward metrics and repeatable measurement systems to evaluate progress toward customer experience improvement goals. Start by establishing a baseline and continually measure improvement from that original baseline. Customer satisfaction, also referred as CSAT, or net performer scores (NPS) are useful and proven methods. Keep your goals at the center of your measurement and reporting. Deliver insights on progress that help the organization make necessary improvements to enhance customer experience.

Fifty percent of consumers think that brands have missed the mark and failed at online expectations, while 65 percent of people surveyed said they will abandon a brand over poor customer experience.[20] Here there is a tragic disconnect: 87 percent of marketers truly believe they are providing their customers an engaging experience.[21] This finding alone poses more questions than answers for many professionals. Despite investing more than ever before on online solutions, the divide between strategy and satisfaction seems to be as wide as ever before.

Using digital media as a strategy for customer care doesn't differ that much from delivering excellence in face-to-face customer service. As mentioned in the brands above, the best experiences are those that have the consumer as the heart of the strategy, using empathy as a North Star, all while utilizing technology to aid in delivering seamless and positive customer experiences. As the landscape becomes increasingly competitive and saturated, organizations will have to use data to break silos and leverage their assets to create more cohesive and satisfying customer experiences.

LushUK: Can a Brand Survive without Social Media?

Introduction

Measurable return on investment—by highlighting how customers are the center of an organization and how organizations can use social media to build strong relationships over time—is essential. This case study will illuminate how a vegetarian and cruelty-free cosmetics brand, LushUK, inventors of the bath bomb, dumped social media in the hopes of refocusing their service model from mass communication (one to many) to person-to-person communication, in order to create more relative content and better one-to-one service to their consumers. Can a brand really survive without social media?

In 2018, LushUK's Facebook and Instagram channels were turning 42 percent growth month after month.[22] Most people would consider that to be a successful social media result, indicative of soundly reaching audiences with content that resonates with the target audience; however, LushUK maintained that social media was making it harder and harder for their staff to talk to their audience directly. The company issued the following statement on Instagram and Twitter:

> We're switching up social. We are tired of fighting with algorithms, and we do not want to pay to appear in your newsfeed. So we've decided it's time to bid farewell to some of our channels and open up the conversation between you and us instead. Lush has always been made up of many voices, and it's time for all of them to be heard. We don't want to limit ourselves to holding conversations in one place, we want social to be placed back in the hands of our communities—from our founders to our friends. We're a community and we always have been. We believe we can make more noise using all of our voices across the globe because when we do we drive change, challenge norms and create a cosmetic revolution. We want social to be more about passions and less about likes. Over the next week, our customer care team will be actively responding to your messages and comments, after this point you can speak us via live chat on the website, on email at wecare@lush.co.uk and by telephone: 01202 930051. This isn't the end, it's just the start of something new. #LushCommunity—see you there.[23]

LushUK didn't have to stop using its Facebook or Twitter feeds altogether to achieve this goal; they could have just stopped paying for placed ads or promoted content in order to decrease their budget in this area and moved to organic content. Oddly, the company is still answering messages via Facebook Messenger, so they are still using the platform to communicate in some ways.

LushUK choosing influencers over spending on social media advertisements is risky. What a company gets in return for paid media, or spending on social channels is undervalued digital advertising and some of the most powerful targeting options advertisers have ever seen, allowing them to get their message in front of exactly the right people.

Social media is not just a push business, so the idea of *we don't want to pay* is likely going to impact the brand's ability to listen to its consumers as well, decreasing their listening power. Unless Lush is switching to a more environmental scanning tactic than content approach, they will get lost in the noise of social. Consumers will still look to engage with LushUK on their official social media pages. Without these pages, brand engagement leaves a lot to be desired. Consumers expect to go online and search for brands, not to call and wait for a reply. People will still look to social media for answers, as way to engage with the brand, to close the feedback loop, and of course, to complain. So, could this actually work? Generational research suggests that one-on-one communication can make an impact. Generation Z, in particular, is starting to crave more phone conversations and face-to-face small talk.[24] Based on this, pushing customers to reach out to Lush via a phone call may be intriguing to some.

LushUK stopped responding to social media channels across all platforms and wanted to shore up its one-on-one communications with consumers through more direct and relevant content means, influencers, but does that leave a service hole? Influencers, while not actual employees of LushUK, have always been a large part of their marketing model; however, this new approach to social media—focusing on their already existing market of "Lush personalities," "brand advocates," and empowering employee spokespeople—is another way of saying they are going "all in" on influencers.[25] Will this compromise the LushUK brand promise? Should organizations force consumers to bend to connect with their brand, on brand terms, not their own? If there is no place for user-generated content to live, will this hurt the brand's ability to watch, learn, and listen from their consumer?

Using the LUPE model, the aim of this case study is to examine whether customer service through social media is a necessary component of a LushUK's digital future. You'll have a critical role in this case study: conduct research of your own, and write the ending. Evaluate the scenario and determine whether you think LushUK leadership primed itself for success when it eliminated social channels for customer care.

Listen and Learn

In the LUPE model we begin with *Listen and Learn*. This stage frames and uses research as discovery to identify and rank risk; understand the significant, dangerous, or beneficial aspects of the issue at hand; and create the agenda for priorities in the most effective research to outline the true scope of the problem or opportunity. Additionally, listening techniques are used for monitoring primary and secondary markets to assess consumer attitudes through mining public discourse, evaluating sentiment, and discovering trending topics necessary for strategic planning. A thorough understanding of the "big picture" during this stage saves time and money, and decreases the risk associated with strategy creation.

LushUK has taken a large risk to eliminate social for customer care on their brand channels. This decision came at the heels of two polarizing events: first, the 30th anniversary of the bath bomb, which included a viral hashtag #WetheBathers and the release of bath bomb products along with unique content online across all social channels, a combined following of 1.2 million,[26] and second, a viral ad campaign that drew attention to the so-called UK spy cops scandal.[27]

(continued)

This second event featured a store window poster of a man in split frame, one side dressed a police officer and the other in plain clothes, alongside the words "PAID TO LIE." Mock police tape running across the shop window read, "POLICE HAVE CROSSED THE LINE." Lush previously said it aimed to highlight "this small and secretive subset of undercover policing that undermines and threatens the very idea of democracy."[28] The company added that it "is not an anti-police campaign." While this was an in-shop social justice campaign, the backlash on social media was felt. LushUK suspended the in-store campaign before the original end date but did not issue an apology, but the hashtag #FlushLush began circulating the Internet because of the Police Federation creating a fuss online immediately thereafter.[29]

LushUK soon announced they would close their corporate their channels; however, they would continue to allow local UK store accounts.[30] In a follow-up announcement divulging that they were in the midst of developing their new strategy, LushUK committed to starting initial conversations, contradictorily while slamming on the brakes:

Although we will no longer be posting on 6 of Lush UK's main channels (Lush, Lush Kitchen, Lush Times, Lush Life, Soapbox and Gorilla Arthouse), we will be continuing conversations through #LushCommunity (and other familiar hashtags such as #Lush, #LushLabs and #LushMakeup to name just a few) via staff, friends and our shop social media accounts across Instagram, Twitter and Facebook.

As this is the first exploratory step by Lush UK, we are not suggesting other Lush markets follow suit. We are sparking an initial conversation.

We will be relying on the expertise of our current social media teams to develop and implement the new strategy. As well as this they will be continuing to create and publish content for our own platforms and those of the community.[31]

Lush North America remained fully functional, even issuing a statement on social channels that they were sticking with social media.

Completing the *Listen and Learn* stage, it is essential to understand the following:

- Powerful social trends of target audiences
- Economic factors at play across an industry sector
- Types of tactics that could be used to connect with audiences

- History of social media response for the brand
- Methods to communicate change to stakeholders

Without the insights gathered in the *Listen and Learn* stage, the brand could not have corroborated audience research, nor tapped into a strong sentiment among the target audience to arrive at this decision. This research allowed for influencer discovery and definition to create a network of influencers who could carry their brand without native social media. Without this knowledge, the agency could not have moved into the next stage of the LUPE model: *Understand*.

Understand

The *Understand* stage from the LUPE model provides major intel gathered from the previous stage to analyze and construct strategies; it also typically uses those to write SMART objectives. Drawing from the data regarding influencers, audiences, mission, and purpose, we can identify their strategy as follows:

Goal: To increase user-generated content (UGC) and cultural authenticity to create loyal audiences.

Objective 1: To increase brand awareness through creating brand advocates out of in-store staff and "Lush personalities."

Objective 2: To maintain or increase sales and improve customer service through one-on-one authentic relationships with current and future customers through Q4 2019.

With goals and objectives in place, the brand then moved on to the next stage, *Plan* to develop a robust action plan to support the achievement of the goals and objectives identified in the *Understand* phase, aided by research.

Plan

Creating the *Plan* as articulated in the LUPE model, LushUK would use behaviors and buying patterns of the target audience, ascertained from the *Learn* and *Understand* phases, to apply specific messaging, strategies, and channel and communication preferences while developing a plan of tactics, timeline creation, and budget formulation based on these elements.

Claiming a $0 advertising budget, Natasha Ritz discussed her strategy on the podcast *The CMO Show:*[32]

> We don't advertise above or below the line. We don't spend money on TV campaigns, on celebrity endorsements. We don't promote social media posts. So, everything we do is organic. Every Facebook post is organic. We have no budget to push behind it.

She went on to comment,

> We've got internal brand advocates, which are our staff, and they are our customers, too. They buy our product and we help service them as a communications department to know what other great messages they can be sharing. And then they create brand advocates on the shop floor by sharing those messages, pampering people, making them feel really good about coming in.

And finally, in a written statement by LushUK pursuant to the social media breakup, the brand promised an increased emphasis on influencer marketing. "You'll start to see the rise of Lush personalities online. This isn't a replacement for the brand channels but an opportunity for our customers to connect one-on-one with people within Lush based on the various categories."[33]

(continued)

The announcement coincided with the closing of their Facebook, Twitter, Instagram, Lush Kitchen, Lush Times, Lush Life, Soapbox, and Gorilla accounts. They did not shut down any local UK store accounts.[34] Because Lush already had a dedicated group of popular brand champions in the ever-growing cosmetics and beauty community on Facebook and Instagram, and this strategy followed their mission to establish and grow communities of influence that are emboldened by their core company values, this did not deviate from their brand message. For example, one of their most popular "Lush personalities," AllThingsLushUK on Instagram, has had a long-standing relationship with Lush, consistently posts product reviews, and runs a Lush product-dedicated blog.[35]

LushUK announces their departure from social media.

Today, people are familiar with the term "influencer." Instagram, TikTok, and Snapchat feeds are full of influencers. So, when it comes down to it, "Lush personalities," or brand advocates as they are called across mediums, is just another name for social media influencers. We know social media influencers to be trusted personalities, usually within a specialized field or niche, who maintain an active and authentic relationships with their followers or audience.[36] As a result of solid relationships, social media influencers enable brands to introduce and maintain relationships with their followers regarding their brand or service. Per Federal Trade Commission law, if an endorsement is present and the influencer gained that product through any type of sponsored or compensated means, the influencer has a responsibility to disclose, in a transparent and obvious manner, the relationship present to establish that a "material connection" or reciprocal relationship is established between a brand and the influencer. A "material connection" to the brand includes a personal, family, or employment relationship or a financial relationship—such as the brand paying the influencer or the influencer is receiving free or discounted products or services.[37] Product promotion can come in a variety of ways: some influencers may promote a brand or product because they genuinely like the product, or they hope to get sponsored by the product brand, or they at least receive something free from the company they are promoting.[38]

According to the company, "Lush's dedication to advocacy resonates with the tech-savvy Generation Z; they respect the company's values around transparency in its supply chain and the investment into where they source their products."[39] Further they noted "The move coincides with talk of a mass exodus of regular everyday humans from mainstream social platforms. According to a 2018 study of over 1,000 Gen Z (individuals born after 1994) Americans, 64 percent are taking a break from social media, and 34 percent are quitting altogether."[40] LushUK's move to cut back on social media could be appealing to GenZ consumers which make up over 64 percent of their spending base and are the demographic with the largest increase in spending power.[41] With the *Plan* stage established, the brand continued on to the next phase of the LUPE model, *Execute*.

Execute and Evaluate

Risks with influencers are plenty, *Social Media Today* lists the top dangers of influencer marketing:[42] (1) influencer engagement is nearing an all-time low, (2) brands are using inauthentic partnerships and content, (3) the Federal Trade Commission (FTC) is cracking down, (4) ethical considerations are present with brand relationships to spokespersons and could cause conflict, (5) follower farms are falsely inflating follower and engagement numbers, and (6) ethical implications of influencer labor are surfacing. This final point is one that is often overlooked. When influencers are being treated more like a commodity than a human being, there's a risk that they will simply quit without obligation because unless contracted, they have no obligation to Lush—or any other company for that matter.[43]

Arguably LushUK's largest influencer, All Things Lush, stopped her Lush social media use in October 2019, just seven months after Lush began going all in on influencers and with the holiday season forthcoming. The dedicated blogger, Jen Wright, had been writing about LushUK since 2013. In her October 24, 2019, final blog, she wrote,

> It was almost seven years ago that I made the choice to dedicate my time and energy into creating the most definitive Lush blog that I possibly could. Little did I know just how much money and time would be needed to fulfil this dream and create something that has grown and flourished as much as it has over the years. . . .
>
> However, change is inevitable and I have reached a stage in my life where I want to explore far more of this world, and in doing so dig far deeper into my own consciousness. This means that I need to let go of the things that are no longer serving me and begin to walk a new, exciting path, and see what life has to offer me when I do.
>
> For this reason, I will be stepping away from updating this blog completely and will no longer be reviewing Lush products on this platform. This blog will remain out there to hopefully inspire and inform new, wide-eyed Lush fans who are looking for a solid reference point to start from, as well as serve as a memory of my time over the last seven years.[44]

The *Evaluate* stage of the LUPE model involved first assessing whether the effort met its overall goal and SMART objectives, and then evaluating other ancillary data to determine if "quitting" social media "worked."

Objective 1: To increase brand awareness through creating brand advocates out of in-store staff and "Lush personalities."

Company-authored data obtained by The Drum, a global media platform and the biggest marketing website in Europe, shows that since closing its own social channels, LushUK's social traffic has dropped only by 4.8 percent. Independent data obtained by The Drum, however, showed that traffic on Lush.co.uk dropped by 7.2 percent from April 2018 to August 2019.[45] Despite the drops in site traffic,

(continued)

there was an increase in site engagement with the average customer spending 10.6 percent more time on Lush.co.uk than before they pulled out of social and pages per visit went up by a quarter. Organic searches for the Lush website went up 2.6 percent. Additionally, the #LushCommunity hashtag, which was promoted during the dropping social announcement, had more than 171,976 posts as of October 2019.[46]

With the focus moving to organic search strategies, comparisons done between January and March and between April and August of 2019 show that organic search was, in fact, up by 2.6 percent.[47] Furthermore, a Google Trends report showing interest over time from April 2018 to December 2018 and April 2019 to December 2019 seems to indicate that 2019 data has actually improved in search in the United Kingdom in Q4 and growing over the popular holiday season in relationship to Lush search terms.

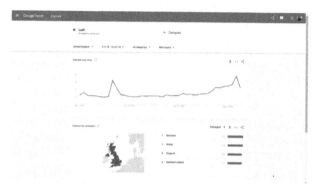

Lush Google Trends, interest over time, April 2018 to December 2018.

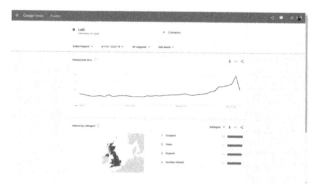

Lush Google Trends, interest over time, April 2019 to December 2019.

Objective 2: To maintain or increase sales and improve customer service through one-on-one authentic relationships with current and future customers through Q4 2019.

Similarly, year-over-year data in 2018 and 2019 indicate a rise and drop during the 2018 holiday season, in contrast to 2019, when interest over time continued to trend positively, surpassing organic search interest in 2018.

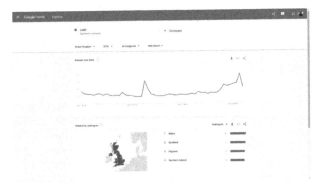

Lush Google Trends, interest over time (2018).

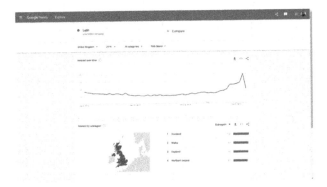

Lush Google Trends, interest over time (2019).

Without access to actual sales data, since Lush is a privately held company, search numbers could then be a key indicator of whether or not the company's sales are increasing.[48]

Goal: To increase user-generated content (UGC) and cultural authenticity to create loyal audiences.

After examining the year-over-year comparison of the top four LushUK hashtags, it seems that the goal of increasing UGC from 2018 through 2019 was achieved.

Using Nuvi, a social experience brand management platform (https://nuvi .com/), we created dashboards to monitor testing of the top four LushUK hashtags: #WeTheBathers, #Lushie, #LushUK, and #LushCommunity. This shows the most prominent hashtag over time in FY 2018 to be #LushUK, with the campaign launch of #LushCommunity not occurring until the following April 2019. Overall traffic seems to have decreased over time on all hashtags based on the x-axis result and range of measurement; however, the #LushCommunity hashtag has risen to prominence from obscurity in 2018 based on the deliberate launch post "social media breakup."

Quitting Social Media

This case study represents the radical notion that a multinational cosmetic brand could quit social media, go "all in" on influencers, and still survive—even potentially

(continued)

thrive—in a one-to-one model. In the *Listen and Learn* stage, LushUK would have paid close attention to the following:

- Powerful social trends of target audiences
- Economic factors at play across an industry sector
- History of social media response for the brand

This would have been done to *Understand* the target audience and ensure appropriate messaging, not to mention to determine if the move to vacate most social media channels would have been a risk worth taking. In *Plan*, LushUK proved that it learned and understood the identity of the target audience, and went to those who impact buying decisions the most and who prove to be most influential in the brand category, and changed social media channels to reflect those that the target audience spend time on and value the most. For example, LushUK left all other channels but still kept Facebook Messenger still in communication for those more perplexing service needs. In the *Evaluate* stage, LushUK understood which evaluation methods would yield metrics to show that their objectives were an important part of the overall strategy in understanding whether their plan to eliminate social media impacted the target audience positively or negatively.

CONCLUSION

Today most purchasing decisions are made based on a customer's experience with a brand. Smart companies are paying attention because they know that even an average customer experience can increase revenue by $823 million over three years.[49] Imagine the revenue stream of an outstanding experience. Offering personalized engagements, developing user-centric designs, and talking to customers helps brands develop an experience appreciated by customers.

DISCUSSION QUESTIONS AND EXERCISES

1. Discuss how social media has enabled consumers to reach brands more directly.
2. Considering consumers' changing expectations about accessing brands' customer care directly through social media, what opportunities and challenges has this brought to companies and organizations?
3. Given that consumers use social media to seek recommendations and reviews, how do brands need to engage differently? Do you think customers embrace being part of the conversation or feel that this can this be off-putting?
4. Debate the most common consumer expectations in customer experience brought about by social media, and highlight the benefits that social media provides in delivering personalized customer care.
5. This chapter highlighted various impacts social media has had on customer service. Using a before-and-after approach, illustrate the organizational alignment impacts of social media.
6. *Small group exercise:* Assess how organizations have had to reorganize functional areas of responsibility to meet the growing demands of consumers

expecting to receive superior customer service through social media. Illustrate organizational alignment pre– and post–social media. Explain the organizational changes and why the post–social media structure you've illustrated supports the delivery of customer care in an improved, non-siloed approach.

KEY TERMS

customer experience (CX)

customer service

social customer care

social media monitoring

NOTES

1. Yafit Mor and Jae Baer, "Why Customer Experience Is the Ultimate Marketing Tool," Convince and Convert, accessed January 3, 2020, https://www.convinceandconvert.com/online-customer-experience/why-customer-experience/.

2. Dan Gingiss, *Winning at Social Customer Care: How Top Brands Create Engaging Experiences on Social Media* (self-pub., CreateSpace, 2017).

3. Ibid.

4. "About Us," Eptica, July 9, 2019, https://www.eptica.com/about-us.

5. "US Retail Multichannel Customer Experience Study 2015," Eptica, October 4, 2018, https://www.eptica.com/500_retail_study_2015.

6. Acquia, "Closing the CX Gap: Customer Experience Trends Report 2019," Acquia, last modified 2019, accessed September 25, 2019, https://www.acquia.com/resources/ebooks/closing-cx-gap-customer-experience-trends-report.

7. Ibid.

8. Joey Chan, "Social Customer Service: Lessons from 5 of Our Favorite Brands," *Mention* (blog), 2019, accessed August 19, 2019, https://mention.com/blog/social-customer-service/.

9. "Episode 31—Spotify Is Hitting All The Right Notes in Social Customer Service," SoundCloud, May 11, 2016, https://soundcloud.com/focus-on-customer-service/episode-31-spotify-is-hitting-all-the-right-notes-in-social-customer-service.

10. Veena Ramakrishnan, "How Netflix's Social Media Strategy Dominates the Online Streaming Industry," *Unmetric* (blog), June 20, 2019, accessed September 9, 2019, https://blog.unmetric.com/netflix-social-media-strategy.

11. Ibid.

12. Ibid.

13. Harvard Business Review, "HBR Analytic Services Survey Highlights How Leaders Are Winning in the Digital Economy," DXC Technology, accessed January 8, 2020, https://www.dxc.technology/innovation/insights/143902-winning_through_change_in_the_digital_economy.

14. Susan Moore, "Gartner Says 25 Percent of Customer Service Operations Will Use Virtual Customer Assistants by 2020," February 19, 2018, https://www.gartner.com/en/newsroom/press-releases/2018-02-19-gartner-says-25-percent-of-customer-service-operations-will-use-virtual-customer-assistants-by-2020.

15. Jess Burns, "Consumer Connection: Effective Approaches to Customer Service," *Aberdeen Group* (blog), March 4, 2018, https://www.aberdeen.com/cmo-essentials/consumer-connection-effective-approaches-customer-service/.

16. Ibid.

17. "Measuring Social Media in the Contact Center: Metrics & ROI for Social Customer Care," TELUS International, 2015, https://www.telusinternational.com/media/Contact-Center_SocialCare_Metrics_rev2015.pdf.

18. Chris Wood, "Under the Tree for 2019: Customer Experience & Beyond," DMNews.com, December 28, 2018, https://www.dmnews.com/customer-experience/article/21038168/under-the-tree-for-2019-customer-experience.

19. Moore, "Gartner Says 25 Percent."

20. Acquia, "Closing the CX Gap."

21. Ibid.

22. J. McCarthy, "Christmas 'Make or Break' for Lush UK's Social 'Switch Up' Strategy," *The Drum* (blog), October 25, 2019, accessed September 23, 2019, https://www.thedrum.com/news/2019/10/25/christmas-make-or-break-lush-uk-s-social-switch-up-strategy.

23. LushLTD, Twitter post, April 8, 2019, https://twitter.com/LushLtd/status/1115147751648571392.

24. L. Stinson, "It's Not Just You—the Lowly Phone Call Is Making a Comeback," *Wired* (blog), June 3, 2017, accessed October 29, 2019, https://www.wired.com/2017/05/phone-call-renaissance/.

25. Ibid.

26. O. Petter, "Lush Is Quitting Social Media," *The Independent UK*, last modified April 10, 2019, accessed September 27, 2019, https://www.independent.co.uk/life-style/fashion/lush-quit-close-social-why-accounts-gone-twitter-instagram-a8861836.html.

27. "Lush Drops 'Anti-spy Cops' Campaign," *BBC News* (blog), June 8, 2018, accessed August 17, 2019, https://www.bbc.com/news/uk-44413586.

28. Ibid.

29. Ibid.

30. K. Benjamin, "Lush Ditches UK Social Media Accounts," *PRWeek* (blog), April 10, 2019, accessed September 9, 2019, https://www.prweek.com/article/1581596/lush-ditches-uk-social-media-accounts.

31. LushUK, "We're Switching Up Social," LushUK, April 15, 2019, accessed May 29, 2020, https://uk.lush.com/article/were-switching-social.

32. "The Organic Growth of Lush Cosmetics with Natasha Ritz," *The CMO Show*, audio podcast audio, November 9, 2017, accessed August 21, 2019, https://thecmoshow.filteredmedia.com.au/lush-cosmetics-organic-growth/.

33. McCarthy, "Christmas 'Make or Break.'"

34. K. Benjamin, "Lush Ditches UK Social Media Accounts."

35. J. Wright, "Let the Good Times Roll," *All Things Lush UK* (blog), October 24, 2019, accessed November 7, 2019, http://allthingslushuk.blogspot.com/2019/.

36. C. Newberry, "Influencer Marketing in 2019: How to Work with Social Media Influencers," *Hootsuite* (blog), May 2, 2019, accessed October 28, 2019, https://blog.hootsuite.com/influencer-marketing/.

37. Federal Trade Commission, "Disclosures 101 for Social Media Influencers," Federal Trade Commission, last modified November 1, 2019, accessed December 1, 2019, https://www.ftc.gov/tips-advice/business-center/guidance/disclosures-101-social-media-influencers.

38. Influencer Marketing Hub, "What Is an Influencer?," *Influencer Marketing Hub* (blog), February 1, 2019, accessed August 28, 2019, https://influencermarketinghub.com/what-is-an-influencer/.

39. Hill Holliday—Origin, "Meet Gen Z: The Social Generation Part 2. A Report on the First True Generation of Social Natives and the Next Generation of Mass-Market Consumers,"

Origin (blog), 2019, accessed November 2, 2019, http://387c234b056784d14ee9-444ab69a763c675d9d74b1fe398cebbd.r57.cf5.rackcdn.com/factsheets/2019-Gen-Z-Report.pdf?__hstc=16060841.b01d5e37365ed9dfdb9e181f0ff82f7c.1575210704 248.1 575210704248.1575210704248.1&__hssc=16060841.1.1575210704248.

40. Ibid.
41. Ibid.
42. Stinson, "It's Not Just You."
43. O. Iurillo, "6 Dangers of Influencer Marketing," *Social Media Today* (blog), July 11, 2019, accessed October 5, 2019, https://www.socialmediatoday.com/news/6-dangers-of-influencer-marketing/558493/.
44. Petter, "Lush Is Quitting."
45. J. Wright, "Let the Good Times Roll."
46. John McCarthy, "Lush Abandons Social Media: It's 'Getting Harder' to Talk to Customers," *The Drum* (blog), April 9, 2019, accessed September 23, 2019, https://www.thedrum.com/news/2019/04/09/lush-abandons-social-media-its-getting-harder-talk-customers.
47. Ibid.
48. Ibid.
49. Yafit Mor and Jae Baer, "Why Customer Experience."

CHAPTER 10

Crisis Communications in a Data-Driven World

KEY LEARNING OUTCOMES

Identify what constitutes a crisis.

Understand how data is used to anticipate a crisis in the
social sphere and develop a response strategy.

Assess the role that crisis communications management
can play within an organization.

Recognize the role public relations, marketing, and advertising
practitioners play in crisis communications management.

Understand the typical stages of crisis communications
and how they are changing because of social media.

Discover the elements of a modern-day crisis
communications plan.

MODERN-DAY CRISIS COMMUNICATION PLANNING

Public relations, marketing, and advertising practitioners know that it's a matter of *when*, not *if*, in crisis communications planning. Organizations are not immune to crises, which means it is important to prepare for the inevitable. In the moments when a crisis unfolds, an organization's response preparedness can determine the long-term impact on the company. To ensure agility, speed, and successful crisis communications remediation, organizations must develop crisis communications management protocols in advance. A study conducted by Pentland Analytics and AON concluded that how a company responds when a crisis hits could add 20 percent value to their organization, or, just as quickly, lose up to 30 percent of their company value, depending on their crisis preparedness and management during the immediate aftermath of a crisis. The study outlined four relevant facts of high priority for any company today:[1]

1. Company size or reputation offer little protection against loss in reputation, revenue, or value.
2. Reputation recovery matters even more with the introduction of social media.
3. Corporate social responsibility plays a critical role in response.
4. Crisis communication must be instant.[2]

Everyone Is Global

The Internet and social media created an environment whereby all organizations that have a website or a presence on the social web are equally accessible in the eyes of the consumer. When news goes viral on social media, organizations must determine the response plan quickly to effectively minimize reputational risks. Regardless of whether the business is a small e-commerce retail shop on Etsy.com, a bakery on Main Street, or a major fashion brand like Burberry, the Internet knows no boundaries, which means that every organization has a global presence. Failure to respond to a communications crisis on social media may bring harm to a company's image, damage its relationships with stakeholders, and negatively affect revenue.

As defined by the Cambridge Dictionary, **crisis management** is "the actions that are taken to deal with an emergency or difficult situation in an organized way."[3] Crisis management can be divided into five phases:[4]

- *pre-crisis:* prepare in advance;
- *origin isolation:* understand where the crisis began and on which social channel it broke first;
- *impact evaluation:* take inventory of what is happening;
- *crisis management:* management responds to a crisis; and
- *post-crisis:* learn from the crisis by seeking ways to better prepare for next time while also taking stock of what went well and what did not during this crisis.

Let's look at each of these phases closer.

Pre-crisis

According to the Institute for PR, preparing in advance means that companies need to understand known risks that can lead to a communications crisis.[5] Having a crisis communications plan in place is key, and the plan must include distinct protocols that take social media into account. Including a specific section in the plan that covers social listening and conversation monitoring of an organization's social mentions is vital to identify and mobilize quickly, should a crisis response be necessary. Using data-driven insights from conversation mining for share of voice allows practitioners to identify inconsistencies or spikes of brand mentions within social media dialogue. **Share of voice** is the percentage of conversations taking place both online and in mainstream media that mention the organization or brand by name versus the percentage of conversation about an entire product category that is non-branded.[6]

Origin Isolation

By using social listening, a company can then conduct an audit to see what is being said about the brand and also isolate when, where, and on which channels the crisis is unfolding. Setting up a social media dashboard using social media monitoring software such as Meltwater, Crimson Hexagon, Social Studio, or countless other social listening and monitoring platforms, organizations can see when a crisis may be emerging. During the crisis, active social listening and monitoring can help practitioners develop keyword strings based on the issue(s) so they can be tracked and analyzed, providing an understanding of what is being said and by whom. In addition, companies need to build dashboards for specific issues, monitor the frequency with which the brand is being mentioned and in what context, and then formulate a response in real time based on the data coming through.

Paramount in determining the nature of the crisis communications remediation plan, practitioners must identify and actively monitor relevant conversations fueling the communications crisis, the people engaging in the conversation, and which social channels are most predominant. When practitioners understand the genesis of the communications crisis, they can better assess and determine options on how best to respond. Proper identification, which also helps an organization determine whether a full communications crisis is unfolding on social media, is invaluable as teams decide next steps and formulate the response strategy.

Impact Evaluation

Constant monitoring is essential to ensure that practitioners can assess a communications crisis and evaluate the potential impact. Teams triaging the crisis should create a log to determine what issue(s) are of highest priority and require immediate attention versus those that are less urgent. The two primary audiences that brands should pay close attention to are those directly impacted by the crisis and those whose attitudes about the organization could be influenced.[7] Determining which group is being impacted more directly will help guide decisions when constructing a plan of action.

Practitioners handling the communications crisis need to continually use social listening insights to assess if the engagement plan is working or if any new issues are arising. Jeff Hunt, author of *Brand Under Fire*, says that there has been a shift from the 24-hour news cycle to what he calls the "nanosecond news cycle."[8] In this nanosecond news cycle, organizations are not always prepared and therefore lose control of the situation and the narrative. Brands are unnerved. CEOs lose their jobs. Companies dissolve. By continually monitoring social media and evaluating conversations and discourse, teams can assess the issues and manage the crisis with precision. And in today's world, that means having the skills and tools to harness insights from social data and analytics capabilities that will support teams in making informed decisions.

Crisis Management

Acting fast and responding to issues as they arise, often in real time on social media, is the job of today's crisis communications practitioner. Establishing an initial response is key, but then the focus should shift toward ensuring there is continuity of messages across all traditional and social channels. Social media has become an unrelenting threat to organizations as it allows the public to spread information to a larger audience at a much faster rate. What we love so much about social media on any ordinary day—people sharing our products or telling others about our good deeds—becomes a detriment to our brand during a crisis. Through social media, people have the power to voice their opinions; however, they may also intentionally (or not) circulate rumors, false information they may have thought to be true, all leading to misinformation sharing and proliferation.

To deal with these inevitable circumstances, it is essential that organizations establish crisis communications protocols in advance. Having a "war room" that serves as the command and control center allows the team to focus on what's happening. Team members involved in crisis communications remediation should clearly understand their roles and responsibilities, to ensure swift and coordinated response triage actions during a crisis. Some steps to consider: create a content plan that include key messages, identify influencers who may be able to work with you to get messaging out, cultivate a list of traditional media partners, and develop a schedule of who's doing what and when.

Post-crisis

When the crisis subsides, it is time for the team to conduct a retrospective to evaluate the actions taken, assess what worked well, and understand how to modify to improve protocols in preparation for the next issue. Conducting a post-crisis review and synopsis include the following elements:

- Executive summary—recap what happened in enough detail so that C-level executives can understand the severity and implications of the issues.
- News and social media cycle analysis—summarize the news cycle and how the crisis unfolded on both traditional and social media.
- Engagement analytics—provide an analysis of the effectiveness of the engagement and execution plan. For example, examine emails sent, offline media coverage garnered, company statements, and all social mentions—including tweets, snaps, blog comments, pins, videos, Facebook updates, and any other online media mentions.
- Actions taken—summarize what was accomplished to remediate and triage during the crisis. Include everything from who was on the crisis communications management team to individual pieces of content sent.
- What happens next—outline the "new normal" for the company. There is a notion that companies will simply "return to business as usual" after a crisis. This does not exist. There is no "normal." There is, however, a *new normal.* So, explain in detail what that is and what that means for the organization moving forward.[9]

Crises are stressful. They do, however, present an opportunity for brands to understand their resilience in the face of adversity. Not all brands can rise to the challenge. See what happened to Papa John's when they fell under public scrutiny.

Papa John's Fumbling to Recover

The goal of every business is, at the end of the day, to be profitable. But a crisis hit when John Schnatter, CEO of famed pizza company Papa John's, began criticizing the NFL for their lack of aggressive response to players taking a knee during the national anthem, and their stock fell more than 33 percent. Schnatter's comments were not received well by those on the social web: the public believed that racism was behind them. The company began fumbling to save their reputation and minimize damage. They released this series of tweets to apologize for Schnatter's comments:[10]

> "The statements made on our earnings call were describing the factors that impact our business and we sincerely apologize to anyone that thought they were divisive. That definitely was not our intention."
> "We believe in the right to protest inequality and support the players' movement to create a new platform for change. We also believe together, as Americans, we should honor our anthem. There is a way to do both."
> "We will work with the players and league to find a positive way forward. Open to ideas from all. Except neo-nazis—[middle finger emoji] those guys."[11]

However, the damage was done. The apology was in vain. In the end, Schnatter stepped down after admitting during a conference call that his comment was indeed a racial slur, but not before the company suffered severe reputation damage as well as a loss in profits.

ANTICIPATING CRISIS WITH ANALYTICS

This chapter shows that brands have the ability to predict when a crisis might occur on social media, or at least see abnormalities brewing in the social sphere. Implementing the LUPE model, let's take a closer look at a how Starbucks used data to turn their crisis into an opportunity.

Turning Crises into Opportunities: Examining the Effectiveness of Starbucks' Responses to Its Philadelphia Crisis

By Yang Cheng, Ingrid Laprea, and Haddon Mackie, North Carolina State University

Starbucks was founded by Howard Schultz in 1971 in Seattle, Washington with one location and selling only high-quality coffee beans.[1] In 1987, the owners sold Starbucks to Howard Schultz, who quickly expanded and soon after started selling a selection of premium brewed coffees as well as coffee beans, drawing his inspiration from Italian coffee houses.[2] Starbucks, as an iconic global brand with the motto "expect more than coffee," aims to provide customers with a full and rewarding coffeehouse experience and it further expanded its products and services to include a selection of premium teas, fine pastries and "other delectable treats to

---

[1]"About Us," Starbucks, https://www.starbucks.com/about-us/company-information.

[2]Starbucks, Starbucks.com.

please the taste buds."[3] Total revenue in 2017 was over $22 billion.[4] Howard Schultz retired in 2017, and Kevin Johnson is currently the CEO.[5]

Listen and Learn

Starbucks ranks high in brand recognition and is highly visible on social media around the world.[6] This company actively apply social media to listen to what consumers are saying about their brand, products, and the market trends. As Reuben Arnold, Starbucks' vice-president of marketing and product in EMEA said, "Listening outside our own channels is important."[7] Social media platforms allowed Starbucks to monitor the direction of conversations, timely understand consumers, and make strategic decisions accordingly. Effective social listening helps Starbucks to learn from their recent Philadelphia crisis and react quickly via social monitoring, intelligence gathering, and sentiment analysis.

On April 12, 2018, a video of two African-American men being arrested in a Starbucks store located in Philadelphia went viral. The video was first posted by a witness on Twitter, where the public perceived the incident as an act of racial prejudice. The incident immediately sparked public outrage, triggering heated protests outside the store and called for a boycott.[8] A more extended video was posted on YouTube that reached approximately a million views.[9]

RESEARCH GOALS: Based on the context of this above-mentioned crisis, this case study aims to investigate Starbucks' crisis responses, strategies, and effectiveness during and after this crisis. As a supplement to the ongoing social media listening that Starbucks was conducting, this research demonstrates that it is essential for a brand to invest in social listening and monitoring to track, engage, and manage online conversations with customers. Furthermore, it supports the argument that ongoing social media monitoring that Starbuck was conducting can help to react to a crisis timely and repair its brand image on the right track.

PRIORITIZE REQUIREMENTS AND FIELD THE RESEARCH: Results from social media sentiment and content analyses of online conversations on Twitter identified both corporate financial and social media performance during and after the crisis. Findings demonstrated the important role of Chief Executive Officer's (CEO) personalities in corporate social-mediated crises by specifically examining the unique response via his crisis prevention strategies. Results of this study also enhanced students' understanding of the impact of social media coverage on corporates' core values and policies, and the importance of timely responses to tackle crises.

---

[3]Starbucks, Starbucks.com.

[4]Starbucks, Starbucks.com.

[5]Starbucks, Starbucks.com.

[6]"Starbucks Hits Lowest Perception Mark in 25 Years after Philadelphia Incident," BrandIndex, 2018, accessed December 11, 2018, http://www.brandindex.com/article/starbucks-hits-lowest-perception-mark-25-years-after-philadelphia-incident.

[7]S. Vizard, "Starbucks Explores Dark Social for Market Research," MarketingWeek, 2019, accessed October, 22, 2019, https://www.marketingweek.com/starbucks-social-market-research/.

[8]Siegel, R and Horton A. (2018, April 17) Starbucks CEO Meets with 2 Black Men Arrested at Philadelphia Store. The Chicago Tribune https://www.chicagotribune.com/nation-world/ct-starbucks-ceo-meets-with-arrested-men-20180417-story.html

[9]Guardian News, "Social Media Video Shows Arrests of Black Men at Philadelphia Starbucks," April 15, 2018, YouTube, https://www.youtube.com/watch?v=xWBVxTEgoYk.

(continued)

Understand

ANALYSIS: Before the crisis, Starbucks kept their daily monitoring brand items such as customer sentiments and engagement, emotions toward the brand, and follower counts in the current and new markets etc.[10] The preliminary analysis found that 89 percent of posts maintained neutral or positive orientation toward Starbucks within one month before the crisis. During the incident, 106,920 mentions of #BoycottStarbucks were posted across social platforms such as Facebook, Twitter, and Instagram between May 26–29.[11] Starbucks announced an unprecedented response: 8000 Starbucks' stores would be closed on May 29 to conduct unconscious racial bias training.[12]

GOALS: This study aims to investigate Starbucks' crisis responses and measure effectiveness during and after the crisis. Social media sentiment and content analyses should be used to identify both corporate financial and social media performance.

OBJECTIVES: Since the building of this brand, Starbucks focuses on providing high-quality products and exceptional customer service. Starbucks' corporate culture is welcoming everyone. Today the organizational goal remains the same: "inspire and nurture the human spirit—one person, one cup, and one neighborhood at a time."[13] Starbucks locations strive to be a place for people to not only enjoy wonderful coffee but a place to connect with one another: "We make sure everything we do is through the lens of humanity—from our commitment to the highest quality coffee in the world, to the way we engage with our customers and communities to do business responsibly."[14]

Plan

TARGET AUDIENCE: Today Starbucks has 28,218 locations distributed in 77 countries and 238,000 employees.[15] They serve near to one hundred million customers a week.[16] The product selection has expanded to include coffee beverages, smoothies, tea, baked goods, and sandwiches as well as 8 subsidiary brands.[17] To repair images during and after this Philadelphia crisis, Starbucks' target audience includes current customers and prospective customers, especially those who are victims in the crisis.

CRISIS STRATEGIES AND TACTICS: Only two days after the incident, Starbucks posted an apologetic response on social media.[18] From the beginning, every

---

[10]S. Vizard, "Starbucks Explores Dark Social."

[11]C. Zara, "Here's How Quickly "Boycott Starbucks" Spread Across the Internet," *Fast Company*, April 18, 2018, accessed December 2, 2018, https://www.fastcompany.com/40560741/heres-how-quickly-boycott-starbucks-spread-across-the-Internet.

[12]D. Arkin, "Starbucks Will Temporarily Close 8,000 U.S. Stores for Racial-Bias Training," NBC News, April 17, 2018, accessed December 2, 2018, https://www.nbcnews.com/news/us-news/starbucks-will-temporarily-close-8-000-u-s-stores-racial-n866746.

[13]Starbucks, Starbucks.com.

[14]Ted Marzilli, "Starbucks at 10-Year Workplace Reputation Low, Yougov.com, May 29, 2018, accessed December 2, 2018, https://today.yougov.com/topics/food/articles-reports/2018/05/29/starbucks-10-year-workplace-reputation-low.

[15]Starbucks, Starbucks.com.

[16]Starbucks, Starbucks.com.

[17]Starbucks, Starbucks.com.

[18]Starbucks, "A Follow-Up Message from Starbucks CEO in Philadelphia," Facebook, https://www.facebook.com/Starbucks/videos/10156348146748057/.

Starbucks Coffee ✔ @Starbucks · Apr 14, 2018

We apologize to the two individuals and our customers for what took place at our Philadelphia store on Thursday.

> We apologize to the two individuals and our customers and are disappointed this led to an arrest. We take these matters seriously and clearly have more work to do when it comes to how we handle incidents in our stores. We are reviewing our policies and will continue to engage with the community and the police department to try to ensure these types of situations never happen in any of our stores.

○ 16.3K   ⟲ 15.4K   ♡ 18.6K   ⬆

Starbucks crisis responses on Twitter

Starbucks' communicative approach centered on the purpose of apologizing and they stood on the side of the victim, which let the stakeholders know that Starbucks was actively trying to keep this incident from happening again.

CEO Kevin Johnson took full responsibility for the incident and stated: "this is a managerial issue, and I am accountable for it."[19] Starbucks continued to reiterate this message in its responses posted on social media, which clearly demonstrates that they did not condone or try to justify what happened. Starbucks proceeded to respond to all comments that were posted, regardless of the comments sentiment or position, reiterating the fact that the actions and larger issue were to be taken seriously, Starbucks was in the wrong, and voiced continued support for the victims of racial bias.

COMPENSATION TO THE VICTIMS. After meeting with the mayor, police chief, Starbucks' CEO, and other city leaders, the two men that were arrested reached a confidential financial settlement with Starbucks. The men also received a symbolic $1 each and a $200,000 pledge to fund a program for young entrepreneurs from the city of Philadelphia.[20] The program aims to teach youth "not only about entrepreneurship, but also etiquette and financial literacy."[21] In an interview with ABC's *Good Morning America* on May 2, Nelson, one of the two men explained that they would be participating in Starbucks' company-wide racial bias training on May 29.[22] Nelson emphasized the response being made by commenting: "The fact that we have a seat at the table, to work on reforms, to be included in racial bias

---

[19]Ibid.

[20]A. Jenkins, "'We Took a Negative and Turned It into a Positive': Black Men Arrested at Starbucks Speak Out After Reaching Settlement," *Fortune*, May 3, 2018, https://fortune.com/2018/05/03/black-men-starbucks-philadelphia-settlement/.

[21]Ibid.

[22]Arkin, "Starbucks Will Temporarily Close."

(continued)

**Joint Statement from
Starbucks ceo, Kevin
Johnson, Donte Robinson
and Rashon Nelson**

May 02, 2018 · 2 min read

SHARE f ✶ in ☷

PHILADELPHIA (MAY 2, 2018) –
After constructive conversations, and mediation before a retired
federal judge in Philadelphia, Donte Robinson, Rashon
Nelson and Kevin Johnson, ceo of Starbucks Coffee Company
(NASDAQ:SBUX) reached a settlement agreement earlier this week
that will allow both sides to move forward and continue to talk and
explore means of preventing similar occurrences at any Starbucks
location.

The agreement between the parties stems from the arrest of
Robinson and Nelson at a Starbucks store in Philadelphia on April 12
and includes a confidential financial settlement as well as a
commitment to continued listening and dialogue between the
parties as a means toward developing specific actions and
opportunities.

As Johnson said previously, "I want to thank Donte and Rashon for
their willingness to reconcile. I welcome the opportunity to begin a
relationship with them to share learnings and experiences. And
Starbucks will continue to take actions that stem from this incident
to repair and reaffirm our values and vision for the kind of company
we want to be."

Robinson and Nelson intend to focus the public reaction to their
arrest toward providing opportunities for young people from
underserved communities.

Joint Statement from Starbucks CEO Kevin Johnson, Donte Robinson, and Rashon Nelson From Starbucks Stories, May 2, 2018, https://stories.starbucks.com/press/2018/joint-statement-from-kevin-johnson-donte-robinson-and-rashon-nelson/.

training, and hopefully other companies will take what Starbucks is putting into perspective, and [they'll] follow."[23]

TRAINING DAY. On May 29, 2018, Starbucks mandated that 175,000 employees should participate in the mandatory racial bias education and training program that was conducted at thousands of U.S. locations. "Gathered around a few iPads at locations around the nation, Starbucks employees watched nearly two dozen videos featuring the rapper Common, documentary filmmaker Stanley Nelson, Starbucks executives and other prominent figures, while participating in wide-ranging discussions about race and identity with their colleagues."[24] "They reflected by themselves, in pairs and as a group, on the meaning of bias. They privately jotted down thoughts in a customized notebook outfitted with prompts about identity and race. They ran through scenarios that may elicit a

> *"Our hope is that these learning sessions and discussions will make a difference within and beyond our stores. After May 29, we will make the curriculum available to the public and share it with the regions as well as our licensed and business partners. Starbucks is a company built on nurturing the human spirit, and it's on us to harness our scale and expertise to do right by the communities we serve. May 29 isn't a solution, it's a first step. By educating ourselves on understanding bias and how it affects our lives and the lives of the people we encounter and serve, we renew our commitment to making the third place welcoming and safe for everyone."*

Starbucks crisis response on May 29, 2018 From D. Wienner-Bronner, "Starbucks Racial Bias Training Went Down," CNN.com, May 29, 2018, https://money.cnn.com/2018/05/29/news/companies/anti-bias-training-starbucks/index.html.

---

[23] Jenkins, "We Took a Negative."

[24] J. Calfas, "Was Starbucks' Racial Bias Training Effective? Here's What These Employees Thought," *Time*, updated May 30, 2018, http://time.com/5294343/starbucks-employees-racial-bias-training/.

biased reaction. They practiced welcoming behaviors and committed to changing their habits for the better."[25]

Once the training was completed, the company made the curriculum available to the public via the website www.starbuckschannel.com. There, Starbucks posted the whole presentation, along with the activities of the employees from that day. The curriculum was developed with the guidance of several national and local experts on confronting racial bias, including "Bryan Stevenson, Founder and Executive Director of the Equal Justice Initiative; Sherrilyn Ifill, President and Director-Counsel of the NAACP Legal Defense and Education Fund; Heather McGhee, President of Demos; former U.S. Attorney General, Eric Holder; and Jonathan Greenblatt, CEO of the Anti-Defamation League."[26] "Starbucks will involve these experts in monitoring and reviewing the effectiveness of the measures we undertake. Closing our stores for racial bias training is just one step in a journey that requires dedication from every level of our company and partnerships in our local communities," Johnson said in an official statement.[27]

THE THIRD-PLACE POLICY. Before the incident, Starbucks had an unclear policy about space usage. For instance, it did not specify whether it was prohibited from customers to use restrooms or if patrons could sit inside without making a purchase, and it allowed individual stores to set their own rules.[28]

On May 19, Starbucks announced an update of their customer policy: *"After investigating what happened, we determined that insufficient support and training, a company policy that defined customers as paying patrons—versus anyone who enters a store—and bias led to the decision to call the police. Our CEO, Kevin Johnson, met with the two men to express our deepest apologies, reconcile and commit to ongoing actions to reaffirm our guiding principles."*[29]

Howard Schultz stated in a letter posted on the newsroom's website: *"The incident has prompted us to reflect more deeply on all forms of bias, the role of our stores in communities and our responsibility to ensure that nothing like this happens again at Starbucks. The reflection has led to a long-term commitment to reform system-wide policies, while elevating inclusion and equity in all we do."*[30]

TIMELINE OF STARBUCKS' CRISIS RESPONSES: Starbucks provided different types of responses such as sending the first Twitter post and apology letter between April 13 and May 29, 2018. Below we list details of important dates during and after the crisis.

---

[25]D. Wienner-Bronner, "How Starbucks Racial Bias Training Went Down," CNN.com, May 29, 2018, accessed December 2, 2018, https://money.cnn.com/2018/05/29/news/companies/anti-bias-training-starbucks/index.html.

[26]Starbucks, "Curriculum Released for 'The Third Place: Our Commitment, Renewed,'" Starbucks Stories, May 29, 2018, https://stories.starbucks.com/stories/2018/curriculum-for-the-third-place-our-commitment-renewed/.

[27]Arkin, "Starbucks Will Temporarily Close."

[28]M. Gajanan, "Want to Use the Starbucks Bathroom? These Are Your Rights," *Time*, April 16, 2018, https://time.com/5241671/starbucks-philadelphia-bathroom-rights/.

[29]Starbucks Newsroom, "Starbucks Announces 100 Percent Gender, Racial Pay Equity for U.S. Partners, Sets Global Commitment," Starbucks Stories, March 21, 2018, https://news.starbucks.com/news/starbucks-pay-equity-for-partners.

[30]Starbucks, "An Open Letter to Starbucks Customers from Executive Chairman Howard Schultz," Starbucks Stories, May 29, 2018, https://news.starbucks.com/news/an-open-letter-to-starbucks-customers-from-howard-schultz.

(continued)

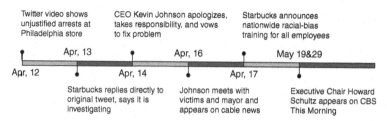

Timeline of the Starbucks crisis

—April 12, a video of two black men being arrested in a Starbucks store located in Philadelphia went viral.

—April 13, Starbucks posted the first response on Twitter replying to the original post: *"We're reviewing the incident with our partners, law enforcement and customers to determine what took place and led to this unfortunate result."*[31]

—April 14, Starbucks posted a new response on its Twitter account apologizing to the two men and to the customers: *"We apologize to the two individuals and our customers and are disappointed this led to an arrest. We take these matters seriously and clearly have more work to do when it comes to how we handle incidents in our stores. We are reviewing our policies and will continue to engage with the community and the police department to try to ensure these types of situation never happen in any of our stores."*[32]

—April 16, Starbucks released the first official letter of apology on its website and Facebook page, in which they conveyed three key aspects: *"First, to once again express our deepest apologies to the two men who were arrested with a goal of doing whatever we can to make things right. Second, to let you know of our plans to investigate the pertinent facts and make any necessary changes to our practices that would help prevent such an occurrence from ever happening again. And third, to reassure you that Starbucks stands firmly against discrimination or racial profiling."*[33]

—April 17, Starbucks posted a follow-up video on Facebook in which Johnson apologizes to the two men arrested, to the community of Philadelphia, and to the Starbucks partners.

- He then states: *"This is not who we are, and it is not who we are gonna be. We will learn from this, and we will be better for it."*[34]

[31] Starbucks, Twitter post, April 13, 2018, https://twitter.com/starbucks/status/984996627759837185?lang=en.

[32] Starbucks, "Starbucks Response to Incident in Our Philadelphia Store," Starbucks Stories, April 14, 2018, https://stories.starbucks.com/press/2018/starbucks-response-incident-in-philadelphia-store/.

[33] Starbucks, "Open Letter."

[34] Starbucks, "A Follow-Up Message."

- He also states the next steps to be taken: *"Changes to the policy, and the practice, additional store-manager training, including training around unconscious bias."*[35]

- Johnson ends the video taking full responsibility for the incident: *"this is a management issue, and I am accountable to ensure we address the policy, practice, and training that led to this outcome."*[36]

The video was viewed more than three million times, shared more than 50,000 times and received more than 12,000 comments.

—April 17, Starbucks CEO met in Philadelphia with the two men arrested, the mayor, police commissioner, and other community members were also present (Associated Press, CBSNews, 4/17/18).[37]

—April 17, Starbucks announced they would close "more than 8,000 company-owned stores in the United States on the afternoon of May 29 to conduct racial-bias education geared toward preventing discrimination in our stores. The training will be provided to nearly 175,000 partners (employees) across the country and will become part of the onboarding process for new partners."[38]

—May 2, Starbucks announces in a press release that they reached a confidential financial settlement with the two victims: *"After constructive conversations, Donte Robinson, Rashon Nelson and Kevin Johnson, CEO of Starbucks Coffee Company reached an agreement earlier this week. The agreement between the parties stemming from the events in Philadelphia on April 12 will include a financial settlement as well as continued listening and dialogue between the parties and specific action and opportunity."*[39]

—May 19, Starbucks announces the updated third-place policy on its website: *"any person who enters our spaces, including patios, cafes and restrooms, regardless of whether they make a purchase, is considered a customer."*[40]

—May 29, Starbucks closes locations for racial-bias training. *"We'll see you tomorrow. Our stores (and mobile ordering) are closing this afternoon. We are closing early as our team reconnect with our mission and each other."*[41]

Execute and Evaluate

SOCIAL MEDIA PERFORMANCE BEFORE AND AFTER CRISIS RESPONSES: The video of the two men being arrested was first posted on Twitter on April 12. The post sparked rapid conversation in response to the issue. Content analysis via Crimson Hexagon found that 48 percent of the comments had a negative sentiment, 38 percent were

---

[35]Ibid.

[36]Ibid.

[37]Associated Press, "Starbucks CEO Meets with Men Arrested in Viral Video," CBS News, April 17, 2018, https://www.cbsnews.com/news/starbucks-arrest-video-company-ceo-meets-with-black-men-arrested-philadelphia-2018-04-16/.

[38]"About Us," Starbucks.

[39]Johnson, Robinson, and Nelson, "Joint Statement."

[40]Starbucks, "Use of the Third Place Policy," Starbucks Stories, May 19, 2018, https://stories.starbucks.com/press/2018/use-of-the-third-place-policy/

[41]Starbucks, "Starbucks Response to Incident."

(continued)

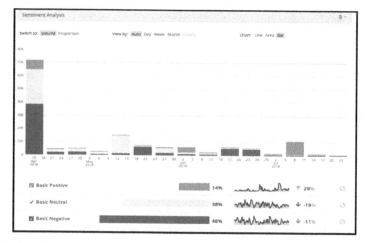

Results of Starbucks social media sentiment analysis showing basic negative responses

neutral, and only 14 percent had positive connotations. Of those negative tweets, the most popular sentiments expressed in the comments was disgust and sadness. After April 17, the conversation decreases from over than 70,000 to less than 10,000.

After the training, the posts were not as abundant, but those that were present had more positive than negative sentiment connotations. However, from the total post, 62 percent had a neutral emotion. After the closing, most comments were either positive or neutral.

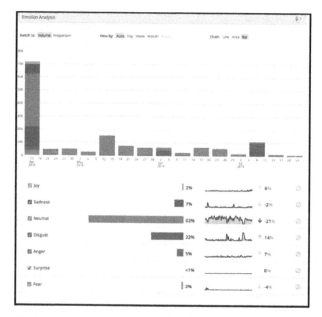

Results of Starbucks social media emotional analysis depicting mostly sadness, neutral feeling, and disgust from the public

Word clouds depicting the most used words related from the incident

In over 135,000 posts from the day the video was posted on Twitter and the following days, the words most related to the incident were #boycottstarbucks, blackmen, pay@starbucks etc. While the typical mentioned word cloud about Starbucks on social media before the crisis (March 11–April 11, 2018) included coffeelover, coffeetime, happy, and fashion. After Starbucks decided to close their stores for unconscious bias training on April 17, 2018, the words were related to the brand such as @Starbucks, wesupport45, training etc.

On April 14, Commissioner Richard Ross gave a statement about the incident: "When police arrived after receiving a 911 call from the Starbucks employees, they asked the two men three times politely to leave because they were trespassing. And instead, the males continued to refuse . . . they continued having the attitude they had with the Starbucks employees, insisting that they were not leaving . . . Policemen were call there for a service. These officers did absolutely nothing wrong, they followed the policy, they did what they were supposed to do. I must say, as an African-American men, that I am very aware of implicit bias, but in this case, they did nothing wrong, they did the service that were called to do."[42]

STARBUCKS' FINANCIAL PERFORMANCE BEFORE AND AFTER THE PHILADELPHIA CRISIS: In 2017, Starbucks was ranked third on *Fortune* Magazine's list of most admired companies in the world and was the number one company in the food service industry.[43] This was the company's highest ranking on the list and it has

---

[42]Philadelphia Police, "Ross just gave a statement on the 4-12-18," Twitter post, April 14, 2018, https://twitter.com/phillypolice/status/985216408991739904?lang=en.

[43]Kate Taylor, "Starbucks Is Set to Lose $12 Million by Closing Stores for Racial-Bias Training, but It's Still a Brilliant Business Idea," *Business Insider*, May 29, 2018, https://www.businessinsider.com/starbucks-racial-bias-training-is-good-business-2018-5.

(continued)

Philadelphia Police ☑
@PhillyPolice

(Seguir)   ⌄

.@ppdcommish **Ross just gave a statement on the 4-12-18 @Starbucks incident. You can watch it here:**

⟳ Traducir Tweet

Philadelphia Police Department
Commissioner Richard Ross gives a statement on the incident that occurred 4-12-18 at the Starbucks at 18th and Spruce Streets
facebook.com

8:01 - 14 abr. 2018

Official Philadelphia Police Twitter response to Starbucks incident

been included on the list every year since 2003. *Fortune* calls the list "the definitive report card on corporate reputations," which it has published since 1983.[44]

In May of 2018, after it closed 8,000 stores for anti-bias training, Starbucks dropped to its lowest reputation metric in 10 years according to the YouGov Brandindex scores.[45] YouGov's BrandIndex surveys 4,800 people each weekday and defines workplace reputation as the positive or negative feelings a person gets when asked if they would want to be associated with a company. In the weeks after the arrests in April of 2018, the brand's purchase consideration, which is defined as a metric concerning the opportunity for sales revenue, also hit lower-than-usual levels. The buzz around Starbucks, or what people are saying about it, took a sharp dive after the arrests, but has since climbed slightly, though nowhere near the level it was before. Ted Marzilli, CEO of YouGov Data Products, said the results are "a tough message for a company that's well-known for its employee benefits and culture" in an article by Diana Pearl published in Adweek.[46] According to Pew social trends report, comparing McDonald's and Starbucks, Starbucks was found to be favored over McDonald's by higher income white consumers.[47]

Starbucks' financial performance over time has remained high, with a slight dip during the controversy in 2015 and the crisis in April of 2018.

HARVEST RESULTS: Through social listening and monitoring, this case study presented Starbucks' crisis communication strategies and examined the effectiveness of those responses during and after the Philadelphia crisis. Results indicated that when the level of dissent around incidences of racial bias in America has sparked intense public backlash, the timely response demonstrated by Starbucks and the level of personal accountability that the CEO presented in the response statements have neutralized negative public perceptions effectively. Additionally, Starbucks took immediate action that sent a clear message that they prioritized this issue

[44] A. Jenkins, "We Took a Negative."

[45] Marzilli, "Starbucks at 10-year Low."

[46] Diana Pearl, "Just Before Closing Stores for Racial-Sensitivity training, Starbucks' Reputation Hit a 10-Year Low," *Adweek*, June 4, 2018, https://www.adweek.com/brand-marketing/starbucks-workplace-reputation-at-10-year-low/.

[47] Ibid.

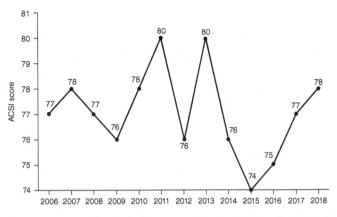

American customer satisfaction index scores of Starbucks in the United States from 2006 to 2018

over profits and public opinion from those that belittled the issue. Shutting down the stores as part of their crisis image repair strategies also doubled as a prevention strategy. This philosophy of crisis management has been consistent with its business operations when Starbucks expanded across the United States and all over the world. Conducting business ethically is an aspect that Starbucks believes is vital to its success. By providing their franchise partners with the resources to make ethical decisions at work, Starbucks asserted its ability to foster a culture that was committed to moral leadership and conducting business with integrity. They did this by encouraging partners to speak up if they had questions and advising leaders on ethical business practices.

Meanwhile, updating third-place policy after the crisis can be seen as an example of effective response to public stakeholders on social media, which influenced the company's core values and policies as well. Similarly, Starbucks' crisis responses such as internal training and educational programs are successfully for image repair and crisis prevention. In sum, due to the significant role that racial injustice has had in American culture and the size of Starbucks, this data-driven case study provides insights into how a CEO and franchise stores can manage and respond to crises of racial bias and policy injustice. Corporations in future crises are recommended to conduct ongoing social media listening and learning to implement and optimize their strategic responses for successful business outcomes.

CONCLUSION

With approximately 36 million negative posts circulating daily on the Internet, it's surprising that brands aren't in crisis mode more often.[12] Using social listening and analytics techniques to make sense of the plethora of data shared on the social web helps practitioners before, during, and after any crisis. Jeff Bodzewski, a contributing author of the edited volume *The New Rules of Crisis Management*, identifies four key sources of web analytics to help practitioners when a crisis happens:[13]

- **Referral Traffic:** A tiered list of all the external websites, including media, influencer and brand sites, where visitors to your website are coming from.
- **Search Traffic:** A complete list of the organic search terms that are taking people to your website.
- **Outgoing Links:** A list of the websites that people visit next AFTER your site, including social, e-commerce, media, law firms and other relevant organizations.
- **Site Visitors:** Demographic, geographic and other data about who is spending time on your website.

Public relations, marketing, and advertising practitioners already know that to succeed on social, media brands must be authentic, transparent, fast, agile, and creative. This does not change during a crisis. Keeping a level head and looking at the data will help the crisis team make sound decisions.

DISCUSSION QUESTIONS AND EXERCISES

1. Explain how analytics and data help in anticipating a crisis.
2. What are the stages of a crisis?
3. What techniques are used to anticipate and manage crisis using analytics?
4. How does a brand's audience factor into modern-day crisis communications?
5. Crisis can take many forms. How can practitioners prepare for the inevitable?
6. *Small group exercise:* Compare and contrast how Starbucks dealt with their crisis versus how Papa John's handled their issue. Ask yourself the following: how do you think each company did in managing their crisis? What suggestions would you have for them in the future should another crisis happen? Then outline what their crisis plan should have entailed. Discuss with a classmate the pros and cons.

KEY TERMS

Crisis management   Share of voice

NOTES

1. AON and Pentland Analytics, *Reputation Risk in the Cyber Age: The Impact on Shareholder Value* (N.p.: AON, 2018), https://www.aon.com/getmedia/2882e8b3-2aa0-4726-9efa-005af9176496/Aon-Pentland-Analytics-Reputation-Report-2018-07-18.pdf?utm_source=aoncom&utm_medium=storypage&utm_campaign=reprisk2018.
2. Ibid.
3. Cambridge Dictionary, "Crisis management," https://dictionary.cambridge.org/us/dictionary/english/crisis-management.
4. Regina Luttrell, *Social Media How to Engage, Share, and Connect,* 3rd ed. (Lanham, MD: Roman & Littlefield, 2016).
5. Institute for PR, "Crisis Management and Communications," Institute for Public Relations, February 20, 2007, https://instituteforpr.org/crisis-management-and-communications/.

6. Chuck Hemann and Ken Burbary, *Digital Marketing Analytics*, 2nd ed. (N.p.: Pearson Education, 2018).

7. Luttrell, *Social Media*.

8. Jeff Hunt, Geoff Levenworth, and Thom Lemmons, *Brand Under Fire* (N.p.: Ordnance Hill, 2018).

9. Regina Luttrell and Adrienne A. Wallace, "The Secret to Modern Crisis Response Success," PR Daily, December 20, 2019, https://www.prdaily.com/the-secret-to-modern-crisis-response-success/.

10. Tory Brecht, "Papa John's: We Didn't Mean to Be 'Divisive' on NFL Protests," *WQAD 8 News*, November 17, 2017, https://wqad.com/2017/11/15/papa-johns-we-didnt-mean-to-be-divisive-on-nfl-protests/.

11. Regina F. Graham, "Papa John's Apologizes for Criticizing NFL Anthem Protests," Daily Mail Online, November 15, 2017, https://www.dailymail.co.uk/news/article-5084157/Papa-Johns-apologizes-criticizing-NFL-anthem-protests.html.

12. RockDove Solutions, "The Role of Data & Analytics in a Crisis Plan," *In Case of Crisis* (blog), accessed 2018, https://www.rockdovesolutions.com/blog/the-role-of-data-and-analytics-in-a-crisis-plan.

13. Ron Culp, ed., *The New Rules of Crisis Management*, 3rd ed. (self-pub., RockDove Solutions, 2018), e-book.

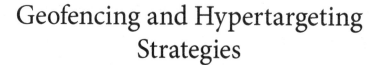

CHAPTER 11

Geofencing and Hypertargeting Strategies

KEY LEARNING OUTCOMES

Describe what it means to "localize" a social media strategy.

Compare and contrast the differences between geo-local and global social media strategies.

Explain how geofencing differs from hypertargeting.

Demonstrate the advantages of using social media hypertargeting techniques.

Explain how the Internet, social media, and mobile device connectivity make geofencing and hypertargeting possible.

Describe how geofencing and hypertargeting can be utilized to drive employee engagement among a geographically dispersed workforce.

HYPERCONNECTED LIFESTYLES

The world has experienced incredible growth from a social standpoint and continues to be increasingly hyperconnected, in large part due to the Internet, expansion in social media platforms, and mobile device connectivity. These capabilities allow individuals to communicate with anyone around the world at a moment's notice. Public relations and marketing professionals are taking advantage of these capabilities to effectively connect with their audiences with increased precision, often in real time. These proficiencies are made possible by techniques known as **geofencing** and **hypertargeting**, which are mobility services allowing users to reach their intended audiences within a specified location, city boundary, or zip code. As implied by its name, a geofence is a virtual perimeter for a real-world geographic area.[1] According to Google, "The geofencing API allows you to define perimeters, also referred to as geofences, which surround the areas of interest. Your app gets a notification when the device crosses a geofence, which allows you to provide a useful experience when users are in the vicinity."[2] A recent Market Research Future report predicts that the global geofencing market will continue to grow, reaching $2.2 billion annually by 2023.[3]

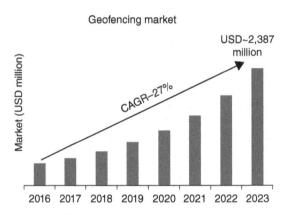

Geofencing market size by million projected to increase through 2023.

LOCATION-BASED MOBILE APPS

Not surprisingly, many top brands are capitalizing on geofencing and hypertargeting technical capabilities through mobile location-based navigation technologies. These platforms allow precision targeting of audiences through social media and popular mobile apps. This chapter explores the fundamentals of how brands and organizations are leveraging and incorporating location-based geofencing and hypertargeting into their localized social media strategies.

Waze: World's Largest Crowdsourced Navigation App

A popular, free navigation-based mobile app, Waze provides users with directions, guidance, and live traffic updates using GPS navigation technologies powered by a community of app users to provide real-time alerts about car accidents, road conditions, police presence, and other hazards. Waze provides public relations and marketing professionals with a straightforward method to implement geofencing and reach an intended target audience. The organization has established a multitude of business partner alliances with well-known consumer brands. Using geofencing strategies, the Waze location-based navigation app even highlights these partners on the guidance map for its users. In fact, Waze uses a brand tagline that conveys their geofencing service as location marketing, made possible by providing brands with the ability to deliver location-based advertising for a business on the Waze map.[4] The application allows a variety of media options that exploit geofencing by serving up advertising within any specified location proximity.

An example of an organization benefiting from Waze geofence targeting is, a popular fuel chain located in California. The brand developed a compelling geofencing campaign called TANK5, in which they targeted California drivers by pinning their recognizable orange and blue logo into the Waze navigation map to alert drivers as they were nearing a 76 fuel station.[5] With the goal of promoting the brand and increasing in-store traffic, the 76 campaign sponsored a contest that gave participants the chance to win a prize at any of the California-based 76 gas stations.[6] As the Waze app detected consumers nearing a 76 station, a message promoting 76 appeared on their display, reminding users of the limited time offer.

Sephora: Personalized Shopping in Real Time

Sephora, a wildly popular beauty brand, appeals to their fashion-forward consumers by offering a retail experience that assists shoppers in discovering the latest in beauty products and trends.[7] By developing an in-store shopping mobile app based on geofencing, called "Store Companion," the brand implemented a location-based solution that presents shoppers with targeted content upon entering a Sephora location, specifically based on each consumer's established preferences.[8] Using this strategy, Sephora can provide individualized discounts or personalized product recommendations based solely on an individual's shopping profile. The mobile Sephora app accesses the real-time location of consumers as they enter a Sephora store and presents shoppers with a variety of options to enhance their overall shopping experience. By leveraging geofencing strategies, the brand aims to influence overall loyalty and satisfaction by providing its target audience with individualized content and location-specific incentives. For example, when a Sephora customer who has an unused gift card enters a particular geofenced location, they will be notified about a nearby store location.

A HYPERCONNECTED WORKFORCE

Hypertargeting allows a brand or organization to target consumers on social media sites through ads that become available only when specific criteria are met.[9] This technological advancement makes precision media targeting possible by leveraging both navigation and location-based services. An individual can be reached based on location even when en route, at any given time, provided they have enabled location tracking in their mobile device.

Furthermore, in recent years, there has been a massive shift in the way that people in the workforce conduct their daily activities. The mobile workforce has arrived and shows no signs of slowing down. As a result of advances in the Internet, social media, and mobile device connectivity, individuals can now essentially work remotely from anywhere with Internet access. Simply put, social technologies have enabled the realities of working remotely by increasing options for staying connected. It should not come as a surprise that since 2005, remote-based working arrangements have been increasingly adopted. A recent study published by Global Workplace Analytics indicated that the instances of remote-based workers has grown 140 percent since 2005, tenfold faster than the growth rate of the entirety of the workforce. Furthermore, these results also highlight a more recent trend related to the widespread adoption of telecommuting, realizing a 22 percent increase between 2017 and 2018.[10] This shift in workplace dynamics has given rise to distributed workforces, which are increasingly commonplace, in which workers rely on the capabilities of the Internet, social networks, and mobile devices to communicate, engage, and collaborate. Organizations, no matter the size, are realizing the benefits of supporting these remote-based work options, such as cost reduction and increased productivity, with social media playing a critical role in this new reality.[11] Social networks are carefully designed to replicate and inspire informal interactions that occur naturally when employees are co-located. Platforms such as LinkedIn, Twitter, Facebook, forums, wikis, and other social networking sites present opportunities for organizations to

- help employees better understand the company's goals, values, and strategy;
- provide managers with simple ways to stay connected with their team members;
- increase the visibility and accessibility of senior leadership;
- allow employees to share ideas and collaborate more effectively; and
- create opportunities for feedback and two-way communication.[12]

More broadly, social media-based technologies provide an opportunity for anyone to join global conversations regarding the latest developments in each industry, profession, or trade. According to a recent Pew Research study, social media platforms promote global connectivity between colleagues and/or organizational resources, oftentimes increasing individual productivity.[13]

One example of an organization that has positively benefited from this evolving workforce by incorporating and utilizing social networking to connect its employees is Sprinklr, a customer experience management software company. Founded by Ragy Thomas in 2009, Sprinklr has experienced rapid growth and proudly identifies itself as a global company with a geographically dispersed workforce. The company provides customer experience management with a unified front-office technology platform across modern social networking channels. Sprinklr's proprietary enterprise software leverages artificial intelligence (AI) and machine learning to support enterprise digital transformation and deliver an enhanced customer experiences (CX).[14]

How Sprinklr Unified Its Globally Distributed Workforce through Hypertargeting to Inspire Employee Engagement

By Dasle Kim, Employee Advocacy Manager, Culture and Internal Communications Strategist at Sprinklr

As the workforce becomes more remote and global, Sprinklr, a provider of customer experience management software, was challenged to engage and activate its network of globally dispersed employees based both remotely and offices locations such as London, New York City, Dubai, and Germany. With the goal of making them feel connected as part of one community and one organization, Sprinklr employed the LUPE model to establish a social media strategy to drive employee engagement and advocacy. Using its own internal advocacy solution, Sprinklr was able to harness the power of its 1,600+ globally dispersed employee workforce to inspire them to actively connect and develop an internal community.

(continued)

This campaign effort is ongoing and based on the promising results, it has proven to effectively enable cross-departmental collaboration and active participation from employees at every level of the organization.

Listen and Learn

Sprinklr began its quest to unify its globally distributed workforce by using its internal social monitoring and listening methodologies to understand what motivates and inspires employees to work at Sprinklr. By tracking public employee sentiment in real-time, Sprinklr was able to use these insights to develop an employment branding and employee advocacy strategy to retain top talent as well as attract new recruits to the fast-growing organization. All employees with @Sprinklr in their Twitter profiles automatically are added to the Sprinklr Employees Profile List. They actively monitor the hashtag #SprinklrLife to listen to employee dialogue as well as other Sprinklr-related hashtags such as location-based hashtags to unify employees in local hubs (e.g. #SprinklrNYC, #SprinklrJP, #SprinklrATX, etc.).

Sprinklr evaluated the state of employee engagement as a bell curve, recognizing their employee base as their target audience and evaluating which social media channels were appropriate to reach the most employees effectively. The team carefully constructed six employee personas. They decided to focus on the largest groups, allowing the hypertargeting effort to leverage the most engaged employees as Sprinklr ambassadors.

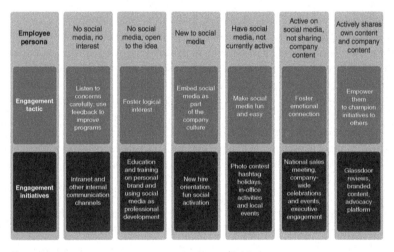

Employee persona	No social media, no interest	No social media, open to the idea	New to social media	Have social media, not currently active	Active on social media, not sharing company content	Actively shares own content and company content
Engagement tactic	Listen to concerns carefully; use feedback to improve programs	Foster logical interest	Embed social media as part of the company culture	Make social media fun and easy	Foster emotional connection	Empower them to champion initiatives to others
Engagement initiatives	Intranet and other internal communication channels	Education and training on personal brand and using social media as professional development	New hire orientation, fun social activation	Photo contest hashtag holidays, in-office activities and local events	National sales meeting, company-wide celebrations and events, executive engagement	Glassdoor reviews, branded content, advocacy platform

Six employee personas, engagement tactics and initiatives

Understand

Analyzing employee conversations to determine unifying attributes trough analysis, Sprinklr mapped the employee community at large to the six personas. This framework would establish a baseline for determining the most impactful engagement tactics for each group.

In order to build momentum, the team needed to understand what would motivate employees from offices located around the world to get involved. What themes would resonate with the culturally diverse employee base to get employees engaged, increase employee participation and brand awareness? What are the unique opportunities that will help the company build a sense of community amongst employees? What would inspire employees to connect internally but also move them to share their employee experience externally in social channels to help build the Sprinklr brand? Initial insights derived through social listening found that Sprinklr employees care deeply about two things: (1) their responsibility to the growth and success of the company and (2) their own pets as well as animals who visit Sprinklr offices.

Plan

To unify employees' shared interests, the team determined that organizing opportunities for employees to take part in events would form both a sense of community and common bond. The team unified around a goal to increase the number of employees (distinct and repeat) engaging with brand handles and hashtags across Sprinklr's social channels. The team developed a strategy oriented around common shared interests in an editorial calendar in which content could be created and distributed according to the theme. Foundational to their strategy was the launch of the photo contest to raise awareness of Sprinklr social channels and make brand engagement with Sprinklr handles a normal routine for employees. Participation rates varied by the type of theme, time of year/business cycle, and the frequency of internal communications. With a goal of reaching a submission target 750 submissions for 2019, the team organized content around key themes:

1. Ongoing: #SprinklrLife and #SprinklrSplash (the Sprinklr onboarding hashtag, named after the Sprinklr new hire orientation called "Splash")
2. February 4—March 31: #SprinklrPets
3. April 14—May 19: #GoTSprinklr (Game of Thrones!)
4. September: #Sprinklr10 (Sprinklr's 10 year anniversary)
5. October: Halloween
6. November: #StacheDontShout (The Sprinklr campaign for the Movember Foundation, nicknamed after one of the Sprinklr company values: "Sprinkle, don't shout.")
7. December: #SprinklrHoliday2019

The team established a plan to create a global Sprinklr birthday celebration that would unite the distributed workforce in the month of September by creating #Sprinklr10. Having a distinct, unique hashtag helped employees to celebrate together their shared purpose and contributions to the company's success. The Sprinklr Culture & Talent (HR) team used insights from social listening to engage employees and motivate them to join in the company's 10th anniversary. They planned birthday parties as office activations, streamed the party on our intranet, and celebrated with colleagues, partners, and customers all over the world. As a result, the teams unified to authentically display the Sprinklr company culture. This resulted in both employee retention by providing each employee with an opportunity to share their unique personal experience and also demonstrated to the world what it's really like to work at Sprinklr.

Execute and Evaluate

Related hashtags such as #Sprinklr10 invited all employees to celebrate the 10th anniversary (birthday) together no matter their location around the globe. Additionally, the Sprinklr team actively monitors employee conversations that specifically mention @Sprinklr and reply to employees from the Sprinklr brand

(continued)

handle, creating a personalized 1:1 connection between the employee and the company. Tactical promotions deployed through social tiles with specific hashtags [e.g., #Sprinklr10].

Social tiles with #Sprinklr10 hashtag

Demonstrated in the accompanying image is an internal Sprinklr Workplace (Facebook @ Work) announcement about #SprinklrPets which was distributed to the employee community through the Company-wide Slack channel and Email.

#SprinklrPets Company Photo Contest

Company Slack message:

Many of you asked, and without further ado, we're excited to announce the very first 2019 theme: #SprinklrPets! 🐷 🐾 🐶 🐹 🐨 🐔 🐱 This is your chance to share your furry (or not so furry) family members in photos while gaining some Sprinklr fame! Please make sure you and/or other Sprinklrites are featured along with your animal friends!

P.S. Special thanks to @evan.bech for the amazing #SprinklrPets graphics! For any questions please contact @Dasle Kim

Company Email message:

Subject: Introducing the #SprinklrPets Photo Contest! 🐷 🐾 🐶 🐹 🐨 🐔 🐱

Ready to see more #SprinklrLife in action?

Thank you for all of your #SprinklrLife photos in 2018—#SprinklrSquad, #SprinklrActive, and #SprinklrGiving! We received 400+ incredible photos and memories of our Sprinklrites that were displayed in our offices all over the world—in real-time!

Many of you asked, and without further ado, we're excited to announce the very first 2019 theme:

#SprinklrPets! 🐷 🐾 🐶 🐹 🐨 🐔 🐱

This is your chance to share your furry (or not so furry) family members in photos while gaining some Sprinklr fame! Please make sure you and/or other Sprinklrites are featured along with your animal friends!

Need some inspiration to get started? Here are some upcoming hashtag holidays you can celebrate this month:

February 20 #LoveYourPetDay

February 22 #WalkYourDogDay

February 23 #DogBiscuitAppreciationDay

February 27 #NationalPokemonDay

Thanks for being a part of our #SprinklrLife. We look forward to your submissions!

From August—December 2018, 415 photo contest entries submitted by Sprinklr employees, with a total budget of $2,650.

Theme	#SprinklrSquad	#SprinklrActive	#SprinklrGiving	Total
Budget ($)	$1,000	$1,250	$400	**$2,650**
# Total Entries	75	226	114	**415**
Twitter	30	53	52	135
Instagram	45	161	39	245
Workplace	N/A	12	23	35

Sprinklr 2018 budget and campaign results.

The newly employed #SprinklrLife related tactics demonstrated a 232 percent increase in unique users of the hashtag within 6 months. Additionally, the content was repurposed for Sprinklr new hire orientation to showcase the company culture during the new employee onboarding process and encourage new recruits to:

- Connect on Twitter + LinkedIn in real-time
- Get introduced to colleagues with shared interest making new hire onboarding more personal and fostering one-to-one connections through direct outreach
- Expedite new hire orientation through quicker, more efficient acclimation techniques and providing new employees to immediately network internally across a distributed workforce
- Inspire long term employees to stay connected throughout their employment at Sprinklr

CONCLUSION

The rise of the Internet and social media make location-based mobile technologies such as geofencing and hypertargeting possible. The ways in which public relations, marketing, and advertising practitioners can tap into the power of location-based abilities to reach audiences with precision are vast. The early adopters of these competencies are effectively integrating these techniques into their strategic development processes to reach their intended target audiences in real time. According to the report Market for Proximity Marketing, the geofencing and hypertargeting markets are expected to be worth upward of $38 billion by 2022.[15]

DISCUSSION QUESTIONS AND EXERCISES

1. Identify and explain the benefits of geofencing and hypertargeting.
2. This chapter covered many aspects of how organizations are inspiring action and employee engagement using hypertargeting. What aspects of using

hypertargeting for connecting a distributed workforce, from the Sprinklr case study, resonated with you most, and why?

3. Using the brand examples provided in this chapter, explain how geofencing provides alternatives to traditional media targeting approaches. What attributes do you believe are most beneficial to reaching audiences with precision?

4. Provide examples of other individuals, organizations, companies, or brands that are utilizing geofencing and hypertargeting in an exemplary fashion. What are the benefits? What is the impact for the consumer?

5. How do you anticipate geofencing and or hypertargeting changing in the future? Explain your reasoning.

6. *Small group exercise:* In groups, valuate a brand that has utilized geofencing and/or hypertargeting to promote either the company or its product/service offerings, and present the benefits the company attained by doing so.

KEY TERMS

geofencing   hypertargeting   location-based

NOTES

1. Google, "Geofencing API," Google Developers, last modified 2019, accessed January 10, 2020, https://developers.google.com/location-context/geofencing.

2. Ibid.

3. "Geofencing Market 2019 Size, Share, Trends and Forecast Report 2023," Market Research Future, accessed December 20, 2019, https://www.marketresearchfuture .com/reports/geofencing-market-4490.

4. "Free Driving Directions and Live Traffic Map App by Waze, a GPS navigation app powered by community. Get driving directions, a live traffic map, road alerts about car accidents, road conditions, police, and hazards," Waze, January 2, 2020, https:// www.waze.com.

5. Marina Kapralau, "Five Examples of Brands Using Geofencing to Great Effect," AList, last modified December 18, 2018, accessed January 10, 2020, https://www.alistdaily .com/technology/five-examples-of-brands-using-geofencing/.

6. Waze, "76 Increased Navigations to Fuel Stations Using a Limited-Time Offer," Waze, last modified 2018, accessed January 10, 2020, https://www.waze.com/brands/ success/76.

7. Andrew Park, "Why Many Brands Are Falling Short on Personalization," Digital Commerce 360, last modified December 9, 2019, accessed January 10, 2020, https://www.digital commerce360.com/2019/12/09/why-many-brands-are-falling-short-on-personalization/.

8. Kapralau, "Five Examples."

9. Raubi Marie Perilli, "What Is Hypertargeting and How Can You Use It to Grow Your Business?," GoDaddy, last modified May 19, 2019, accessed January 10, 2020, https:// www.godaddy.com/garage/what-is-hypertargeting/.

10. Global Workplace Analytics, "A Coworking: A Corporate Real Estate Perspective," Global Workplace Analytics, accessed December 20, 2019, https://globalworkplaceanalytics .com/telecommuting-statistics.

11. Ibid.

12. "Using Social Media to Keep Remote Workers Connected," Davis & Company, accessed December 20, 2019, https://www.davisandco.com/article/using-social-media-keep-remote-workers-connected.

13. Cliff Lampe and Nicole B. Ellison, "How Americans Use Social Media at Work," Pew Research Center: Internet, Science & Tech, March 15, 2017, https://www.pewresearch.org/internet/2016/06/22/social-media-and-the-workplace/.

14. Sprinklr, "The First Unified Front Office for Modern Channels," Sprinklr, last modified 2019, accessed January 10, 2020, https://www.sprinklr.com/; "Customer Experience Management & Unified Front Office." Sprinklr, October 16, 2019. https://www.sprinklr.com/.

15. BIA Advisory Services, "2019 U.S. Local Advertising Forecast," BIA Kelsey, last modified January 2019, accessed January 10, 2020, http://www.biakelsey.com/wp-content/uploads/2019/01/BIA-Briefing-Q1-2019.pdf.

CHAPTER 12

Future Implications
of Data-Driven Decisions

KEY LEARNING OUTCOMES

Understand how data will continue to influence
public relations and marketing.

Establish key data-driven factors that impact an ever-evolving field.

Learn how ethics, big data, and the continued importance
of GDPR will impact brands and consumers.

Assess ethical standards and the persistent emphasis on the field.

Analyze and apply standards of Federal Trade Commission
guidelines for influencer engagement to social media posts.

Evaluate insights from professionals in the field.

A LOOK AHEAD

Technologies will continue to evolve and advance at an unprecedented rate. According to the Chicago Analytics Group, 25 percent of companies cite faster innovation cycles as being the number one factor when using data analytics, followed by improved business efficiencies (17 percent), more effective R&D (13 percent), and an overall impact on product and services (12 percent).[1] Take Netflix, for example. The company saves $1 billion a year maintaining customer satisfaction by mining its immense customer data.[2]

The need for data **big data and analytics (BDA)** to drive public relations and marketing initiatives is paramount for today's practitioners. Due in large part to the advancements in cloud-based software as a service (SaaS) development, the ability to collect, track, and analyze data in real time helps practitioners adjust their campaigns accordingly. As organizations delve deeper into the data-driven aspects of the communications industry, there are several key areas that will undoubtedly impact the future of public relations and marketing.

Ethics in the Profession

Ethics is eminently collective. The voice of reason cannot fall to one person or one department. Collectively, brands, organizations, and businesses—big and small—must be custodians of ethical principles and practices that drive action. As we explored in Chapter 1, the proliferation of data, analytics, and AI has brought about ethical dilemmas for today's marketing and public relations professionals. As AI becomes more deeply embedded in daily life one, must consider the ethical implications.

One overarching argument is that that communications departments should serve as ethical consciences for their organizations.[3] Tech giants Google, Apple, IBM, Microsoft, Amazon, and Facebook are part of nonprofit research consortium called the Partnership on AI. The group attempts to promote and understand the ethical use of artificial intelligence and consumer interface. Eric Horvitz and Mustafa Suleyman, founding co-chairs of the coalition, created the organization because they believe that society is "at an inflection point in the development and application of AI technologies. The upswing in AI competencies, fueled by data, computation, and advances in algorithms for machine learning, perception, planning, and natural language, promise great value to people and society."[4] With these promises though, come great challenges and responsibilities. Nick Statt, a reporter for The Verge, which covers Silicon Valley, gaming, and AI, notes that the Partnership in AI is focused on two main initiatives: (1) educating the public about uses of AI and (2) ensuring industry experts are collaborating on AI best practices while receiving outside council from people like researchers or academics.[5] AI is already present in social media—for example, Facebook uses machine learning to identify your face in photos and promote tagging in others' photos, Snapchat hosts augmented reality filters, and LinkedIn uses AI to part the seas of data to determine what jobs or people you might be interested in connecting to. As such, social media is committed to AI for creating basic content, analysis of data for recommendations, and advertising audience targeting. As such, discussions regarding ethics should be ongoing and involve multiple parties.

On the global stage, discussions surrounding algorithms, artificial intelligence, and ethics are also ongoing.[6] In France, the Commission Nationale de l'Informatique et des Libertés (**CNIL**) a data protection agency, released its report surrounding these issues. The report highlighted six major areas of ethical concern:

1. Autonomous machines as a threat to free will and responsibility
2. Biases, discrimination, and exclusion
3. Algorithmic profiling
4. Discovering a balance in AI regarding personal data
5. Curating quality data; process should be bias free
6. Safeguarding human identity above artificial intelligence

As you can see, the areas highlighted in this report are concerns observed globally and across teams. The priority for public relations, marketing, and advertising practitioners will be to model principled decision making and help strengthen overall ethics within our digitally driven society as these issues continue to evolve.

As public relations, marketing, and advertising practitioners, we must understand the intricacies and implications that data and AI have on our key target audiences. It is our responsibility to act ethically while keeping the consumer top of mind, serving as the collective conscience of our organizations. Now is the time to have conversations surrounding public trust as it relates to emerging technologies that integrate data-driven intelligence into our brand activities. For brands looking to get ahead in this space, create an educated a workforce embedded with AI technologies, and ensure that AI is accessible across economic classes.

Continued Focus on GDPR and Privacy

Governance initiatives will continue to advance globally. Cambridge Analytica and the great Facebook data dump/debacle of 2017–18 was the grand eye-opener that most people needed—for at least a moment—to become more critical of what happens to their personal information when they ignorantly scroll and click through long, seemingly aimless documents like "Terms of Service" agreements and the like to rush to an app install that will tell them "Which Disney Princess are you?" or maybe even "What Harry Potter character are you?"[7] Do you really know what you just agreed to and how the information you opted into is being used?[8]

We have now likely "learned the hard way" that what we hold so dear (our personal information) can and will be used online for illegal or unethical purposes. The mining of consumer personal data—to the tune of more than 50 million users—has been deemed "just the tip of the iceberg" when it comes to privacy violations. And the parading of Facebook founder Mark Zuckerberg, in front of a shamefully technologically ignorant U.S. Congress, proves not only that most of our elected officials do not understand how the Internet, apps, and privacy work (it seems that is a bipartisan issue to the core),[9] but that we have a lot at stake when vetoing our right to privacy.[10]

Enter the **General Data Protection Regulation (GDPR)**, which was voted into existence and approved by the European Union Parliament in April 2016 (but wasn't officially an *enforced policy* until May 2018), which threatens to levy heavy fines on those who are not in compliance. The introduction of GDPR guidelines pushes organizations to establish uniform compliance policies as they relate to data. If not, substantial fines and penalties are administered. Since the Internet is a global platform, not just local or country-based, GDPR becomes the new standard for many international organizations. It was created to protect and empower all EU citizens' data privacy and to "reshape the way organizations across the region approach data privacy," but it has also had a cascading effect of blanketing the rest of us outside the EU with safer data collection processes by companies doing business. The implications are significant. In short, the GDPR protects anyone who does business within the borders of the EU or does business with EU data subjects—and that is pretty much everyone in a digital world.

Not long ago, 70 percent of businesses failed to fulfill requests by users wanting a copy of their personal data.[11] This prompted tougher and more stringent follow-through. The GDPR has the power to impose a fine of over $1 million per violation.[12] Noncompliance can be considered a violation—even if a breach of data has not occurred. This should be an eye-opening consequence. Brands considering all implications should look beyond these hefty fines and understand that at the heart of GDPR rests their customers. GDPR empowers customers, which means that brands need to adhere to these established guidelines to build trust with their target audiences.

People-Centered Design

Public relations, marketing, and advertising practitioners will need to focus more attention on human-centered approaches to their campaign strategy. This means truly resonating with a brand's core, target audience. These are the types of products and campaigns today's consumer wants to experience. According to Don Normana, cofounder of the Nielson Norman Group, "We can't get into the heads and minds of millions of people, and moreover we don't have to: we simply have to understand what people are trying to do and then make it possible."[13] Chatbots, voice command, visual search abilities, and touch interfaces are all examples that can provide the customer with this type of enhanced digital experiences they are searching for.

Chatbots

The fallout from Cambridge Analytica's role in global elections has given **chatbots** a bad reputation. However, chatbots can be an effective tool for public relations, marketing, and advertising practitioners. Chatbots are software applications that interact with people using natural language processing.[14] Chatbots take on humanlike mannerisms but are interactive software platforms that reside in apps, live chat, email, and SMS.[15] In conjunction with AI they can enhance communication—from answering basic questions to scheduling appointments, to ordering food, to simply entertaining customers—and chatbots offer an array of on-demand options. In a survey of businesses conducted by Oracle, 80 percent of the 800 respondents said they already used or planned to increase their use over the next few years.[16] The challenge facing practitioners will be striking the right balance between automation and human interaction.

Regulation of Influencers

While the Federal Trade Commission (FTC) of the United States doesn't expressly define the term "influencer," it certainly has an opinion on the disclosure requirements that are required to avoid what it calls 'misleading consumers or acting in a manner deemed unfair or deceptive advertising' under the Federal Trade Commission Act, 15 U.S.C. §§ 41-58 (the "FTC Act"). First, in 2009 the FTC revised its Endorsement Guides, or the "guides concerning the use of endorsements and testimonials in advertising," to include then-current techniques in marketing, public relations, and advertising, which were mostly relegated to the blogging world and word-of-mouth activities. Then, in November 2019, the FTC released a new guide and video designed to take the questions out of what constitutes the previously friendly advice of "advertising should be truthful and not misleading."[17] Adding to what some communications professionals deem flexible or nonspecific in nature came the first two public actions concerning the guidelines in September 2017 when the owners of CSGO Lotto, Inc., an online gambling platform, settled the FTC's first formal complaint against their online influencers. The FTC said that they were not properly disclosing that their ownership of the company, and they were promoting by posting videos of themselves winning virtual currency on their website and then encouraging others to do the same. No fines were levied in this action; instead, the commission simply ordered the owners and their paid influencers to clearly disclose any material connections with endorsers and promoted products.

So, who cares? According to the *Harvard Business Review*, nearly 20 percent of all consumers have admitted to purchasing a product within the last year based on promotion from a social media influencer.[18] Double that in consumers 25 years and younger. Influencer campaigns earn about $5 in free exposure on social media for every $1 paid to influencers.[19] If a prominent influencer is working with a brand, then the number triples. As calculated by *Forbes* in 2018, companies were on track to spend at least $3 billion on influencer social media marketing in 2019.[20]

We will be watching closely to see how organizations leverage macro- and micro-influencers to support brand strategies, as well as enforce the guidelines of the FTC.

Woke Brands (Corporate Social Responsibility and Brand Activism)

Are brands running purpose-driven campaigns, or are they "**woke-washing**"— a trend that seems to straddle the fine line between *do good for the public* and *do good for the bottom line of a company without the commitment or authenticity related to and concerning the actual cause*?

We have hit the age of "**woke**" advertising, and for some brands, it's a hit (hat tip to you, Nike and Proctor & Gamble), and for other brands, a total disaster (we're looking at you, Pepsi and Kendall Jenner). Somewhere in the midst of "woke" transforming from black activist watchword to teen Internet slang incorporating various social issues and current affairs, brands capitalized on the awakening, by integrating "woke" into their brand perspective,[21] a move that has not proved to be totally inauthentic.

Perhaps the first successful authentically "woke ad" was run in 2014 by Proctor & Gamble brand Always, in their award-winning #LikeAGirl campaign.[22] Others soon followed. Leading the "woke" resurgence were powerhouse brands like Nike, featuring Colin Kaepernick, activist and former National Football League stand-out, forever known as "the guy that took a knee" in support for Black Lives Matter in the Nike "Dream Crazy" ad,[23] which soon morphed into a campaign series. Nike was seen as "all in" with regard to social justice, a move that critics thought was, well, crazy, until their stock price for online sales jumped 31 percent following the Kaepernick campaign and a 17 percent year-over-year gain.[24] Nike has since built upon the "Dream Crazy" campaign, featuring other social justice issues like "Mamba Forever" and "You Can't Stop."[25]

Proctor & Gamble continued to take a stand, even winning Cannes Lion and Emmy Awards for their work relating to unconscious bias in "The Talk" (2017) and "The Look" (2019) ads.[26] These ads addressed the controversial issue with mixed results, but have successfully launched a total effort, proving it's not "just for sales" but for change. Gillette has followed closely, calling out toxic masculinity in the #MeToo era, generating over 33 million views with #TheBestMenCanBe, a short film/advertorial regarding bullying and harassment in a call-out, asking, is this the best a man can get?[27]

As it turns out, we care if a brand is "woke." We are very much aware of how our purchasing decisions impact the world, and we perceive a brand's commitment to a social cause in terms of its alignment with our own value system. Additionally, these factors influence our buying decisions even more than price does, according to a survey done by Washington, DC– based firm Clutch.

"The beliefs and values that drive a company's brand are becoming increasingly important as people are more aware of the impact their buying decisions can have on the world around them."[1] Research firm Clutch surveyed 420 consumers in the United States to discover if corporate social responsibility (CSR) influences how people perceive brands and where they choose to shop. They discovered that yes, people think it is important for businesses to demonstrate social responsibility and take stances on current social movements. Here are the key findings from the report:[2]

1. Three-fourths of people (75 percent) are likely to start shopping at a company that supports an issue they agree with.

2. Fewer people (44 percent) say price is among the most important attributes of a company compared to environmentally friendly business practices (71 percent), social responsibility (68 percent), and giving back to the local community (68 percent).

3. Seventy-one percent of people think it is important for businesses to take a stance on social movements.

4. Twenty-nine percent of people think that businesses support social movements to earn money; slightly fewer people (28 percent) think it is because businesses care about the issues a movement can address.

5. More than half of people (59 percent) are likely to stop shopping at a company that supports an issue they disagree with.

6. Seventy percent (70 percent) of Generation Xers (ages 35–54) and 54 percent of millennials (ages 18–34) are likely to stop shopping at a company that supports an issue they disagree with, compared to 37 percent of baby boomers (ages 55+).

---

[1]Toby Cox, "How Corporate Social Responsibility Influences Buying Decisions," Clutch, last modified January 7, 2019, accessed December 29, 2019, https://clutch.co/pr-firms/resources/how-corporate-social-responsibility-influences-buying-decisions?utm_source=hs_automation&utm_medium=email&utm_content=68755276&_hsenc=p2ANqtz-9xSzoFg7t9xD6H7gF0lvW_WIXzOhBYZo-lmgh4-d9xRdOc3zk0awFGS0x7_NnlV3eG1hvD_O-sKxUYl3uFXf0jg8ZwFg&_hsmi=68 755276.

[2]Ibid.

As baby boomers begin to slip out of the purchase market and other generations come forward with the majority of purchase power, it makes sense to continue to observe and relate to brand attributes and social responsibility, and to continue to develop meaningful and authentic connections with social justice issues—just not at the expense of brand authenticity.

More Videos and Photos

Listen to the numbers—videos make up 82 percent of all Internet traffic, according to Social Media Today.[28] Videos and photos are engaging. It's as simple as that. Practitioners should center on creative, engaging storytelling through visual elements that capture the customer's attention within seconds. According to Deep Patel, "Social media platforms, including Facebook, Instagram and Snapchat, are already pushing brands to produce video content through Story Ads, in part because these ad campaigns often see higher click-through rates than traditional News Feed ads. Twitter is also jumping into the fray with six-second video ads. Personalized content will take this trend to the next level."[29]

Higher Focus on Search: The State of Search Marketing

By Jason Dodge, BlackTruck Media & Marketing

Google's mission since its founding was to "organize the world's information and make it universally accessible and useful,"[1] and over the last 20 years, they've done this many times over.

In our current search landscape, just over 3.5 billion searches are performed every day on Google.[2] Sixteen percent of those searches are BRAND NEW, meaning Google has not ever seen them before. So, search is growing, booming, and Google is changing in response.

Search "back then" and search now are very, quite different things. We've moved well beyond the original "10 Blue Links," and the complexities that make up search continue to morph with the growth in machine learning and AI. The accompanying image shows just a few examples of what might turn up on search results pages.

Experience Shifts in Search Results

Now, we see the search experience getting better (some might argue worse), and Google will continue to do what they want to do.

Know this: Google is very much okay with disrupting their own revenue stream (Google Ads) if it means a better user experience. Google wants to provide us with the answer before we ask the question. Hence the shift toward becoming an "answer engine," and answering more search queries right on their own page.

Is Search Engine Optimization Dead?

Don't panic! SEO is not dead; it's evolving. Organic search still has a lot of reach, especially for more complex queries that can't be easily answered by Google. And organic search still attracts clicks. Specifically, for every 1 paid click, there are about 20 organic clicks happening. So yes, organic search is still relevant, and organic search is valuable!

Some other stats to consider:

- Five percent of clicks happen on Ads—but that space gets 90 percent of marketing dollars.
- Ninety-five percent of the clicks happen on organic—but that space only gets 10 percent of marketing dollars.

Time to re-prioritize!

Also, worth noting is that in 2017, organic search overtook social media as the top source of referral traffic sent to websites. That happened for the first time since 2013.

What to Do? Focus on the Human Factor

Now and moving forward, your organization should be paying attention to site security, performance, and user experience. These are all very powerful elements that should be reviewed and optimized. Plus:

---

[1]"Our Approach to Search," Google, last modified 2018, accessed January 5, 2020, https://www.google.com/search/howsearchworks/mission/.

[2]Ibid.

(continued)

IT'S (NOT) ALL ABOUT THE KEYWORDS These days, optimizing for search is less about those individual, single keywords you're ranking for, and more about the theme of those keywords. So, you're going to need to get away from focusing in on that single phrase and start to go deeper. Developing the "what" is always easy, but uncovering the "why" is more difficult, but much more lucrative.

That leads us to content.

CREATING QUALITY CONTENT Search results continue to become more competitive, and in that environment, high-quality content and highly-relevant content will win out. Period.

What should you consider?

Is your content thin?

It's time to revisit your content strategies. If you have content that is very light, like a paragraph without much depth, and that's it … it's likely this could be viewed by Google as "thin content." Thin content isn't very valuable to people or search engines, especially if your competitors are sharing more insights. There's no specific word count to aim for; however, as Google says, there should be enough main content to "satisfy the needs of the user."

E-A-T

This acronym is taken right from the Google Quality Rater Guidelines. It stands for Expertise, Authoritativeness, and Trustworthiness. Your website should demonstrate these qualities through its main content to show Google you are a worthy source to show. Another way to think about this: Your site should also be an authority on the subject/topic being discussed to be considered a quality site. Are you going to have a positive reputation in the market for something you don't even do or isn't closely related to your business? Probably not. Stick with what you know and do and build strong information that will help you lead.

YMYL

This stands for Your Money, Your Life—another acronym from the Google Quality Rater Guidelines. If your brand has anything remotely connected to a person's financial well-being (careers, financial advice, etc.), health (medical, physicians, hospitals), or legal needs, this concept applies to you.

Because of the impact the published information could have on a visitor, these types of sites/brands come under scrutiny far more than many others, and they saw the greatest impact from one of the most recent Google algorithm updates.

FUTURE-PROOF YOUR CONTENT How can we future-proof our content? Create human-centered content. Start developing content strategy for the person behind the keyboard, and not the robot.

WHAT ABOUT VOICE SEARCH? Voice search has been a constant topic of conversation, but the truth is, we're not quite there yet, as far as replicating a typed search journey or making purchases from true "voice search." The bulk of what is perceived as voice searches are not voice search at all. They're more aligned with Personal Assistants, such as using your Google Home/Google Assistant, Siri, Amazon Echo, etc.

We're asking these devices things such as, "What's the weather going to be tomorrow," or "What's on my schedule on Thursday?" or "Ok Google—call Nicole mobile." None of these are remotely tied to the search engine itself, but to your mobile device and the apps on the device.

Voice search has its place and is used more in re-order situations, but rarely for "Hey Google, find me a size small t-shirt ..."

What's the future of voice? It's "natural language" searches. When you ask Google something and it understands and reads back the answer to you, it's reading directly from the featured snippet on a search results page, which could be from your website. You have some control over this. To be effective here, content needs to be written in a format that's human-centric. It reads as naturally as you and I would speak to one another.

<small>REPRINTED WITH PERMISSION FROM BLACKTRUCK MEDIA & MARKETING.</small>

Blurring of the Lines

Like it or not, more integration between public relations, marketing, and advertising will continue to happen. Public relations has historically been centered on building relationship with internal and external audiences—people-focused. Marketing has historically been focused on advertising efforts and bottom-line numbers. In today's consumer-centric atmosphere, the two professions need to work even closer together. Finding balance and respect between the two professions is essential. Marketing practitioners can learn from PR experts, and public relations practitioners can learn from marketing folks. Consumers are in the social sphere and therefore so are a brand's PR and marketing efforts.

DATA-DRIVEN DISCUSSIONS: PROFESSIONALS SHARING INSIGHTS

We asked several practicing professionals in public relations and marketing what they see as trends within the industry and how data drives their campaign planning and execution. Here is what they had to say.

Jeff Bodzewski, Chief Analytics Officer, M Booth
Is a Third Winter for AI Next? Will Regulations, Understanding and Fear Extinguish the Hype?

Everyone always wants to know what's next. Countless books, posts and videos over the last few years have focused on how technology will transform every aspect of our lives from the way we travel because of autonomous unmanned vehicles, wearable technology predicting likely medical emergencies and of course how much personally sensitive (and embarrassing) information advertisers know about you. As of this writing, data certainly supports the explosive growth with AI controlling an estimated 60 percent of stock trades, accounting for 80 percent of customer service interactions and forecast to be the single largest growing area of investment for many companies.[30]

AI taking our lives is hardly guaranteed as I came to appreciate when chairing an event on the topic in 2018 where hundreds of the industry leaders responsible for implementing and adopting AI expressed concern whether reality will match hype. AI already has gone through two "winters," most recently in the late 1980s, where the expected results did not meet that era's expectations. In the sake of adding a contrarian opinion rather than simply adding to the body of positive predictions, here are three reasons AI may retreat into a third winter.

- Increased Data Regulations and Restrictions: It's no secret that AI needs not only large quantities of data, but large quantities of good data to be effective. Only two years ago the sheer number of data collection points seemed likely to grow exponentially. The Cambridge Analytica reveal and implementation of GDPR in the EU marked turning points where people were no longer complacent about how their data is being used. Companies quickly found their advertising targeting options decreased and even entire countries shut off to them because of these new restrictions. The California Privacy Law (CCPA) enacted in 2020 brings many of those restrictions to the United States that are likely to dramatically reduce both the type of data that can be collected as well as how a company may use it.
- Lack of Human Understanding: For decades the financial industry worked on creating and refining algorithms to govern their equity trading. When an investor asked the simple question of "why" a trade was performed or the firm felt confident in recommending a stock, there was always a clear rationale by those who created the algorithm. Hard AI, or more sophisticated problems, increasingly are adapting and evolving in ways that their creators are unable to understand. In one well-publicized case, two AI programs created their own language to communicate that its own creators were unable to understand. Continued advances in AR will test the human ability to accept not knowing why an action was taken and likely never receiving a complete explanation.
- Human Fear: Finally, the uncertainty of a large enough segment of society shifting from full employment to potentially millions of jobs eliminated in favor of AI has the power to halt any number of advances whether through policy or other means. Concepts such as guaranteed income and skills retraining have had limited success in their initial pilots and the fear of job loss is no longer limited to the blue collar workforce as the same specter that once haunted marketing, financial and HR industries with offshoring now faces the same threat from AI.

None of these factors individually may stall the growth of AI and the endless stream of data collection but combined it may lead to a third AI Winter. The greater likelihood however is that data collection will grow in sophistication and scope through smart home hardware, wearable technologies and even brain chip technologies in their nascent stages. The result is likely to be a marketer's dream in knowing an individual's preference and the unique time and message to reach them with, but a consumer minefield.

Jessica Collins, M.S., Virginia Commonwealth University
There Can't Be a Yin without the Yang: Understanding the Importance of How Qualitative Research Can Really Bring Your Data-Driven Marketing Decisions to Life

A quick Google search (and some intuitiveness) can lead anyone to the undeniable importance of data-driven marketing and how it impacts overall business objectives. You cannot mention data-driven anything without stepping straight "Top Trend" list that mentions the following data-driven issues:

- **The Facebook Fear Factor:** AKA the rise of ethical data collection.
- **Staying Up Close and Personal:** Optimizing every campaign to meet personalized consumer needs.
- **Multichannel Mastery:** Creating a seamless marketing campaigns across a variety of consumer channels.
- **Keeping It Real with Artificial Intelligence:** Utilizing AI to create real-time consumer leads and response times.
- **Getting Pretty Predictive:** Figuring out what the consumer wants before he/she finishes typing.
- **Serving Up SEO:** Capturing the correct consumer catchphrases.

A lot of consumers might say are we talking about "Big Data" or "Big Brother"? But what saves consumers from the depths of a George Orwell 1984 repeat is the trend often at the bottom of the list that does not get as much air time.

We are talking about the yin to quantitative data: the more chatty, more opinionated yang of qualitative research. In our quest to make sure we are making the right decisions, we often forget about the peace of mind a little qualitative texture can add to the process. It gets easy to get caught up in the statistical measures like audience analytics and usage metrics without doing a simple gut check in the actual voice of the consumer. Remember that person?

Armed with a "Top Trend" list of its own, you can be ready to answer the following questions about qualitative research when your client or company is insistent upon using only quantitative methods:

1. **Can't we just find out everything we need to know through quantitative data?**
   Sure, if you just want to know the "what," but not the "why" and the "how." Real conversations with real people add to the facts on the spreadsheets and take us past just identifying the problem.

2. **Isn't it more cost-effective to just do the research quantitatively?**
   New online qualitative platforms are emerging every day that make it easier to recruit and have conversations with consumers without the cost of travel. More importantly, the rise of online platforms and mobile devices are allowing consumers to answer questions in their natural habitat (i.e.: in the moment in the grocery store aisle) which makes their answers even more powerful—and realistic.

3. **Isn't it better to have MORE data—aka quantity over quality?**
   Normally more is better. But big data has become so mainstream now that companies are spending time collecting data that isn't even useful. It's so easy to create online surveys now that many companies aren't even considering the value of the research.

This isn't the Qualitative and Quantitative Battle Royale. Quantitative data is important. Qualitative data is important. But in the era of "Big Data," taking the time to figure out if you need the yin (quantitative) or the yang (qualitative)—or a combination of both—will lead to the biggest and best results.

Derek DeVries, M.S., Director of Digital & Social Strategy, Lambert & Co.
The Importance of Data in Marketing and PR

Impressions. Clicks. Unique visitors. Engagements. Conversions. Return on ad spend. Customer lifetime value. This trajectory of modern digital metrics was enabled by the combination of (1) data and (2) the burning need of communicators to know what works (and why). In it, we can glimpse the outline of the future of marketing.

If a human activity can be documented and quantified, it can contribute to a richer understanding of the motivations of each individual member of one's publics. That understanding can inform a cascade of decisions about how resources are deployed to wring more value from one's investment.

Data by itself is not helpful—it requires scale and context to produce insights that are actionable. The **exabytes** of data created every single day by billions of Internet users can only be pressed into service by assistive technologies like algorithms and automation.

As the ecosystems that enable the collection of user data have grown (tracking users through platforms, by geography, over time, and across devices), so too have the algorithmic tools for parsing and applying that data.

What we can see in the hazy edges of the future of digital marketing are three implications for advertisers, marketers and public relations practitioners:

1. Analytical Literacy: Everyone needs a strong command of statistical concepts and research methodology. We won't need to know the cumbersome equations, rather we'll need to be able to analyze our strategies (and results) through the lens of theoretical frameworks.

2. Continuous Learning: Digital platforms and technology will eventually solve for the gaps in our current understanding, so we need to be ready to incorporate these new insights into our strategies and tactics. We need to be ready to apply an e-commerce mindset (and its ruthless devotion to real-time efficiency) to virtually every activity. For example, it's currently difficult to track online activities through to a conversion point in the "real world" (say a purchase at a retail location, or attendance at an event). Eventually the two separate databases that hold the answers will speak to one another and if you sell toothpaste at grocery stores

3. Creative Thinking: As assistive technologies handle more of the grunt work of setting up tracking systems, crunching numbers, or analyzing sentiment, humans are freed to spend their energy on creativity and problem solving. The performance of our campaigns will mostly be limited to our ability to think differently about our publics, and to produce a healthy variety of messages and multimedia to communicate most effectively to increasingly atomized audiences.

This future is not guaranteed, however, as the spectrum of privacy regulation hangs heavy over the promise of technological advancement. If social media platforms and tech companies continue to be poor stewards of their customers data, or they continue to allow malicious actors to undermine democratic processes and commercial markets—governments will step in (with anti-trust regulation or onerous privacy protections) or users will abandon the platforms.

Betsy Emmons, Ph.D., APR, Samford University
The Influence of Data on Public Relations and Marketing

Data, and data analytics, sound daunting to many marketing and public relations practitioners. Those of us who remember faxed press releases and scissor-clipped newspaper ads are especially vulnerable to feeling overwhelmed by the endless stream of data that we now have access to. Many of us also argue that the current obsession with data ignores some fundamental aspects of strategic communication. Data gives us excellent information and better access to the success of our messages than ever before, but data can show that a terrible message resonated (such as an insensitive tweet) as much as a great message (such as a clever meme), and we do not always know if data truly tell us what we need to know. For example, is #blessed trending because people feel genuinely "blessed," as in spiritually favored, or is #blessed trending because we are feeling collectively sarcastic and using the hashtag to mock ourselves or our situations? Data will generally not tell us this. As with similar tools, data only helps through the study of context and interpretation. This is the interesting space where marketing and public relations practitioners have new opportunities to move the needle via data analytics.

Data allow us to do our jobs better in many ways. While there are countless examples, here are three key ways data matter in modern marketing and public relations:

> **Improving relationships with journalists:** Which recent story by a journalist garnered the most comments? A quick view of data such as comments to an online news story, social media comments, likes, or shares can tell you what a resonating topic is. This is a big help if you have context or addition to the story to add. Alternatively, what interesting data jumped out from your recent sales spreadsheet that would be intriguing to a reporter? Data can help tell stories in new ways—if you notice an unusual piece of information in your sales data or usage data, a reporter might find it interesting, too.
>
> **Anticipating trends.** Watching spikes in online activity or other data can help anticipate trends. One recent example is TikTok. Within the past year, enormous spikes in downloads and increased chatter on other social media suggested that TikTok was jumping in usage. Since the app is most popular with children and teens, it took keeping a pulse on data for brands to decide to join the app and tap into the moment. Makeup brands, sports leagues, fashion brands, and young influencers have jumped on TikTok as a new way to reach young consumers as other apps like Instagram age.
>
> **Use data to acknowledge what data misses.** It can be easy to get wrapped up in what data is able to show us, but we also can use it to show us our blind spots. Data tell us if sites are more visited by women than men, if people from certain geographic regions are over or under-represented, and how old users are. We now know that we will need to use other channels to reach the demographics we are missing. Maybe mail would be a better way to reach your target audience, or maybe there is an in-person way you can reach your stakeholders? Gaps in data tell us where we need to tweak or refine our messages.

Imran Mazid, Ph.D., Grand Valley State University
Importance of Data on PR

The current digital media ecosystem generates a treasure trove of consumer data that can be deployed to develop a strategic blueprint to achieve business goals. On average, every consumer generates 1.5 Gigabytes of data per day through actions like web browsing, sharing content, online search, and other activities.[31] Brands are leveraging big data technologies, artificial intelligence, and data analytics tools to collect, analyze, and visualize real-time data about digital audience behavior. Such use of technologies and data help brands to secure a strategic advantage. Data-driven business decisions often foster innovations, transparency, and collaboration. Global brands like Google, Amazon, Walmart, Netflix, and others have embraced a data-driven strategy to innovate and influence business transformation. Digital data can be used to develop effective public relations initiatives, including but not limited to discovering new audiences, measuring public sentiment, tackling crisis communication, developing competitive intelligence, and promoting social change.

More specifically, public relations professionals use digital data to formulate campaign strategy, examine public opinion, and evaluate performance. Analysis of social media conversations help organizations to illuminate people's attitudes toward social practices. Then, the public relations team can use such insights to develop a campaign strategy. For example, Sport England wanted to address the gender gap in sports and planned a national campaign to inspire women to participate in sports. It analyzed more than a million tweets to examine women's attitudes toward sports. The analysis of twitter data revealed that women do not participate in sports because of the fear of judgment. Sport England used such insight to develop a national campaign that resulted in a considerable increase in women's participation in sports.

Public opinion plays a critical role in public relations practices. Digital data help organizations to investigate public opinion in real-time, and the public relations team can develop a plan to ensure favorable public image. The advancement of Natural Language Processing (NLP) tools supports the analysis of enormous data corpus to mine public sentiment about brands. Organizations can use such tools to measure the pulse of public opinion and take necessary action to mitigate any adverse public sentiment. Also, computational topic modeling techniques are used to analyze large online data sets to generate insights about relevant themes of online public dissuasion. Such data-driven insights can be used to maintain a favorable public image and mitigate any tensions between organizations and the publics.

Organizations also use digital and social media data to evaluate their campaign performance. Web analytics and social media analytics tools provide necessary insights about campaign performance. For example, if a brand launches a digital campaign, then digital traces of all campaign data can be tracked, analyzed, and reported to evaluate performance. Organizations can use data analytics tools to learn about the target demographic and their online behavior to maximize their efforts. Public relations teams use digital data for time-series analysis to see the impact of their campaign. They can calibrate their actions to reach the optimum outcome.

Overall, digital data reshaped public relations practices. Organizations need to be data-savvy to survive in the emerging digital economy and strengthen their impact in the marketplace. Seasoned public relations professionals need to develop a "digital-first" mindset to optimize their communication efforts. Academia needs to train the new generation of public relations students in data analytics, data mining, and data visualization to tackle the challenges of the digital world.

Christopher J. McCollough, Ph.D., Jacksonville State University
Big Data: Valuable Tool for Research in Marketing and Public Relations, When Used Strategically

Data is the dominant form of preliminary research and evaluation of public relations and marketing strategy. The predictive value that large bodies of data present in identifying potential attitudes, feelings, and beliefs present marketing and public relations professionals with resources that enhance preliminary research and assessment of campaigns. Given that best practices in strategic communication espouse thorough research, practitioners clearly depend on data and analytics to research, design, execute, and evaluate successful campaigns.

The growth and impact of data on marketing and public relations is clear. Big data has expanded landscape analysis in public relations and marketing functions to explore the current state of the organization, its competitors, and larger economic and societal factors, as it enables professionals to have more intuitive perspective on their audiences. Setting objectives in marketing and public relations work now reflects the incorporation of data, enabling assessment of meaningful impact on organizational success (recruitment, retention, profit, and cost efficiency). Tactics are now more intuitive at the individual level and reflect a larger sphere of impact, which empowers practitioners to define and demonstrate how essential public relations and marketing practices are valuable to organizational success. Data enables a nimble, effective approach to incremental evaluation and adaptation that better ensures campaign success and stewardship of client resources. This has only grown with the emergence of real-time data collection and analysis in cloud-based computing. Data illustrating organizational function now better establishes the connection between marketing and public relations functions and organizational success, strengthening summative evaluation and practitioners' arguments for the value and marketability of their work.

Data analysis and integration presents some concerns and challenges for strategic communication work. Vanity metrics in data, particularly in organizational social media analytics are too often upheld as essential for measuring impact in social media campaigns. Counting Facebook fans, Twitter followers, blog post views, email open rate, and number of subscribers offer a snapshot that are not indicative of the actual engagement, application, value to user, or direct relationship to conversion. Given the breadth, depth, and real-time value of data being derived in strategic communication work, practitioners stand the risk of undermining the value of their work by not establishing the purpose, effectiveness, and value of strategic communication work. Practitioners need to drill down to analysis that articulates conversion to relationships and consumers to thoroughly establish the impact and value of campaign work.

Data in strategic communication also presents emerging ethical concerns in professional practice. Concerns about privacy, access, and transparency related to disclosure of and access to sensitive client and user information, matters of consent, and inaccurate analysis and representation of data are growing areas of debate among strategic communication professionals and scholars. Recent scandals at Facebook, Twitter, and related to organizations like Cambridge Analytica highlight concerns related to leveraging data without consent in strategic communication. Effectively striking the balance will enable professionals to be dynamic in practice, to enhance their professional reputation and relationships, and to enhance the reputation and relationships of clients and organizations with consumers, stakeholders, and investors.

John Palmer, M.A., APR, Director of Media & Public Relations, The Ohio Hospital Association
Big Data Getting Bigger Leading to Greater Precision for Effective Public Relations and Marketing Strategy

Public utilization of technology is growing at an unprecedented rate requiring organizations to set new approaches to compiling and assessing large amounts of data generated every day. Social media utilization, online purchases, Internet searches (worldwide there are 5 billion searches a day) are all contributing to the daily generation of data about consumers, stakeholders and many other audiences. Every industry, non-profit, not-for-profit, corporate and government are all looking to incorporate robust data with their strategic planning. The USC Annenberg Center for Public Relations and the Association of National Advertisers conducted a study where respondents (public relations and marketing professionals) stated big data and social listening are the leading influencers for the future of the field.[32]

Effective organizational strategy depends on reliable, accurate and understandable data. Public relations and marketing professionals are often the stewards of data analysis and reporting to guide the overall planning process. According to McKinsey Global Institute, organizations are exploring how large volume data can be usefully deployed to create and capture value for individuals, businesses, communities, and governments.[33] There are about 10 billion galaxies in the observable universe per the University of California's National Science Foundation. UCNSF claims "the number of stars in a galaxy varies, but assuming an average of 100 billion stars per galaxy means that there are about 1,000,000,000,000,000,000,000 (that's 1 billion trillion) stars in the observable universe."[34]

So, there is a lot of data and it's getting bigger and more complex. PR and marketing professionals are challenged to locate, analyze and mine the appropriate data such as: survey data, social media data, customer relationship management data, consumer purchase data, website utilization data and more.[35] To formalize and rationalize the large amounts of data, dashboards are developed to allow for more robust and in-depth discussion and consideration at the planning level. Every aspect of public relations and marketing is transforming with the data being generated today including content strategy, event planning, speech writing, product packaging and distribution, media relations and branding.[36]

An article from Forbes states, "With real-time data being used as an asset, professionals in the PR and media industries are able to provide their audience with content they want, rather than content they find annoying. This helps them eliminate time being wasted on content that won't be received well by their audience."[37] By measuring the impact of a campaign or strategy in real-time (product purchases, consumer feedback, etc.) organizations can make adjustments to tactics and content timelier to obtain desired engagement by consumers and stakeholders.

The digital age is providing a wealth of timely and relevant data on consumers and stakeholders enabling public relations and marketing professionals to engage in more constructive research, greater stakeholder analysis, better content strategy, smarter goal setting and quality strategic planning for organizations. Strategy is also adapting with great frequency by continually to monitor data trends and adjusting to reach goals. As technology advances and organizations align to capture and analyze the data being generated, public relations and marketing professionals are leading efforts to the discovery of new opportunities and possibilities for an organization.

Kate Stewart, University of South Carolina, Public Relations Consultant, Approach Marketing
Despite Access to Big Data, Adoption Remains Far Too Small

Today's marketers are currently entangled in a complex web of consumer and performance data that only an elite few know how to navigate and interpret. And, it's this lack of understanding and action by the majority that will make or break the future of the profession.

We are, without a doubt, racing against the very tools we're using to plan, monitor and analyze our campaigns. Our future selves are begging us to dial in and do better.

Reflecting on a common marketing team scenario, I reference the visual of time, interest and budget plotted along a line graph that rises and then steadily falls throughout the campaign's activation. Enthusiasm and momentum are typically sky-high while planning. Creative ideas fly around the room and undergo revisions for months—if not years—in aspiration of would-be success. We then commit to monitoring for optimization along the way, but most practitioners do not progress beyond reporting context-less statistics to check the box on "measurement."

Fast forward to a program's conclusion and teams are often spent of energy and budget to conduct a true post-mortem analysis, let alone use it to inform a future initiative. Analytics and Intelligence teams are growing but not nearly where they should be in most corporations. Is it any surprise, then, that a sobering 80–85% of fast-moving consumer goods still fail to launch successfully? Most fails I can recall are swept under the rug as quickly as possible rather than truly digested. Repeat the process.

Marketing and related departments (communications, digital media and public relations) are routinely vying for company budget over sales or operations. The C-suite may perceive that it's impossible to measure marketing effectively or easy to automate on the cheap—thanks to the stack of useless reports we spew out from subscription tools.

There is a related knowledge-time-cost challenge to data interpretation because it's presently mastered by so few. This will be critical to overcome as we progress into the next decade. Ideally, the points of time, interest and budget in *analysis* along the activation line graph will be equal to higher than the program's counterparts of planning and implementation. This will keep marketing in the game.

Is There Room for Poor-Performing Marketing in the Future?

Even with marketers more in-tune with data, I can't help but wonder if we are shifting into an era where predictive analysis makes it easier to curb—or prevent—marketing flops to the degree we've experienced.

Think about it. Tools and connected devices have the ability to capture details on most aspects of our day. Social media algorithms can determine what content resonates most with users. Is it possible that machines will soon serve to marketer's failsafe product concepts that fall into our hands to materialize, refine and support with complementary offline strategies? Why couldn't they also tell us the product's predicted lifespan, allowing us to plan and budget accordingly?

By the same token, social media platforms are already able to summarize which of our pre-scheduled, auto-posted content performed the best among the most engaged audience profile. Is this another area of marketing where failure becomes obsolete?

There is no denying that marketing and data go hand-in-hand. However, in order for us to realize these potential advances, we must first get more hands-on with it.

Kate Stewart, Auburn University
Data, Data, Data

Data-driven results are viewed as concrete evidence to show that methods you are using in your strategies and tactics work or not. It is not all about having backing of your project in the boardroom though, the importance boils down to being able to do what is best for your clients to have profitable returns from the work that you are doing for them.

When clients and businesses go out on the limb to invest money into marketing or public relations, they expect for it to have some type of positive effect on their company whether that be social impact, branding and reputation, or increased profits. Marketing and public relations can help in each of these three areas depending on your clients' vision or goals they are trying to accomplish by bringing you onboard. Data helps you stay on budget for clients and helps you make realistic goals when it comes to campaigns, instead of guessing. Both elements will help your clients feel more secure about investing in marketing and public relations. Also, it helps them visualize success and visualize the improvements you are making for their company. Data and marketing and public relations are intertwined even more so now that social media has become the dominant source of communicating with publics and target audiences. Also, as technology continues to advance, professionals must pay attention to the data to ensure their methods are not outdated.

Public relations and marketing professionals can monitor their advertisements and social media posts for clients to see how many people are being reached and if the people that interact with the content are a part of their intended target audience, how much engagement is received, and what type of posts do better for the clients' potential customers. Following this data over time help professionals create content that is best for the clients and helps you report to your clients on a monthly, six month, or yearly basis how social media and advertising are helping grow their presence.

Incorporating data into a crisis communication plan can allow you to better prepare for what is to come in a clients' future in case an issue arises that you may need to handle. This data will help you follow the conversation around a crisis if it does happen. Tracking the positive and negative conversation that is revolving around the crisis allows you to create a narrative to help the outcome be more positive for your client.

These results also allow you to keep working toward being more creative and more innovative in your approaches when dealing with client work. Data helps you create more intentional strategies, allows you to produce more effective campaigns for your clients, and better collaborate with the online community.

Caitlyn Tuzzolino, Senior Marketing Manager, Amplience, United Kingdom
The Importance of Data on Marketing

Data-driven marketing is extremely important because it allows marketers to monitor the performance of programs, efforts, traffic, and more. As a senior level marketing professional, it's important to gain insights into which campaigns work well and which don't. It is crucial that as practitioners we understand the data and then adjust accordingly with future efforts. In my role, if something works well, I repeat it. Using analytics, I can determine why a campaign was less successful than we anticipated and then fix it. For example, with an email campaign, was it the subject line that did not catch the attention of the recipient? Or was it the call-to-action button? With A/B testing, a method of comparing two versions against each other (in this case, of a subject line or a call-to-action button), it allows marketers to determine which version performs better. That is just one example of data-driven marketing that my company uses on a regular basis.

Another example of data-driven marketing that I use for email campaigns is demographic data. Let's say I want to send an email campaign to the top 200 prospects in my company's database. With specific filters, I can pull that information based on engagement scores and other criteria. I could refine it further—based on each contact's gender, job title, company revenue, location, and more. Why is this important? The different criteria that I set could aid in the success of the campaign. If the goal of the campaign is to convert the prospect into a new client, I need to make sure the message is reaching the right people. Job titles, for example, could play a huge role in that. If the message is reaching an Administrative Assistant when really it should be reaching a Chief Marketing Officer, chances are, it will not be effective.

There are hundreds of examples of why data is so important to marketing. The bottom line is, over time, data helps with making smart marketing decisions. Collecting data from previous programs, campaigns, and different types of marketing efforts will allow you to refine your data-driven marketing campaigns moving forward.

One final thought on the importance of data on marketing: it helps improve marketing return on investment (ROI). Without data, it is impossible to measure ROI. That is what all C-level executives care about. Otherwise, what is the point of marketing? You should not just throw stuff at the wall and hope it sticks.

You should use data to solve challenges, gain insight on your target audience, identify interesting trends, and again, increase marketing ROI.

CONCLUSION

From ethics to privacy, to embracing being "woke," so much is impacting industry. Further developments in data, analytics, and the use of AI will continue. The evolution of the industry is clear. Using data to improve public relations and marketing efforts is impactful for brands—big and small. Rising to the call will be more important than ever.

DISCUSSION QUESTIONS AND EXERCISES

1. The founders of the Partnership on AI identified concerns such as "safety and trustworthiness of AI technologies, the fairness and transparency of systems, and the intentional as well as inadvertent influences of AI on people and society."[38] What does this mean to marketing and public relations professionals? Should they serve as an integral part of an organization's ethical conscience? Watch the short video *Moral Code: The Ethics of AI* (http://bit. ly/HPAtlanticEthicsAI), and learn more about the Partnership on AI (https://www.partnershiponai.org/about/).

2. General Data Protection Regulation also requires companies outside the European Union to safeguard personal data. This means companies inside United States are impacted. Often public relations and marketing campaigns collect a customer's data. Put your practitioner hat on—how would you advise your manager on how to be GDPR-compliant as you roll out your next social media campaign?

3. What are the ethical implications of AI, and what role should practitioners play? How should marketing and public relations practitioners incorporate ethics into their campaign strategy—particularly one that relies on data?

4. Social media is noted as the number one area that companies are planning to increase their investment in big data analytics. Think about what you have read throughout the book while considering the implications and the future of data. Develop a checklist to be used by practitioners when developing a public relations and marketing campaign.

5. Assess your favorite brand on social media. See if you can identify any paid or partner influencers connected with your brand. Are their disclosures in line with the 2019 FTC guidelines for social media influencers? Do you think these guidelines matter? Why or why not?

6. *Small group exercise:* After you finish question 5, now it is time to get to work. What makes for a legal and compelling social media influencer post? Using your favorite brand on social media from question 5, create a post as if you were an influencer for that brand. Review the FTC press release, video, and guide (https://www.ftc.gov/news-events/press-releases/2019/11/ftc-releases-advertising-disclosures-guidance-online-influencers) as well as this "101"

document (https://www.ftc.gov/system/files/documents/plain-language/1001a-influencer-guide-508_1.pdf) before and in conjunction with creating your #Ad. Use a creative platform like Canva.com to mock up your ad. Distribute to your team to review, discuss, and evaluate. Want to up the difficulty level? Have your instructor select one of your group members to play the outlier—to knowingly create a "bad" ad—one in violation of any of the core guidelines from the FTC. Can you spot it? Evaluate each ad's disclosure for compliance with FTC regulations.

KEY TERMS

big data and analytics (BDA)

chatbots

Commission Nationale de l'Informatique et des Libertés (**CNIL**)

exabyte

General Data Protection Regulation (GDPR)

woke

woke-washing

NOTES

1. Allan Jay, "11 Big Data Trends for 2020: Current Predictions You Should Know," *Finance Online Reviews for Business* (blog), December 2019, https://financesonline.com/big-data-trends/.

2. Ibid.

3. S. A. Bowen, R. L. Heath, and J. Lee, "An International Study of Ethical Roles and Counsel in the Public Relations Function" (paper presented at the annual meeting of the International Communication Association, Dresden, Germany, 2006).

4. Eric Horvitz and Mustafa Suleyman, "Introduction from the Founding Co-chairs," Partnership on AI, September 28, 2016, accessed January 20, 2019, https://www.partnershiponai.org/introduction-from-the-founding-co-chairs/.

5. Nick Statt, "Facebook, Google, and Microsoft Team Up to Pacify Fears about AI," The Verge, September 28, 2016, accessed January 20, 2019, https://www.theverge.com/2016/9/28/13094668/facebook-google-microsoft-partnership-on-ai-artificial-intelligence-benefits.

6. "Algorithms and Artificial Intelligence: CNIL's Report on the Ethical Issues," CNIL, May 28, 2018, accessed January 20, 2019, https://www.cnil.fr/en/algorithms-and-artificial-intelligence-cnils-report-ethical-issues.

7. Kevin Granville, "Facebook and Cambridge Analytica: What You Need to Know as Fallout Widens," *New York Times*, last modified March 19, 2018, accessed January 5, 2020, https://www.nytimes.com/2018/03/19/technology/facebook-cambridge-analytica-explained.html.

8. WZZM, "Online Quizzes Can Gather Your Personal Information," WZZM-13, last modified March 23, 2018, accessed January 5, 2020, https://www.wzzm13.com/article/money/consumer/online-quizzes-can-gather-your-personal-information/69-531393400.

9. Kurt Wagner, "Congress Doesn't Know How Facebook Works and Other Things We Learned from Mark Zuckerberg's Testimony," Recode, last modified April 11, 2018, accessed January 5, 2020, https://www.recode.net/2018/4/11/17226742/congress-senate-house-facebook-ceo-zuckerberg-testimony-hearing.

10. Nicolas Thompson and Fred Vogelstein, "Inside the Two Years That Shook Facebook— and the World," *Wired*, last modified February 12, 2018, accessed January 5, 2020, https://www.wired.com/story/inside-facebook-mark-zuckerberg-2-years-of-hell/.

11. Jay, "11 Big Data Trends."

12. Focal Point Insights, "The GDPR in 2019: Enforcement and Penalties around the Globe," *Focal Point Data Risk* (blog), January 2019, https://blog.focal-point.com/the-gdpr-in-2019-enforcement-and-penalties-around-the-globe.

13. Dana Kachan, "5 Trends of Dynamic Human-Centered Design in 2019," Muzli, July 21, 2019, https://medium.muz.li/5-trends-of-dynamic-human-centered-design-in-2019-abc3743f9089.

14. Abbi Whitaker, "How Advancements in Artificial Intelligence Will Impact Public Relations," *Forbes*, March 20, 2017, https://www.forbes.com/sites/theyec/2017/03/20/how-advancements-in-artificial-intelligence-will-impact-public-relations/.

15. Business Insider Intelligence, "80% of Businesses Want Chatbots by 2020," Business Insider, December 14, 2016, https://www.businessinsider.com/80-of-businesses-want-chatbots-by-2020-2016-12.

16. Ibid.

17. Federal Trade Commission (FTC), "Disclosures 101 for Social Media Influencers," Federal Trade Commission, last modified November 2019, accessed January 5, 2020, https://www.ftc.gov/system/files/documents/plain-language/1001a-influencer-guide-508_1.pdf.

18. Alice Audrezet and Karine Charry, "Do Influencers Need to Tell Audiences They're Getting Paid?," *Harvard Business Review*, last modified August 29, 2019, accessed January 5, 2020, https://hbr.org/2019/08/do-influencers-need-to-tell-audiences-theyre-getting-paid.

19. Ibid.

20. Tom Ward, "The Influencer Marketing Trends that Will Explode in 2019," *Forbes*, last modified December 18, 2018, accessed January 5, 2020, https://www.forbes.com/sites/tomward/2018/12/18/the-influencer-marketing-trends-that-will-explode-in-2019/#54903ea02786.

21. Charles Pulliam-Moore, "How 'Woke' Went from Black Activist Watchword to Teen Internet Slang," Splinter News, last modified January 8, 2016, accessed January 5, 2020, https://splinternews.com/how-woke-went-from-black-activist-watchword-to-teen-int-1793853989.

22. Always, "Always #LikeAGirl," YouTube, June 26, 2014, accessed January 5, 2020, https://www.youtube.com/watch?v=XjJQBjWYDTs.

23. "Colin Kaepernick JUST DO IT Nike Commercial 2018 Feat LeBron James & Other Athletes," posted by Yt Godski, YouTube, October 17, 2018, accessed January 5, 2020, https://youtu.be/wyHI3IrJOR8.

24. Ciara Linnane, "Nike's Online Sales Jumped 31% after Company Unveiled Kaepernick Campaign, Data Show," MarketWatch, last modified September 17, 2018, accessed January 5, 2020, https://www.marketwatch.com/story/nikes-online-sales-jumped-31-after-company-unveiled-kaepernick-campaign-2018-09-07.

25. "You Can't Stop Sisters," YouTube video, 1:00, posted by "Nike," August 31, 2020, https://www.youtube.com/watch?v=lqQdXlHWiL8.

26. Proctor & Gamble, "Let's Talk about Bias," United States Proctor & Gamble, last modified 2019, accessed January 5, 2020, https://us.pg.com/talkaboutbias/.

27. Gillette, "We Believe: The Best Men Can Be | Gillette (Short Film)," YouTube, last modified January 13, 2019, accessed January 5, 2020, https://youtu.be/koPmuEyP3a0.

28. Erica Perry, "2020 Video Marketing and Statistics: What Brands Need to Know," Social Media Week, October 30, 2019, https://socialmediaweek.org/blog/2019/10/2020-video-marketing-and-statistics-what-brands-need-to-know/.

29. Deep Patel, "12 Social Media Trends to Watch in 2020," *Entrepreneur*, December 20, 2019, https://www.entrepreneur.com/article/343863.

30. Jacques Bughin et al., "How Artificial Intelligence Can Delivery Real Value to Companies," McKinsey Global Institute, June 15, 2017, https://www.mckinsey.com/business-functions/mckinsey-analytics/our-insights/how-artificial-intelligence-can-deliver-real-value-to-companies.

31. C. Hemann and K. Burbary, *Digital Marketing Analytics: Making Sense of Consumer Data in a Digital World* (U.S.A.: Pearson Education, 2018).

32. USC Annenberg, "Global Communications Report 2017," USC Annenberg School for Communication and Journalism, 2017, http://annenberg.usc.edu/sites/default/files/KOS_2017_GCP_April6.pdf.

33. "Data Privacy: What Every Manager Needs to Know," McKinsey & Company, July 21, 2018, accessed January 5, 2020, https://www.mckinsey.com/business-functions/risk/our-insights/data-privacy-what-every-manager-needs-to-know.

34. "About How Many Stars are in Space?" Materials Research Laboratory, UC Santa Barbara, Question Date: February 19, 2013, scienceline.ucsb.edu/getkey.php?key=3775

35. Heaviside, "The Future of Public Relations: Trends, Skills, PR vs. Marketing: Study," Heaviside Group, July 2, 2019, https://www.heavisidegroup.com/marketing/the-future-of-public-relations-trends-skills-pr-vs-marketing-study.

36. Mark Weiner and Sarab Kochar, "Irreversible: The Public Relations Big Data Revolution," Institute for Public Relations, accessed November 5, 2020, https://instituteforpr.org/wp-content/uploads/IPR_PR-Big-Data-Revolution_3-29.pdf

37. Bernard Marr, "How Much Data Do We Create Every Day? The Mind-Blowing Stats Everyone Should Read," *Forbes*, September 5, 2019, https://www.forbes.com/sites/bernardmarr/2018/05/21/how-much-data-do-we-create-every-day-the-mind-blowing-stats-everyone-should-read/#20b0f99f60ba.

38. Horvitz and Suleyman, "Introduction."

Glossary

Advertising The action of calling something to the attention of the public especially by paid announcements

Advocate One who supports or promotes the interests of a cause or group

Algorithmic Bias Algorithms can deepen the echo chamber by spreading fake information and can discriminate against people or perpetuate bias by constructing data sets based on perceived identities and stereotypes.

Algorithms An algorithm is a finite sequence of well-defined, computer-implementable instructions, typically to solve a class of problems or to perform a computation.

Analytics The discovery and communication of meaningful patterns in data.

Artificial Intelligence The capability of a machine to imitate intelligent human behavior.

Association for Measurement and Evaluation of Communication (AMEC) The world's largest media intelligence and insights professional organization [organization], representing organizations [organization] and practitioners who provide media evaluation and communication research.

Audience Analytics A deeper understanding of their current and potential customers to improve marketing strategy, customer experience, and brand perception.

Audience Segmentation The process of dividing website visitors into subgroups based on a common set of characteristics such as behavior, psychographics, demographics, and customer type.

Authenticity The quality of being authentic; of undisputed origin; genuine.

Barcelona Principles Identify the importance of goal setting, the need for outcomes, instead of outputs-based measurement of PR campaigns, the exclusion of ad value equivalency metrics, the validity of quantitative and qualitative measurements, the value of social media, and a holistic approach to measurement and evaluation.

Brand Ambassador A person, especially a celebrity, who is paid to endorse or promote a particular company's products or services.

Brand Awareness The extent to which consumers are familiar with the distinctive qualities or image of a particular brand of goods or services.

Brand Recognition The extent to which a consumer can correctly identify a particular product or service just by viewing the product or service's logo, tag line, packaging or advertising campaign.

Brand Tracking The marketing efforts used to quantify the effects of brand building campaigns on sales and conversions.

Chatbots Pieces of software designed to respond to messages sent on social media, websites and more.

Collaborative Filtering A technique commonly used to build personalized recommendations on the Web.

Content Analysis Analysis of the manifest and latent content of a body of communicated material (such as a book or film) through a classification, tabulation, and evaluation of its key symbols and themes in order to ascertain its meaning and probable effect.

Content Creation The process of generating topic ideas that appeal to your buyer persona, creating written or visual content around those ideas, and making that information accessible to your audience as a blog, video, infographic, or other format.

Content Marketing A type of marketing where brands plan, create, promote and analyze content to meet strategic goals.

Crisis Management The process by which a business or other organization deals with a sudden emergency situation.

Customer Experience The impression you leave with your customer, resulting in how they think of your brand, across every stage of the customer journey.

Customer Service The assistance and advice provided by a company to those people who buy or use its products or services.

Descriptive Analytics The interpretation of historical data to better understand changes that have occurred in a business.

Digital Natives A person born or brought up during the age of digital technology and therefore familiar with computers and the Internet from an early age.

Dual Coding Theory Proposed by Paivio attempts to give equal weight to verbal and non-verbal processing. The theory assumes that there are two cognitive subsystems, one specialized for the representation and processing of nonverbal objects/events (i.e., imagery), and the other specialized for dealing with language.

Engagement Public shares, likes and comments for an online business' social media efforts.

Exabyte a unit of information equal to one quintillion (1018) bytes, or one billion gigabytes.

Formative Research Research carried out before and during the campaign to determine and refine the campaign planning process, provides accurate, up-to-date information to strategically develop the campaign on a sound basis.

Federal Trade Commission (FTC) Protects consumers and businesses from practices that can cause markets to become unfair and anti-competitive.

GDPR Gross Domestic Product (GDP) is the total monetary or market value of all the finished goods and services produced within a country's borders in a specific time period.

Generation Z The generation of people born in the late 1990s and early 2000s. the generation reaching adulthood in the second decade of the 21st century, perceived as being familiar with the internet from a very young age.

Geofencing The use of GPS or RFID technology to create a virtual geographic boundary, enabling software to trigger a response when a mobile device enters or leaves a particular area.

Hypertargeting A marketing strategy where you clearly identify a target customer and deliver extremely relevant messages in the places where they will be most likely to see it.

Influencer Someone in your niche or industry with sway over your target audience.

Influencer Identification The ability to map business goals downward to the people who can help your brand achieve them.

Influencer marketing A type of marketing that focuses on using key leaders to drive your brand's message to the larger market.

Infographics A chart, diagram, or illustration (as in a book or magazine, or on a website) that uses graphic elements to present information in a visually striking way

Keywords Significant words from a title or document used especially as an index to content

Linguistic Analysis The analysis of language or its structure; (Philosophy) analysis that takes language itself, rather than its subject matter, as the primary focus of study.

Location-based real-time geo-data from a mobile device or smartphone to provide information, entertainment or security by using a smartphone's GPS technology to track a person's location, if that person has opted-in to allow the service to do that.

Machine Learning An application of artificial intelligence (AI) that provides systems the ability to automatically learn and improve from experience without being explicitly programmed.

Market segmentation The process of dividing a market of potential customers into groups, or segments, based on different characteristics.

Marketing The action or business of promoting and selling products or services, including market research and advertising. Also, the process or technique of promoting, selling, and distributing a product or service.

Marketing Mix Modeling A technique which helps in quantifying the impact of several marketing inputs on sales or Market Share.

Millennials A person born in the 1980s or 1990s who reached young adulthood in the early 21st century.

Natural Language Processing The automatic manipulation of natural language, like speech and text, by software.

Objective Part of goal setting, an objective is a specific measurable statement of what needs to be achieved.

Omni-Channel A multi-channel sales approach that provides the customer with an integrated customer experience.

Organizational Silos The isolation that occurs when employees or entire departments within an organization do not want to, or do not have the adequate means to share information or knowledge with each other.

Personalized Customer Engagement AI-based bots can learn and adapt to customer preferences, they can arguably outdo humans at anticipating customer needs and personalizing their responses accordingly.

PESO Model A strategy, developed by Gini Dietrich, that touts the integration of paid, earned, shared, and owned media to deliver integrated marketing programs, extend reach, and establish brands as leaders within their industry.

Point of Sale Of or relating to the place (such as a check-out counter) where an item is purchased.

Predictive analytics Category of data analytics aimed at making predictions about future outcomes based on historical data and analytics techniques such as statistical modeling and machine learning.

Prescriptive analytics A type of data analytics—the use of technology to help businesses make better decisions through the analysis of raw data.

Public Relations Public relations is a strategic communication process that builds mutually beneficial relationships between organizations and their publics.

Rapid Response Specifically designating a team or unit of people who are deployed to deal with an incident or situation as soon as possible.

Real Time the actual time during which something takes place

Reputation Management The effort to influence what and how people think of a brand or person.

Research Systematic collection of data used to understand phenomena.

Return on Investment (ROI) Measures the gain or loss generated on an investment relative to the amount of money invested.

SMART Objectives Acronym for specific, measurable, achievable, realistic and time-oriented.

Search Engine Optimization (SEO) The process of maximizing the number of visitors to a particular website by ensuring that the site appears high on the list of results returned by a search engine.

Search Engine Results Page (SERP) Web pages served to users when they search for something online using a search engine, such as Google. The user enters their search query (often using specific terms and phrases known as keywords), upon which the search engine presents them with a SERP.

Search Engine A program that searches for and identifies items in a database that correspond to keywords or characters specified by the user, used especially for finding particular sites on the World Wide Web.

Semantic Analysis Describes the process of understanding natural language–the way that humans communicate–based on meaning and context.

Share of Conversation The percentage of mentions the particular brand receives in relation to the broader conversation.

Social Consumer A new breed of engaged and informed customer and that means every industry, every vertical and ultimately every business is going to be rethought in a social way.

Social CRM The integration of social media channels into Customer Relationship Management (CRM) platforms.

Social Customer Care Company proactive in meeting customers' needs before a customer reaches out to you about a product or service.

Social Media Forms of electronic communication (such as websites for social networking and microblogging) through which users create online communities to share information, ideas, personal messages, and other content (such as videos).

Social Media Monitoring The process of collecting social conversations and messages into a database of useful information.

Social Media Optimization (SMO) Techniques and strategies for promoting awareness of a brand, publication, product, etc., on social media, especially by encouraging the sharing of content that attracts people to a particular website.

Social Networks An online service or site through which people create and maintain interpersonal relationships. Networks involve individuals (such as friends, acquaintances, and coworkers) connected by interpersonal relationships.

Social Sphere The broad network of interactive digital and social media channels that collectively create a new form of public sphere.

Strategy General approaches used to achieve objectives.

Summative Research A process of evaluating the final or near-final state of a feature, a website, or an application at the end of a project or development cycle. It helps evaluate whether a design, feature, or application/website meets the user goals.

Tactic Tactical elements of a campaign such as a press release, social media post or website.

Target audience The intended audience or readership of a publication, advertisement, or other message catered specifically to said the intended audience.

Typography The style, arrangement, or appearance of typeset matter

User-Created Content (UCC) Any content that has been created and published by unpaid contributors. Also known as User Generated Content (UGC).

User-Generated Content (UGC) Is any form of content, such as images, videos, text, and audio, that has been posted by users on online platforms such as social media and wikis.

Visual Storytelling A story told primarily through the use of visual media.

Woke-Washing The appropriation of ethical and progressive values as a form of advertising just to make more profit while hiding the dark side of conventional capitalistic business management.

Woke Alert to injustice in society, especially racism. A term which originated in the United States and it refers to a perceived awareness of issues which concern social justice and racial justice. It derives from the African-American Vernacular English expression "stay woke", whose grammatical aspect refers to a continuing awareness of these issues.

Index

1-9-90 Rule, 78–80

A/B testing, 109, 110–111
Ace Hardware, 10
Accreditation in Public Relations
(APR), 26
Adobe, 172
Adobe Spark, 112
advertising, iii, 2, 11, 12, 14, 21, 29, 34,
35, 39, 41, 49, 61, 62, 64, 70, 71,
87, 88, 135, 143, 160, 167, 175,
177, 205, 216, 218, 219, 223, 224,
232, 234
Advertising Standards Authority
(ASA), 88
AI, see artificial intelligence
algorithm(s), 8, 13, 18, 29, 44, 45, 47,
52, 60
algorithmic bias, 18
Always, 219
Amazon, 10, 72, 124, 216, 228
Amazon Alexa, 8
Amazon Echo, 222
Amazon Mechanical Turk, 152
Amazon Prime Video, 166
American Advertising Federation
(AAF), 14
American Marketing Association
(AMA), 14

Ambassador, 77, 102, 208
brand ambassador, 1, 42, 90, 155
Amplience (UK), 233
Answer the Public, 56
Analytics, v, 2, 3, 14, 25, 33, 36, 43, 45,
59, 60, 77, 78, 83, 87, 161, 172,
188, 190, 201, 202, 216, 231,
233, 234
audience analytics, 21, 225
big data analytics, 215, 234, 235
data analytics, 108–109, 227,
228, 229
digital analytics, 35
engagement analytics, 189
Google Analytics, 36, 40, 41, 61, 64
language analytics, 5
predictive analytics, 7, 12, 36, 43
descriptive analytics, 36, 43
social media analytics, 20, 34,
42, 61, 75, 77, 81, 82, 85, 90,
109, 229
web(site) analytics, 109, 201, 228
AON, 186
Apple, 8, 129, 216
Approach Marketing, 231
Apps, 158, 205, 217, 218, 227
Artificial intelligence (AI), iii, ix, 1, 2,
4, 5, 7, 9, 11, 13, 14, 20, 21, 207,
216, 225, 228